SILVER SEASONS

Four leaping Red Wings during spring training before the 1940 season.
Courtesy of the *Democrat and Chronicle/Times-Union*.

Silver Seasons

The Story of the Rochester Red Wings

Jim Mandelaro
and
Scott Pitoniak

With a Foreword by Joe Altobelli

SYRACUSE UNIVERSITY PRESS

First Edition

96 97 98 99 00 01 02 03   6 5 4 3 2 1

This book is published with the assistance of a grant from the John Ben Snow
Foundation.

The paper used in this publication meets the minimum requirements of American
National Standard for Information Sciences—Permanence of Paper for Printed Library
Materials, ANSI Z39.48-1984. ∞™

Library of Congress Cataloging-in-Publication Data
Mandelaro, Jim.
    Silver seasons : the story of the Rochester Red Wings / Jim
Mandelaro and Scott Pitoniak ; with a foreword by Joe Altobelli.—
1st ed.
        p.   cm.
    Includes bibliographical references (p.   ) and index.
    ISBN 0-8156-2703-3 (alk. paper).—ISBN 0-8156-0379-7 (pbk. :
alk. paper)
        1. Rochester Red Wings (Baseball team)—History. I. Pitoniak,
Scott.   II. Title.
GV875.R63M35   1996
796.357'64'0974788—dc20   95-50078

Manufactured in the United States of America

To the memory of my father, Albert (1922–77), my first baseball hero, and to my mother, Connie, who remains the heart of my order.

—Jim Mandelaro

To Susan, Amy, and Christopher, the wind beneath my wings, and to the memory of my dad, Andrew (1913–71), the first person to take me out to the ballgame.

—Scott Pitoniak

Jim Mandelaro is a Rochester native and a graduate of St. John Fisher College. He has worked for the Gannett Rochester Newspapers since 1982 and has covered the Red Wings since 1991. Mandelaro was named Sportswriter of the Year by the Monroe County American Legion and the Rochester Press-Radio Club in 1995. His work has appeared in the *Washington Post,* the *Baltimore Sun,* the *Charlotte Observer,* and several national baseball magazines.

Scott Pitoniak, an award-winning sports columnist and feature writer for the Gannett Rochester Newspapers, has covered the Red Wings off and on for the past eleven summers. He is the author of two best-selling trivia books about the Buffalo Bills, co-hosts a weekly cable television sports talk show and teaches journalism at St. John Fisher College. A 1977 magna cum laude graduate of Syracuse University, Pitoniak has received more than fifty national and regional journalism honors. His work was cited in the book *The Best American Sportswriting, 1992.*

Contents

Illustrations

Foreword

JOE ALTOBELLI

At a time when fans and commentators lament the state of our great national pastime, I know a place where baseball thrives—as it has for more than a century.

Baseball has been an integral part of the fabric of Rochester for more than one hundred years. Today, the spirit of the game is as alive as ever in the Flower City. Through championship seasons and last-place finishes, this community and its ball club have shared a special bond, one I first felt when I came to Red Wing Stadium as a visiting player in the 1956 Junior World Series. To this day, the feeling is the same as I pass through the gates at 500 Norton Street.

As a player, coach, manager, and front office executive, I have been fortunate enough to spend nearly half a century in baseball. And while my career has taken me across America, for the last thirty years I have called Rochester my home and the Red Wings my family.

What minor-league city can claim a tradition so rich? There are Hall of Famers like Stan Musial, Bob Gibson, and Jim Palmer and Hall of Famers-to-be like Cal Ripken, Jr., and Eddie Murray. There are local heroes like Luke Easter, Estel Crabtree, and Jim Fuller, who may not have made it to Cooperstown, but who thrilled Rochester fans like few others. And there are the off-field superstars like Morrie Silver, who gave so much and asked nothing in return to make the Red Wings Rochester's team.

In *Silver Seasons,* Jim Mandelaro and Scott Pitoniak have done far more than compile a complete history of the Rochester Red Wings franchise: the great players, the great teams, and the great memories they have provided. They have succeeded in the even greater task of capturing the essence of the game in Rochester. In these pages, the personalities again come to life, and the great moments are relived as if we were reading about them in the morning paper.

I hope you enjoy reading *Silver Seasons* as much as I, and thousands of others through the years, have enjoyed living them.

Preface

It would be hard to find a city with a richer minor-league baseball tradition than Rochester, New York. The game's roots here can be traced all the way back to the early nineteenth century, when baseball was played on a meadow not far from the banks of the Genesee River. The Flower City fielded its first all-professional team in 1877, and since that time the oldest member of the International League has captured eighteen pennants.

But the true story of the Red Wings can't be measured by numbers alone. It's in the names of the men who wore the uniforms. Billy Southworth, Stan Musial, Bob Gibson, Jim Palmer, Joe Altobelli, and Cal Ripken, Jr., learned their trade here. Ron Shelton was a supporting player on the 1971 championship club, but became a heavy hitter in Hollywood, directing movies such as *Bull Durham, White Men Can't Jump,* and *Blaze.* Morrie Silver never threw a pitch—or swung at one—but he was the ultimate franchise player.

From Estel Crabtree's miracle homer in 1939 to Finigan's Rainbow in 1961; from the Cardinals to the Orioles; from Southworth to Altobelli; from Rip Collins to Jeff Manto—it's all here.

More than a century's worth of Silver memories.

Enjoy.

Jim Mandelaro and Scott Pitoniak

September 1995
Rochester, N.Y.

Acknowledgments

S pecial thanks to Lary Bump, whose tireless research stretched into the ninth inning, and to Glenn Geffner, who was always there with a name, a number, and a helping hand.

The authors also wish to acknowledge the following: Joe Altobelli, Priscilla Astifan, Andy and Maureen Baxter, George Beahon, Frank Bilovsky, Greg Boeck, Bob Brown, Jack Buck, Tom Callinan, Jim Castor, George Christoff, Fred Costello, Joe Cullinane, Elliot Curwin, Tom Decker, Carl Desens, Blaise DiNardo, Jeff DiVeronica, Ellen Flynn, Christine Frost, Gannett Rochester Newspapers, Jamie Germano, John Gibson, Carolyn and Dan Guilfoyle, Kevin Higley, Reed Hoffmann, Joe Horrigan, Ralph Hyman, John Ignizio, Bill Koenig, John Kolomic, Josh Lewin, Len Lustik, David Mack, Sal Maiorana, Connie Mandelaro, Doug Mandelaro, Dan Mason, Bob Matthews, Jim Memmott, Keith Moyer, Paul Pinckney, Susan Pitoniak, Robyn Reville, Rochester Community Baseball, Inc., Mike Roman, Karen Schiely, Naomi Silver, Patti Singer, Terry Slaybaugh, Curt Smith, Syracuse University Press, Michael Ward, Eric Washington, Tony Wells, Ginny Wheeler, Lisa Winston, and Harold "Tiny" Zwetsch.

SILVER SEASONS

1

A Game Rooted in Rochester

*The thing that keeps recurring in my research is
how significant Rochester's role has been in the evolution of baseball.*
—*Priscilla Astifan,* baseball historian

Rochesterians weren't clamoring
for the Baseball Hall of Fame to
relocate to their fair city, nor were they demanding that Cooperstown
take down its "Birthplace of Baseball" signs. But author Stephen Fox's
contention that the game's roots can be traced to Rochester did spark
some interesting discussion and underscored again the city's significant
role in baseball's evolution. In his 1995 book, *Big Leagues,* Fox wrote:

> A child's game of ancient and obscure origins, baseball was
> first played by adults on a regular basis around 1825 in the booming
> village of Rochester, New York. A young printer in Rochester,
> Thurlow Weed, later remembered those games played in Mumford's
> meadow, an expanse of eight or ten acres bordering the Genesee
> River. "A base-ball club, numbering nearly fifty members, met every
> afternoon during the ball-playing season," Weed recalled. "Though
> the members of the club embraced persons between eighteen and
> forty, it attracted the young and the old." Among the best players,
> Weed listed eight names: a merchant, three doctors, and four law-
> yers. In those particular players and place, the essential elements of
> nineteenth-century baseball were already visible.

In those days, Rochester was a gigantic village in the midst of giddy
expansion. At the intersection of the Genesee River and the Erie Canal,

it was perfectly situated to take advantage of the waterway traffic flowing west to Buffalo and Lake Erie, and east to Albany, the Hudson River, and, eventually, New York City. The town's growth was reflected in its census figures, which revealed a population explosion from 331 residents in 1815 to 7,669 by 1827. Many of Rochester's early citizens were transplanted New Englanders looking to take advantage of economic opportunities in a new frontier. The largest immigrant group, though, was composed of Irish laborers who had remained after completing their work digging the Erie Canal.

In its formative years, Rochester baseball was an elitist game usually played by the community's movers and shakers. Weed arrived in Rochester in 1822 and learned the newspaper business from a local editor. In later years, as editor of the *Albany Evening Journal* and mentor to William H. Seward, the man most responsible for the purchase of the Alaskan territory, Weed would become one of the nation's shrewdest and most powerful political bosses. Thomas Kempshall, one of Weed's baseball teammates, came to Rochester as a penniless British immigrant and worked his way up as a carpenter. He eventually purchased the dry-goods store in which he had started as a clerk, and later joined forces with Ebenezer Beach to build the nation's largest flour mill. He went on to become mayor of Rochester and to serve in Congress. Fred Whittlesey, one of several lawyers to participate in the Mumford meadow games, also became a congressman, and Addison Gardiner and his law partner, Samuel Selden, became judges. "All these men," wrote Fox, "worked at self-bossed, sedentary jobs that allowed them the energy and flexible schedules to go play baseball on pleasant summer afternoons."

In time, the popularity of the game spread to the masses, supplanting baseball's European ancestors such as cricket, wicket, and rounders as the people's sport of choice. Rochester baseball historian Priscilla Astifan wrote that "by the onset of the Civil War, teams [in Rochester] were made up of merchants, grocers, small shopkeepers, clerks, bookkeepers and mechanics. In spite of long hours in an office, at a machine or at heavy labor, the workers gathered at the ball fields after work, or on Saturday afternoons or even mornings so early they had to wait for the sun to come up."

In the early years of Rochester baseball, there weren't any official playing fields, so players, to the annoyance of many, would transform public squares and quiet neighborhoods into ball diamonds. Initially, ministers questioned the morality of such recreational endeavors, especially on the Sabbath. But in time, baseball came to be seen as a healthful pastime.

The exhilaration of green fields and pure air will supplant the morbid and pernicious cravings for tobacco and rum . . . Baseball playing would be a time for fathers and mothers and friends to share a common interest.
—*Rochester Democrat and American,* 1858

Astifan's research discovered that private baseball clubs in Rochester were organized according to neighborhoods, vocations, economic standing, religious affiliation, and race. One of the star players on one of Rochester's all-black teams was Frederick Douglass, Jr., whose father was a former slave and the leading voice of the Abolitionist movement. A local newspaper in 1858 estimated there were at least a thousand baseball clubs in the Rochester area, although later research suggests that figure may have been exaggerated. There were no sports sections in daily newspapers in those days, so recorded information about the games was hard to come by. Baseball announcements often were tucked amid notices of mill accidents, robberies, court proceedings, suicides, and even murders, but as the game grew in popularity, the coverage devoted to it increased. According to Astifan, the first formal public baseball game in Rochester that received any substantial newspaper coverage was held on June 18, 1858. An account of that game years later in the *Rochester Evening Express* reported that "the day was fine and carriages lined up in the street, and the youth and beauty of the town were there to see the first game of baseball played here."

Three months later, the Buffalo Niagaras defeated Flour City 30–20, in what is believed to be the first intercity match for a Rochester baseball club. The *Union and Advertiser* reported that "thousands watched the game with intense interest." Such high scores were common in this era before the advent of the baseball glove. A few weeks later, a rematch was held in Buffalo, and thousands of Rochesterians took advantage of the special half-price round trip offered by the railroad. Flour City lost again, this time by six runs. The National Association, baseball's loosely organized governing body, required that the winning team host the losing team at a banquet after an intercity match. Following the Niagaras' second win over Flour City, they toasted their opponents, and Buffalo's J. R. Blodgett presented the visiting team with the sheet music from his "Baseball Polka." As part of the National Association of Professional Baseball Players' code of etiquette, each team serenaded its opponent with a postgame cheer.

That same year, the Live Oaks, under the guidance of player-

Baseball became popular after the Civil War, with games played almost daily in squares, parks, and meadows. Courtesy of the *Democrat and Chronicle/Times-Union.*

manager James Backus, became Rochester's first official baseball champions, defeating Genesee Valley 39–7 in a game hosted by the Monroe County Agricultural Society. As a reward, Backus and his players were invited to a tea party where they were asked to help in the judging of breads, cakes, and native wines produced by members of the agricultural society.

Although the rules of nine innings per game and three outs per half-inning were in effect, the guidelines of mid-nineteenth-century baseball differed greatly from those of today's game. Balls caught on the first bounce were outs. Pitchers stood forty-five feet, rather than sixty feet, six inches, from the plate, and usually delivered the ball underhand or sidearm, often while on the run. Batters could request where they wanted the ball thrown; walks were rare and usually only awarded if the umpire felt the hitter was being too picky in his pitch selection. Early bats resembled long, heavy clubs. Occasionally, players would use whittled-down wagon wheel tongues. The baseball often consisted of nothing more than a tightly wound ball of yarn with a rubber core, and unlike today there was not an endless supply of them. The same ball usually was used the entire game. Protective equipment was unheard of, so to soften the blow of receiving balls bare-handed, catchers often positioned themselves a good thirty to forty feet behind home plate. Despite such precautions, catchers and other fielders often played with bruised, bloody hands and broken fingers. Said one player from that era: "It was not a game for weaklings."

Rochesterians' increasing interest in baseball was evident on January 16, 1860, when nearly one hundred spectators showed up to observe an eight-inning game played on ice skates on Irondequoit Bay, north of the city. The following year, on New Year's Day, another baseball game was played on the frozen bay, this time before an estimated crowd of 2,500.

During the summer of 1860, the Brooklyn Excelsiors came to town during what is believed to be the first national tour in baseball history. The Excelsiors were regarded as the best team in America, and they did nothing to jeopardize that standing while in Rochester. They whacked Flour City 21–1, then defeated the Live Oaks 27–9. The *Democrat and American* applauded the efforts of the hometown teams, reminding readers that the local clubs played the Excelsiors not to win, but to improve their skills by observing the experts. It also was noted that the Excelsiors were known to devote considerable time to baseball, and that some of their players might even be considered professional, though compensation to players in any way was strictly forbidden by the National Association.

As the Civil War neared, baseball in Rochester began to lose its innocence. The jumping of star players from team to team became more prevalent, and gamblers frequented games, probably bribing players, umpires, and managers. In November 1860, in one of the last contests before most of Rochester's prominent players headed off to war, a game was staged between supporters of the two presidential candidates: Abraham Lincoln and Stephen Douglas. The Douglas team won the game, but lost the election. Baseball continued to be played in Rochester during the war years, but the quality of the games suffered. Occasionally, soldiers home on furlough would take part. During the 1864 New York State Fair in Rochester, the Atlantics of Brooklyn pummeled the Canadian national baseball champs 75–11. Wrote the *Rochester Evening Express:* "Their presence here has infused some of the base ball fever among our citizens." In reality, Rochester's interest in the sport wouldn't take off again until several years after the war.

Although it was rumored that players on the 1860 Brooklyn team that visited Rochester were being compensated for their ballplaying, professional baseball didn't officially come out of the closet until nine years later when the Red Stockings of Cincinnati announced to the world that they were paying all their athletes. Their willingness to offer monetary compensation enabled them to assemble the finest team in the land. The Red Stockings took their show on the road, playing before relatively large crowds at each stop. On Friday, June 4, 1869, a day after clobbering the Buffalo Niagaras 46–6, the Red Stockings' barnstorming team arrived in Rochester. Despite rainy weather, nearly three thousand spectators showed up at Jones Square and watched the Rochester Alerts make a game of it before losing to the Red Stockings 18–9. The *Rochester Evening Express* was effusive in its praise of the visitors: "We have never seen a finer set of men, physically. Their heavy batting showed that they have plenty of muscle, and know how to use it. Their daily practice for several weeks past has bronzed their countenances and given them a rugged, stubborn look." The game was Cincinnati's most tightly contested to date, prompting the decidedly biased Rochester newspaper to claim: "Had [the Alerts] had the practice of the [Red Stockings] we think the result would have been in favor of our boys." The Red Stockings' visit whetted Rochester's appetite for its own professional baseball team. It would be eight years before those yearnings would become reality.

In 1877, a team sponsored by the Rochester Baseball Association joined the International Association, believed to be the first minor league ever. Led by Nat Pond, who served as president, manager, and player, Rochester finished in third place in its rookie season but dropped out of the league the following summer after placing seventh among twelve teams. The team featured two notable baseball figures: third baseman Ned Hanlon, who was credited with numerous innovations, including the hit-and-run, the intentional pass, and finger signs from catchers to pitchers, and second baseman Sam Crane, who would later gain fame as a syndicated baseball writer whose reports on the New York Giants "spread the gospel of baseball as did no other reporter."

After a year without a team, professional baseball was revived in Rochester by Asa Soule, whose company manufactured Hop Bitters, a tonic that claimed to cure all ailments. According to Rochester baseball historian Bill McCarthy, the Hop Bitters were forced to cease operations during the season after the manager of the club absconded with several hundred dollars—big money in those days. Soule put police on the manager's track, but he was never apprehended. Rochester was without a professional team for the next three summers, a fact that pleased many who continued to feel that baseball was an immoral and wretched pastime. This clearly was the editorial position of the *Union and Advertiser*, which criticized the rival *Democrat and American* for devoting too much coverage to the sport. "Ball playing is an amusement and only immature critics think it necessary to treat it as a matter of gravest importance," preached the *Union and Advertiser.* "Thought should be reserved for other matters."

Albert Reinhart and William Deininger apparently disagreed with the *Union and Advertiser's* stance, because in 1885 they formed a new team and joined the New York State League, the forerunner to the modern-day International League. For the next five summers, Rochester fans or "cranks," as they were called in those days, would be entertained, and in some cases annoyed, by colorful players who played hard—on and off the diamond. Those out to prove baseball was immoral could cite the renegade 1887 Rochester club as Exhibit A. Wrote McCarthy in his 1950 book *Rochester Diamond Echoes:* "Jack Humphries, catcher-manager, had little control over off-diamond activities of this aggregation. Rollicking Rochesters flirted with hops and barley, and were the drinkingest fish yet spawned in International pool. Always in hock to management and town bar-keeps, they were known as the good time Charleys of a riotous league. Magnates [owners] constantly fined and suspended players for following the primrose path." Fred Lewis, the team's top party animal, was also its top hitter, batting .412 during a time when averages were inflated by bases on balls counted as hits. Lewis's teammate, John (Monk) Cline, hit .398, but was better known for his hilarious antics during games. Some regard him as a nineteenth-century version of Max Patkin, who retired as the Clown Prince of Baseball in 1994.

For the next two seasons the team would be paced by Big Bob Barr, a rubber-armed right-hander whose one hundred career victories remain a Rochester record. Barr's greatest year came in 1888, when he won twenty-nine games while recording a 1.58 earned run average and 216 strikeouts. His primary victims were Syracuse and Toronto; he defeated each team seven times. The summer of '88 also saw two other noteworthy pitching performances. In the season opener, local hero Will Calihan struck out sixteen London, Ontario, hitters, establishing a Rochester record that would stand for seventy-eight years. Nearly two months later, on July 6, George Hays pitched the first no-hitter in the city's professional baseball history, blanking that same London club, 6–0, at Rochester's Culver Field.

In 1889, another Calihan would make news that, according to McCarthy, "turned the town topsy-turvy and brought about a reorganization that reached into the directorate." Tom Calihan, Will's brother and teammate, reportedly blew his top after being fined $25 for his poor infield play. He was then docked another $25 for not accepting the first fine gracefully. Tom and Will quit the club, and Bob Barr and Chub

Collins asked to be sold to another team. As a result of the mutiny, manager Harry Leonard resigned his position, Tom Calihan was released, and his brother, Will, and Collins were traded to Buffalo. Barr stayed put, and wound up having another outstanding season, recording another club-leading twenty-nine victories. The "Calihan Affair," as the story became known, was big news that summer, but an even bigger story would unfold in the off-season, one that would have significant historical ramifications for Rochester baseball.

In the summer of 1889 major league baseball was in a state of disarray that was every bit as tumultuous and confusing as the disputes that would force cancellation of the World Series 105 years later. During the 1889 season, team owners announced they would impose a salary cap to limit players' earnings to $2,500 per season, about half what the top stars were being paid. In rhetoric hauntingly similar to that heard in the summer of 1994, owners complained that escalating salaries were outlandish and were threatening to ruin baseball. Incensed leaders of the Brotherhood of Professional Base Ball Players compared themselves to slaves, citing the reserve clause that bound a player to a team unless he was released, traded, or sold. The players' union originally considered striking on Independence Day 1889, but decided against that move after devising a plan far more revolutionary. The Brotherhood opted to wait until the off-season and form its own league. As lawsuits mounted between the Players' League and the two established major leagues—the National League and the American Association—fans became increasingly disillusioned with the perceived greed of the players and the owners.

> *By the late 1880s, "baseball's artists"—today's sportswriters would call them superstars—commanded salaries up to $5,000. That seemed like an astonishing sum of money to Rochester's teachers, who averaged $565 a year, and to the Erie Railroad workers, who earned less than $2 for a 12-hour day. When an agent of the players' union visited Rochester, the* Union & Advertiser *described him as "one of the 'slaves' who desired to be released from the bondage of drawing a salary of $2,000 to $5,000 for six months of baseball playing . . . cheered by the crowds, banqueted, gold-watched and diamond-pinned, and yet talking about slavery."*
>
> *—Bob Minzesheimer,* Upstate 1980

Despite the resultant bad public relations, neither the players nor the owners would budge from their positions, and the union went ahead with its plans. The game's best players left the established leagues, and the American Association wound up losing franchises in Cincinnati, Baltimore, and Kansas City. In a scramble to replace those teams, they contacted several minor league baseball cities, including Rochester. General Henry Brinker, a Prussian-born businessman who made a fortune in American railroads and breweries, willingly forked over the $8,000 league entry fee, as did the owners of teams in Syracuse and Toledo. Brinker saw Rochester's move up to the big leagues as a golden business opportunity. He planned to sell his beer at the ballpark and also figured that one of his railroads would reap the benefits of transporting spectators to Windsor Beach, on the shores of Lake Ontario, where the team was scheduled to play its Sunday home games. Minzesheimer noted that "the nucleus of the team would come from Rochester's minor league team, but Brinker vowed, as new owners have vowed ever since, to have the strongest team money can secure." Several big city newspapers scoffed at the idea that such "villages" as Rochester could be in the major leagues. This despite the fact Rochester had experienced a 54 percent increase in population between 1880 and 1890 and now ranked as the twenty-second largest city in America.

That March, for the first time in Rochester's history, a baseball team headed south to Washington, D.C., for spring training. After its first two exhibition games were snowed out, Rochester scored consecutive victories over the world champion New York Giants, prompting the *New York Herald* to describe the upstaters as "the now famous Rochesters." The giddiness continued as Rochester opened the regular season by winning five of its first seven games on the road before arriving in the Flour City to host Brooklyn on April 28, 1890. An announced crowd of four thousand showed up at Culver Park to watch Rochester defeat the visitors 5–1. Despite fielding essentially the same team it had the year before in the International League, Rochester was holding its own against the big boys. Thanks to the pitching of Bob Barr, who was starting almost every other game, Rochester resided in second place for the first several weeks of the season. In mid-June, the nation's baseball fans took notice of the Rochesters when an engraving of the mustachioed team appeared on the cover of *The Sporting Life,* the nineteenth-century equivalent to *Sports Illustrated.*

The good times wouldn't last, however. Injuries to pitchers Will Calihan and Hook Schaeffer meant an even greater workload for the already overworked Barr. And problems away from the diamond began to surface. Shortstop Marr Phillips was found drunk and was suspended.

After returning from his finger injury, Calihan, a fiery Billy Martin type, punched out the private detective Brinker had hired to trail him and was suspended for several weeks.

The novelty of big-league ball in Rochester faded fast with fans. Newspaper accounts in June reported fewer than one hundred spectators at some games, and farmers and ministers near the park at Windsor Beach were growing increasingly angry about ball being played on the Sabbath.

On Monday, June 9, one day after Rochester hosted Philadelphia, an Irondequoit farmer named Frank Towle swore out an affadavit claiming that the players from each team had violated a state law prohibiting "all fishing, playing public sport, exercise and shows" on Sundays. The players were arrested and taken to jail, and local newspapers informed readers that the teams had been arrested for Sabbath breaking. The players were released on bail in time to play that afternoon, but the issue was far from resolved. Towle and other residents formed the "Law and Order League of Irondequoit." Later that season, during a Sunday game between Rochester and Columbus at the Windsor park, members of the society jumped onto the field and threatened to arrest the players. Spectators angered by the society's tactics also took to the field and surrounded the would-be law enforcers. Fearful of a riot, Rochester manager Pat Powers worked a compromise. If the society allowed them to complete the game, they would appear in court the following day.

For all intents and purposes, Rochester's big-league experiment was doomed a few weeks later when a state Supreme Court judge refused to throw out the indictments against the players. The team owners agreed not to play any more Sunday games, which meant Rochester would lose out on its biggest drawing days. Brinker told reporters "it would be foolish to throw away any more money on baseball," and sold the team. The Players' League folded after just one season, and Rochester, Syracuse, and Toledo returned to the minors, where they would forge rivalries that continue strong more than a century later.

Professional baseball in Rochester continued to be a precarious venture at best. Historian Bill McCarthy wrote that the team's 1891 season ended prematurely in August when players Joe Visner, Alonzo Knight, Bobby Gilks, and Pietro Sweeney left the team because paychecks were three weeks in arrears. Alcohol abuse continued to be a problem during the '92 campaign. George Meakin, who won 23 of 30 decisions for Rochester, was fined $100 for "lushing." He asked forgiveness, and the money was refunded. To celebrate the turn of events, Meakin went on another drinking binge and was fined $200 and released. A more calamitous event occurred a few days after the season finale when Culver Field burned to the ground. Without a place to play, Rochester was forced to withdraw from the league. It would be two years before professional baseball would return.

Charley Leimburger, Charley Englert, and Jim Buckley—three saloonkeepers who became known to local baseball fans as the "Big Three" —purchased the franchise and fielded a team in 1895. They erected a new ballpark on St. Paul Boulevard, across from the spot where the Seneca Park Zoo now resides, and signed several former big-league players, including ex-Brooklyn pitcher George Harper, who accounted for 25 of Rochester's 49 wins. The following season, the Big Three signed Dan "Old Piano Legs" Shannon as the new player-manager and nicknamed the team "Brownies" in honor of George Eastman's new locally produced Kodak cameras. During the summer of 1897, former world heavyweight boxing champion Gentleman Jim Corbett stopped at Rochester's Riverside Park to stage a three-round exhibition bout. While there, Corbett suited up and played first base for the Brownies. He proved he wasn't a slugger on the diamond, going hitless in four at-bats and committing two errors in the field. Later that summer, problems arose again when the Law and Order League arrested six Brownies for breaking the Sabbath. The incident became known as "The Kid Gannon Case" after the Rochester pitcher who was on the mound when the arrests were made. The six were found guilty, and the district attorney agreed to waive the sentences if the Big Three agreed to abandon Sunday ball. Without the Sabbath revenues, the owners decided that running a ball club in Rochester was no longer feasible, and switched the team to Montreal on July 23. Baseball was back in the Flour City the following season, but only briefly. New ownership rebuilt burned-down Culver Field, encircling it with a bicycle track. Before long, cycling outdrew baseball, and that, combined with continued Sunday bans, forced the club to head north of the border again, this time to Ottawa.

Despite its almost antibaseball atmosphere in the late nineteenth century, Rochester didn't lack for entrepreneurs willing to take the risk of fielding a professional team. And so it was again in 1899, when George Sweeney, Edward F. Higgins, and John Callahan formed the team's third different ownership group in as many seasons. In a move that would influence Rochester baseball history, they hired Albert Buckenberger to serve as manager. Sportswriters nicknamed Buckenberger "Silent Chief." The moniker was clearly a misnomer. Buckenberger was

Al Buckenberger's feisty Bronchos literally fought their way to Rochester's first
pennant in 1899. Courtesy of the *Democrat and Chronicle/Times-Union.*

anything but silent, and neither were his players. Although officially
called the Bronchos, the team quickly became known to local fans and
sportswriters as "Buck's Bronchos." Out-of-town writers and fans came
up with other, less complimentary nicknames for the rowdy Rochester
ball club.

Baseball in the 1890s had evolved into a rugged, mean-spirited
game, and no team in the old Eastern League was more intimidating
than Buckenberger's. The Bronchos went to extravagant lengths to bully
opponents and gain an edge. First baseman Harry O'Hagan finished the
season with almost as many fistfights as at-bats. Opponents claimed that
O'Hagan placed a hat pin in his glove with just enough of the point
protruding to "vaccinate" runners as they dived back into first on pickoff
attempts. Despite numerous complaints and inspections, no umpire was
able to find a pin in O'Hagan's mitt. Still, O'Hagan's actions received
Buckenberger's tacit approval and helped set the tone for others to follow. Bronchos center fielder Bill Lush intimidated infielders with spike-
flying slides. Catcher "Fat Bill" Smink walked on the toes of umpires and

opponents, spraying them with tobacco juice through his walrus-like mustache. Sneered one Worcester sportswriter: "The Rochester Raws are a band of chesties who wear their caps on the side of the heads and swagger when they walk." But the Bronchos weren't just mean; they were good. Robert Becker won twenty-two games and Ed Householder batted .350 as Buck's boys posted a 73–44 record and captured the first pennant in Rochester history.

The following summer, Buck's Bronchos continued to entertain. Trips to the ballpark became festive occasions. As McCarthy pointed out: "Cranks who liked the shade and a cool glass of brew—and proximity to the source of supply—could loaf in the pavilion beneath the grandstand and watch the game. If the Broncs were losing, a modicum of good cheer could be whipped up by any group willing to unloosen their celluloid collars and give out with four-part harmony." Bronchos shortstop–second baseman Frank Bonner often gave patrons reason to sing for their beer, and cry in it, too. He committed an astounding 104 errors during the summer of 1900, including five in one game against Syracuse. Perhaps the most incredible fielding play in Rochester baseball history also occurred that season. It involved Eddie Murphy and literally was a case of the Bronchos pitcher using his head. A batter hit a line drive that, according to one sportswriter, "bopped Eddie flush on the forehead, felling him like a poled ox." The ball richocheted off Murphy's noggin and headed back toward home plate, where catcher Eddie Dixon gloved it for an out. Although Murphy suffered a nasty bruise and a severe headache from the beaning, the hard-headed pitcher shook off the injuries and wound up winning 18 of 34 decisions. Late in the season, there was another contact story that attracted headlines. Buckenberger got into a fistfight with Toronto manager Edward Barrow, who would later gain fame as the general manager of the Babe Ruth-led New York Yankees. The Bronchos manager had Barrow arrested for assault and battery, but nothing ever came of the charges.

In 1901, the Bronchos made news for their on-field antics. From August 22 through September 2, they won fourteen straight, a Rochester record that stood until 1953, when the Red Wings won nineteen in a row. King Malarkey, who won four games during the streak, led the pitchers with twenty-seven victories; Lush stole fifty-four bases and scored 137 runs; and Reddy Grey, brother of famed novelist Zane Grey, hit twelve homers as Rochester won its second pennant in three years.

Buckenberger departed after the season, and the team experienced several pitiful years. Harry O'Hagan took over as player-manager late in the 1902 season and pulled off the first unassisted triple play in baseball history. That was one of the few highlights in a season that saw the

Bronchos lose twenty-five more games than they had the previous season, dropping them from first place to seventh. Arthur Irwin, whom some credit with inventing the fielder's glove, took over as manager in 1903, and the team's nickname was changed to the Beau Brummels. But the losing got worse. Irwin was replaced by George Smith in midseason, and the team finished in last place with a 34–96 record, as Frank Leary established a league record for pitching futility with twenty-seven losses. McCarthy wrote that it was a mystery why the Beau Brummels "weren't tossed into the Exchange Street [jail] for masquerading as pro ballplayers."

Although there is room for debate over whether the 1930 or 1971 Red Wings were the best team in Rochester history, there is no debating which team was the worst. The 1904 Beau Brummels win hands down. They won just 28 and lost 105, prompting McCarthy to write: "The Beaus were as gamey as a shirt worn three days running in torrid August. Slugless outfit won booby-record with picayune total of 28 wins. They performed like pullets with noggins decapitated." The team was managed by Heine Smith, who, just two years earlier, while managing the National League's New York Giants, had attempted to convert pitcher Christy Mathewson into a first baseman. Mathewson balked at the move, and wound up pitching himself into the Baseball Hall of Fame.

In an attempt to reverse their fortunes, the owners brought back Buckenberger as manager, but the magic was missing. His 1905–7 clubs finished seventh, fourth, and seventh, and he was fired during a 1908 game and replaced by shortstop Eddie Holly. The team finished last for the third time in six years. The only highlight was the opening of the new Baseball Park on Bay Street. Charles T. Chapin, who headed the group that purchased the team in 1903, had grown tired of the losing, and shortly before the 1909 season, he hired former major leaguer "Big Jawn" Ganzel to manage the team. Ganzel told the owners that they would have to clean house and spend more money on quality players if they were sincere about their desire to revive interest in Rochester baseball. With the owners' grudging approval, Ganzel purchased the contracts of several former big leaguers, and the moves paid dividends, as the newly named Hustlers won their first of three consecutive pennants. The most important acquisition occurred on August 27, when Rochester purchased pitcher Don Carlos Patrick Ragan from the Chicago Cubs. Ragan made six starts in the final nine days of the season, winning them all to help the Hustlers clinch. It was more of the same in 1910 as Ragan, George McConnell, Ducky Holmes, and Ed Lafitte combined for 75 of the team's 92 victories. Interest in the Hustlers became so great that an automatic scoreboard was installed at Genesee Hall, so the fans could

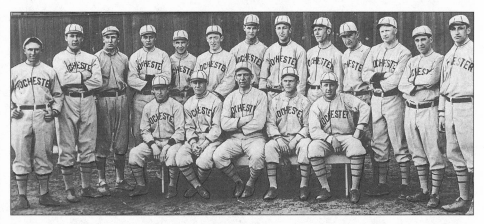

The 1909 Rochester Hustlers captured the first of three consecutive pennants. Courtesy of the *Democrat and Chronicle/Times-Union*.

get up-to-the-minute details when Rochester was on the road. Big Jawn's Hustlers made it three straight pennants in 1911 as George "Slats" McConnell became the only Rochester pitcher to win thirty games in a season. The Hustlers would remain competitive under Ganzel's guidance during the next four seasons, but it would be seventeen summers before another pennant was raised in Rochester. An individual highlight of note occurred in 1913 when George "Hack" Simmons led the league in hitting with a .339 average, making him the first Rochester player to accomplish the feat since Doc Kennedy topped all hitters twenty-eight years earlier. Wally Pipp paced the Hustlers with fifteen homers in 1914 and was sold to the New York Highlanders. Pipp, of course, would become a footnote to history. After holding down New York's starting first base job for eleven seasons, legend has it that Pipp begged out of a game one day because of a headache. He was replaced in the lineup by Lou Gehrig, who stayed there for 2,130 straight games, a record that stood until former Red Wing Cal Ripken, Jr., surpassed it with the Baltimore Orioles on September 6, 1995.

Ganzel and Charles Chapin came to a parting of the ways in August 1915, and several nondescript seasons followed. Carmen Hill, the ace of the Hustlers' 1916 staff, went 14–16, and attracted the attention of fans because he donned glasses during games. He is believed to be the first bespectacled player in Rochester history. The following summer, Al Schacht lost 21 of 33 decisions, but he would later make fans in Rochester and baseball parks throughout America laugh with his goofy antics.

Barnstorming Babe

Babe Ruth made at least four appearances in Rochester: one at the old Baseball Park on Bay Street and three at Red Wing Stadium at 500 Norton Street. Each of the Sultan of Swat's visits left an indelible impression.

In the summer of 1925, Ruth and his New York Yankee teammates pulled into town behind a locomotive and played an exhibition against the Rochester Tribe. Before the start of the seventh inning, Tribe manager George Stallings instructed pitcher Harry Weaver to groove a fastball so the Babe could hit a home run and send the huge crowd home happy. The fiercely competitive Weaver objected at first, but changed his mind when Stallings threatened to yank him from the game. When Ruth stepped to the plate, the Rochester catcher asked him where he would like the pitch. "Belt high," replied the Babe. The pitch was delivered to the requested location, and Ruth drove the ball over the fifty-foot-high scoreboard in right field. The ball did not return to earth until it had also cleared a row of poplar trees and houses across the street. It was the first and only home run in the twenty-year history of Baseball Park to clear the scoreboard. After the game, a 7–3 Yankees victory, Ruth sent Weaver an autographed baseball with the inscription: "Thanks a lot, Harry, Babe Ruth." Later, the Yankees slugger told Tribe right fielder Eddie Murphy: "I believe that is the longest home run I ever hit."

On September 8, 1930, more than fourteen thousand fans watched with rapt attention at Red Wing Stadium as the Babe hit a two-run homer to lead the Yankees to a 7–6 exhibition game victory against the Wings. Wrote former *Democrat and Chronicle* sports editor Joseph Adams: "The fourth inning of the exhibition tilt will linger long in the memory of those fans out to see the great Babe Ruth in action. Ruth hit a home run in that frame off the delivery of 'Lefty' Larry Irvin, who was grooving the ball for the big fellow. Ruth smashed the pellet over the right-field fence, several miles above it and way out into the parking lot."

Ruth and his barnstorming teammates stopped in Rochester again on May 16, 1934. While in town, the Babe headed to Rochester General Hospital to visit Rabbit Maranville, a veteran major-league baseball player who had broken his leg in a home plate collision with Yankees catcher Norm Klein before the start of the season. Maranville, who had married a woman from Rochester and made his off-season home there, was scheduled to undergo surgery and Ruth was hoping his visit might boost his friend's spirits. While at the hospital, the Babe stopped by the children's ward, where he signed autographs and played with the kids for almost an hour. During that afternoon's exhibition game against the Red Wings, neither Ruth nor his home-run-clouting teammate, Lou Gehrig, was able to hit one out. Each slugger was held to three singles, but the fans didn't leave disappointed. Recalled longtime season-ticket holder Carl Desens: "We didn't have television back in those days, so for most of us, our only view of Ruth had been through the photos the newspapers ran. To see him in person was something special."

Ruth's final public appearance in Rochester came on August 15, 1941. He had retired from the game several years earlier and was cutting back on his appearances, but at the behest of Rochester entrepreneur William Raithel, the Babe agreed to take part in the Red Wings' annual charity baseball night. When Ruth arrived at the ballpark that evening, he expressed reservations about participating in a pregame home run derby. "I haven't had a bat in my hands in more than two years and I don't know if I'll even see that apple," he told reporters. Ruth, who was forty-six years old at the time, grabbed one of the heaviest bats in the rack and stepped to the plate. Red Wings manager Tony Kaufmann threw batting practice and the Babe tried futilely to lift a ball out of the park. Finally, on the twenty-fifth pitch, Ruth slammed a line drive over the right-field fence. The fans went wild.

When his pitching career ended, Schacht barnstormed as the original Clown Prince of Baseball. The newly named Rochester Colts finished one game below .500 in 1918, but it could have been worse without Henry Heitman's heroics. The iron-man pitcher won both games of a doubleheader twice in a four-day span, and wound up leading the International League with an 18–6 record and a 1.32 earned run average.

The highlight of an otherwise dreary 1919 season came on June 24, when Rochester trounced Reading 19–0. The star of the day was George "Highpockets" Kelly, who established a Rochester baseball record by smacking four homers in one game. He also had a double and drove in nine runs, as Rochester recorded one of its most lopsided victories ever. The following summer, there would be little to applaud as the Colts lost 106 games. McCarthy laid the blame on owner Chapin. Wrote the historian: "America's national pastime was clearly off the war-time pattern, but Prexy Chapin played ostrich. He foisted a stinkeroo on the town."

Courtesy of the *Democrat and Chronicle/Times-Union.*

Rochester experienced its next baseball renaissance in 1921 when it changed names and managers. George Stallings was the new skipper of the Tribe, and he came to town with impeccable credentials, having managed the 1914 Miracle Boston Braves from a last-place standing at midseason to the National League pennant and World Series title. Many baseball historians regard that turnaround as the most momentous of all time.

Like Big Jawn Ganzel, Stallings liked veteran players. His most famous acquisition was first baseman Fred Merkle. Despite his success in the big leagues—he batted .273 in 1,637 games—Merkle will forever be remembered in baseball lore for one "bonehead" play he made when he was a nineteen-year-old rookie with the New York Giants in 1908. The Giants were locked in a heated pennant race with the Cubs at the time, and Chicago came to town and won the first two games of a crucial series. The Giants appeared to have the third game won when the incident occurred. In the bottom of the ninth, Moose McCormick was on third base and Merkle on first, when Giants shortstop Al Bridwell hit a ball to center field for what looked like the game-winning hit. Merkle ran about two-thirds of the way to second base while McCormick crossed the plate. The crowd poured onto the field, thinking as Merkle did that the game was over. Amid the confusion, Cubs second baseman Johnny Evers, of Tinker to Evers to Chance fame, yelled frantically for the ball. He eventually retrieved it and touched second base. Umpire Hank O'Day called Merkle out, ending the inning and negating McCormick's run. The game ended in a tie, and the teams finished the season deadlocked in first. The Cubs won the make-up game 4–2, and "Bonehead" Merkle would forever be persecuted for that one play that cost the Giants the pennant.

Stallings, however, had come to admire Merkle's stellar play against the Braves through the years, and when the first baseman became available, the manager signed him immediately. He would not regret the move. Merkle would hit .311 or better in his four seasons with Rochester.

The Tribe was a colorful team. The outfield included "Fat" Bob Fothergill, who entertained fans with handsprings, and Maurice Archdeacon, who earned the nickname "The Comet" because of his blazing speed. Before one game, Archdeacon set a world record by zipping around the bases in 13.8 seconds. Reporters referred to him as "The World's Fastest Human."

The '21 team would become the first in Rochester history to win more than a hundred games (101–67). Unfortunately, the Tribe, despite a fifty-six-game improvement from the year before, would be overshadowed by Jack Dunn's dynastic Baltimore Orioles, who finished nineteen and a half games in front of Rochester.

The 1922 Tribe was stronger than the previous edition. Fothergill's 250-pound body wasn't the only thing fat about him. He hit safely in twenty-seven consecutive games and finished with a robust .383 batting average. Merkle batted .347, Archdeacon stole fifty-five bases, pitcher "Big" Jack Wisner went 22–8, and catcher Gus Sandberg threw out three would-be base stealers in one inning as Stallings's boys finished with 105 wins and 62 losses. The impressive record, however, didn't produce a pennant. The Orioles, featuring future major-league pitching star Lefty Grove, won again, this time by ten games.

It was more of the same in 1923. For the third straight season the Tribe won more than one hundred games, and for the third straight season they were beaten out by Dunn's Baltimore club. Adding insult to injury, Clarence Pitt, a player Stallings traded to Baltimore, wound up nipping Archdeacon for the batting title, .35738 to .35736. Wisner won twenty-six and Bill Moore eighteen for the Tribe. Baltimore's dominance

Walter Hagen: Baseball Magnate

Baseball had always been Walter Hagen's first love, so when the golfing great heard that his hometown team, the Rochester Tribe, was for sale in 1927, he instructed business manager Bob Harlow to put in an offer. For $10,000, Hagen became part owner of the team, which had a roster of fifty-three players, including one who had been a high school teammate of The Haig's.

Wrote Hagen in his 1956 autobiography, *The Walter Hagen Story:* "I was beginning to think of myself as a baseball magnate. I intended to forget the advice Larry Fischer gave me when I mentioned the deal to him. He told me, 'Walter, stick to your golf. Don't divide your interests. I approve of your golf manufacturing venture, but not this baseball deal.' Despite Larry's advice I went ahead with the deal. However, my bank balance was far from enough to see me through. I needed a new ball park so I decided to call on my old friend George Eastman."

Years before Hagen became a golf star, he had caddied for Eastman, the founder and president of the Rochester-based Eastman Kodak Company. The two met for lunch, and the film manufacturing giant told Hagen he would mull over the idea during his safari to India and give him an answer when he returned. "I followed through with the Rochester deal as long as I could . . . but my stay [in baseball] was short," Hagen recalled. "My money was fast giving out. I finally got out of the deal after I'd lost $37,500."

Hagen had once been one of Rochester's top semi-pro baseball players. He made $1.50 each game he pitched and helped his team to three straight city championships. He was so good that the Philadelphia Phillies invited him to spring training, but an editor talked him out of it; told him he should pursue golf. It was good advice. Hagen wound up winning seventy-six tournaments, including the PGA five times, the British Open four times, and the U.S. Open twice. He was captain of the U.S. team in the Ryder Cup a record seven times.

would continue during the summer of '24 as the Orioles won their sixth consecutive pennant. The Tribe, weakened by the sale of twenty-five-game winner Walter Beall to the Yankees and Archdeacon to the Chicago White Sox, finished a distant fourth. Jocko Conlon, who would become a Hall of Famer as an umpire, played a solid center field and batted .321.

"Squaw" Moore paced Rochester's pitchers with a no-hitter against the Syracuse Stars.

The most memorable play of the season, though, would involve Merkle, and it would conjure memories of his infamous past. Baltimore was leading 4–2, but Rochester was threatening with two on and two out in the bottom of the ninth. Merkle, who would finish the season with a .350 average, smashed a ball over the center-field fence at Baseball Park, but there would be no joy in Merkleville. Tribe base runner Eusibio Gonzales planted himself on third and watched the flight of the ball. Meanwhile, Birney Griffin began running full force from second. Griffin rounded third and was called out for passing Gonzales. Merkle was deprived of a home run and the Orioles won 4–2. Baltimore would win a record seventh straight league title in 1925, finishing well ahead of the third-place Tribe. Rochester batted .292 as a team and rode the arm of left-hander Carl Yowell, who led the league with an 11–1 record. Some compared Conlon's defense to that of major-league great Tris Speaker. Merkle had another solid season, batting .311.

Rochester's baseball fortunes would decline over the next two seasons under new owner Sam Weidrick. Merkle was dealt to Reading, where he became a manager. Reading, meanwhile, sold pitcher Mose Swaney to Rochester for the then hefty sum of $5,000. Weidrick purchased the ancient pitcher so "he won't beat us any more." To the owner's chagrin, Swaney never reported. The futility of that team was underscored by the revolving door at each of the infield positions. By season's end, the Tribe had gone through five first basemen, five second basemen, five shortstops, and five third basemen.

The Stallings era—which might have been one of Rochester's greatest had it not occurred during Dunn's dynasty—came to an end midway through the 1927 season. Despite a number of star ex-major leaguers, including the fun-loving, basket-catching Rabbit Maranville, the Tribe finished in sixth place under manager George Mogridge. Attendance had dwindled dramatically at dilapidated Baseball Park, and the team, despite prominent investors such as golf immortal Walter Hagen, eventually went bankrupt. It appeared that baseball might flee town again.

Manager Billy Southworth *(left)* and general manager Warren Giles were the brains behind Rochester's four consecutive International League pennants from 1928 through 1931. Courtesy of the *Democrat and Chronicle/Times-Union.*

Southworth had batted .298 in a ten-year National League playing career that included stops in Pittsburgh, Boston, New York, and St. Louis. His finest moments had come with the Cardinals. St. Louis acquired him from the Giants midway through the 1926 season, and the player known as Billy the Kid made an immediate impact, on the field and in the clubhouse. Southworth batted .320 that summer and delighted fans with his "pepper and his hustle." The Cardinals were in the middle of a heated pennant race when dissension threatened to tear them apart. Although a newcomer, Southworth sensed what was happening, and he knew that if the carping didn't stop soon the Cardinals' season would be ruined. One day, he invited the main antagonists to a players-only clubhouse meeting. He convinced them that they were in danger of "fighting themselves out of the pennant race." By the time he had finished with his oratory, the leaders of the various cliques were shaking hands. The Cardinals won their first pennant in fifty years, and then knocked off Babe Ruth's Yankees in the World Series. Grover Cleveland Alexander struck out New York slugger Tony Lazzeri with the bases loaded in the seventh inning of game seven, and then pitched two more scoreless innings to clinch the championship.

The turning point of the season, however, was the clubhouse meeting Southworth had initiated. And that point was not lost on Rickey and Breadon, who began to view Southworth as a prime managerial candidate. When the Cardinals braintrust was looking for a man to manage the Red Wings, they immediately thought of Billy the Kid. They felt he was ready to match wits with such International League managerial legends as Baltimore's Jack Dunn. Southworth knew his playing career was winding down and he wanted to stay in baseball, so he accepted the Cardinals offer.

That 1928 Red Wings club featured several veterans, including graybeard catcher Hank Gowdy, a hero of the Boston Braves Miracle Team of 1914, and Tony Kaufmann, a former pitcher with the Chicago Cubs. Young shortstop Charley Gelbert was the top prospect. He would respond well to Southworth's nurturing and finish with a .340 batting average. Reinforcements would come in July when Rickey sent down second baseman George "Specs" Toporcer, who would go on to become one of the most popular players in Wings history. But for the most part, the team was regarded as fairly run-of-the mill, which made the job Southworth did all the more remarkable.

Led by Billy the Kid's managing and his bat, Rochester set the pace in the International League for several weeks, but that all changed after a disastrous midseason road trip in which several starters were injured. By August 20, the Wings had dropped from first to fifth place. In an

What's in a Name?

On February 5, 1928, the *Democrat and Chronicle* reported that Rochester's baseball club was staging a "Name the team" contest. The winner would receive $50 and a season pass to all home games. The response was phenomenal. During the ten days of the contest, the club received roughly seventeen hundred letters. On February 28, club president Warren Giles announced that the team would forevermore be known as the Red Wings. Three people suggested the name, but Frank Spofford was declared the winner because his letter was received well before the two other backers of the Red Wings moniker. According to the newspaper, Giles had several reasons for adopting Red Wings. He liked the fact that no other team in organized baseball had a similar name. It also conveyed Rochester's position as a unit or wing of the St. Louis Cardinals organization. Lastly, and most simply, Cardinals were birds with red wings. In keeping with the Red Wing theme, Giles envisioned a logo on the team's caps and uniforms where wings protruded from a baseball. A theme built around Rochester's reputation as the Flower City didn't inspire Giles, who saw pitfalls in a floral approach. Reported the *Democrat and Chronicle* on February 28: "Giles and others who aided in selection of the name felt that baseball players might not care to have as part of their uniforms a bud, a carnation or rose emblem."

As it turned out, the nickname continued to work years later when Rochester decided its longtime working agreement with the Cardinals was for the birds. The Red Wings switched affiliations before the 1961 season, signing on with the orange-winged Baltimore Orioles. Before becoming the Red Wings, Rochester switched nicknames about as often as New York Yankees owner George Steinbrenner switched managers. From its inception in 1877 until 1928, Rochester's teams were known at various times as the Live Oaks, Jingoes, Bronchos, Hustlers, Colts, Brownies, Champs, Chiefs, Beau Brummels, Hop Bitters, and Tribe.

attempt to help bolster their burned-out pitching staff, Rickey promoted Laurence Irvin, Willard Ford, and Charles Foreman. The young arms would help invigorate the slumping team. By the start of September, the Wings had climbed within two games of first-place Buffalo with a doubleheader sweep of Dunn's Baltimore Orioles in front of twelve thousand fans at the Bay Street park. Toporcer drove in the tying and winning runs in the bottom of the ninth of the nightcap, and the fans stormed onto the field and carried him to the clubhouse on their shoulders.

Adversity, though, struck again—this time literally—during the final regular season series in Montreal between the Wings and Royals. While returning to their hotel, a taxicab carrying seven Rochester players collided head-on with another car. Starting catcher Bob Morrow, who was hitting .290 at the time, broke a bone and was sidelined for the remainder of the season. The Wings, however, had overcome several injuries throughout the year. Young players had responded before for Southworth, and that would happen again. James "Rip" Collins, a power-hitting first baseman just called up from Danville, made an immediate impact. He hit four home runs down the stretch, helping the red hot Wings keep pace with Buffalo. The race would come down to the final day. If the Bisons won their last game, the Wings would be forced to sweep their doubleheader with Montreal.

Southworth decided to start Herman "Wheezer" Bell, a grizzly pitcher who had paced the Wings with a 19–8 record and twenty complete games. Bell struggled in the early innings but settled down to pitch a three-hitter as Rochester won 5–2. He was supported offensively by Tony Kaufmann's three runs batted in. Kaufmann, a veteran pitcher, had been called upon by Southworth to play the outfield after the Wings were decimated by injuries. He wound up hitting .402 during the final ten days of the season.

News reached Montreal that the Bisons had won, meaning Rochester's only chance of capturing the International League pennant would be by taking the second game as well. In the clubhouse between games, Southworth surveyed his pitching staff long and hard. After what seemed an eternity, Specs Toporcer broke the locker room silence.

"Who will it be, skipper?" he asked the Wings manager.

"Fellows, there's one fellow in this room who can win this one—and the pennant—for us," Southworth said, confidently. "He just can't lose. His name is Wheezer Bell."

The players broke into spontaneous applause.

"Wheezer," Southworth said, putting his arm around Bell's shoulder, "You're the one to sew up the championship for us. . . . Change your sweatshirt and stand them on their heads."

The tired but game Bell took the mound and received plenty of support from his inspired teammates. The Wings staked him to a four-run lead in the first, and Collins added a homer in the later innings as Rochester won 5–0. It was its first pennant in seventeen years, and it had come by the narrowest of mathematical margins: .001. The Wings (90–

74) and Buffalo (92–76) had finished in a tie in the won-lost column, but Rochester had the advantage in the percentage column.

The fact the Wings went on to lose to Indianapolis in the Junior World Series mattered little. The town was smitten with the job Southworth had done and was looking forward to the 1929 season and the opening of its brand new ballpark.

Shortly after Rochester's season ended, St. Louis clinched the National League pennant to earn a spot in the 1928 World Series against the Yankees. The year before, New York's Murderers Row lineup, featuring Babe Ruth and Lou Gehrig, had easily dispensed with the Pittsburgh Pirates in four straight. The same fate would await manager Bill McKechnie's Cardinals. Ruth hit three homers in one game and batted .625 for the series, while Gehrig smacked four homers in four games as the Bronx Bombers swept St. Louis. The ease with which the Yankees handled the Cardinals did not set well with owner Breadon, who publicly criticized McKechnie for pitching to Ruth. In reality, even if the Cardinals had intentionally walked Ruth the entire series, the Yankees would have won. Nonetheless, Breadon was so angry he decided a managerial change was in order. Before the 1929 season, he demoted McKechnie to Rochester and promoted Southworth to St. Louis. But Rochester had not seen the last of Billy the Kid.

3

A Diamond in the Bushes

It was like going from a barn to a palace.
—Spectator *Jack Lustik*
on the Red Wings move
from Baseball Park on Bay Street
to Red Wing Stadium in 1929

The anticipation had been building for weeks. After several years of grumbling about the deteriorating conditions at rickety Baseball Park on Bay Street, Rochesterians were finally getting a new ballpark. And what a park it was! Constructed of steel and concrete, Red Wing Stadium was state of the art, of quality equal to most major-league parks. The price tag for the new "baseball plant," as sportswriters fondly referred to it, was roughly $415,000. The bill was footed entirely by the Wings parent club and owner, the St. Louis Cardinals. There had been some haggling initially over the location of the ballpark, but the Cardinals, Red Wings, and city officials eventually agreed upon a tract of land on Norton Street near where the Ringling Brothers, Barnum and Bailey Circus pitched its big top during its annual visit to town.

In the days leading up to the stadium christening on May 2, 1929, demand for tickets became so great that thousands of bleacher seats were added, boosting capacity to approximately nineteen thousand, about double that of the Bay Street park and nearly eight thousand more than the Norton Street park would hold after its renovation in the late 1980s. The new ballpark was designed by George W. Thompson, one of the nation's foremost stadium architects. Thompson, who hailed from Syra-

29

cuse, also had designed the Cardinals' minor-league park in Houston—after which Red Wing Stadium was modeled—and the new football stadium at the University of Florida. For weeks leading up to the Red Wings home opener, there was concern about whether the project would be completed on time. April had been rainier than normal, delaying certain aspects of the construction, including painting. But thanks to the indefatigable efforts of project superintendent Harrison Dann and his workers, the ballpark was completed just in the nick of time. The day before the opener, Dann shook hands with Red Wings president Warren Giles at home plate and told him: "It's yours, take it. I've completed my job. It's in your hands from now on." Dann couldn't stop worrying about the House the Cardinals Built, however. "He was as nervous as a race-horse at the post all day even though his job was finished," wrote *Democrat and Chronicle* sports editor Joseph T. Adams. "He walked a short marathon as he tried to find something that needed his attention." The players from the Wings and the visiting Reading Keystones who practiced on the field that day were impressed with the ballpark. One of them referred to it as "the Taj Mahal of the minor leagues." The three or four hundred kids who had played hooky from school to take a peek also were in awe. "Wow!" was the word most of them used when asked their impressions by reporters.

The night before the opener, the American Legion of Monroe County held its annual banquet to honor the ball club at Rochester's Seneca Hotel. Branch Rickey, the Cardinals vice president, served as the guest speaker, and he proved once again that he was a master at ingratiating himself to an audience. "I believe [the Cardinals purchase of the Red Wings] is the best investment the organization has ever made," Rickey said, evoking a rousing ovation from several hundred attendees. Rochester baseball fans were primed to christen their new ballpark the following afternoon. Now, if only the weather would cooperate.

In those days, a "game today" flag on top of the Powers Hotel in downtown Rochester informed fans whether Red Wings home games would be played or postponed because of the weather. Hours before Rochester's 1929 home opener, the flag flapped, in the words of venerable *Democrat and Chronicle* columnist Henry Clune, "soggily and dispiritedly from its newly painted staff." In an interview 66 years later, spectator George Christoff said, "I remember being really scared that the game was going to be called off. I wore a green raincoat that day and walked two miles in the pouring rain to get there. I kept my fingers crossed all the way."

Christoff had plenty of company on his way to the ballpark. The streets in and around the stadium were jammed with thousands of peo-

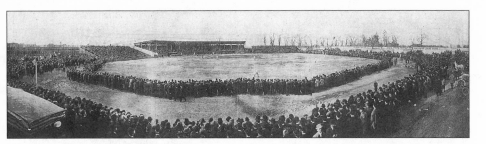

An overflow crowd of thirteen thousand fans—five thousand above capacity—
turned out for the first game at Baseball Park on Bay Street in 1908.
Courtesy of the George Christoff collection.

ple, many of whom had taken the trolley to the station a block from the
ballpark. A parade of nearly one hundred automobiles made its way
north from downtown. In the lead car was Frank Rutz, who, in the
words of one fan, "was the grand marshal of everything. You couldn't
hold a parade unless he was there."

Tickets to the new park ranged from $1.50 for a box seat to fifty
cents for admission to the bleachers. Christoff, a teenager at the time,
invested fifty cents of his hard-earned money for a bleacher ticket. The
memory that investment produced proved priceless. "Outside of family
moments, like my marriage and the birth of our children and grandchil-
dren, walking into that ballpark for its opening was one of the most
moving events of my life," he recalled. "I remember everything being so
green. Even the outfield walls were green. In those days you didn't have
the advertising signs you have all over the place now." Most agreed it
was a significant improvement over the Red Wings' previous home on
Bay Street. "It was like going from a barn to a palace," said Jack Lustik,
whose son, Len, would become the Wings official scorer for more than
two decades. "At Bay Street, everything was wooden: the seats, the
fences, the stands. It was so far behind the times, getting food and everything. [At Red Wing Stadium] you thought you were in a new world."

The outfield fences at Baseball Park had rotted so badly that "young
fans and hoodlums, using crowbars and axes managed to rip holes
through them and stream into games," an unidentified fan said. To guard
against similar shenanigans at Red Wing Stadium that day, the back of
the outfield fences was protected by two rows of barbed wire and additional policemen.

The rainy weather forced the opening day ceremonies to be shortened. Rochester manager Bill McKechnie and his Reading counterpart,

The debut of Red Wing Stadium in 1929 dominated the *Democrat and Chronicle*'s front page. Courtesy of the *Democrat and Chronicle/Times-Union*.

Harry Hinchman, jointly raised the American flag as a marching band played. Newspaper accounts reported that Rochester mayor Joseph C. Wilson was scheduled to throw out the ceremonial first pitch but changed his plans because of the damp, chilly conditions. "He was held in reserve," Adams wrote in the *Democrat and Chronicle*. "George J. Nier, commissioner of public safety, arose after the players had marched to home plate, and tossed out a brand, new baseball. Then, he dropped down to his blankets again." Michael Ward, a spectator that day, recalled the toss in vivid detail decades later. "The guy had a lousy arm," Ward joked. "He rolled the damn thing most of the way."

Columnist Clune captured the soggy day in his inimitable prose in a story headlined: MANY DUCKS SEE OPENER. "Hardy fellows braved the elements without earmuffs and long underwear. Some of them wore mitts, though only on one hand. The Rochester club opened its new park —and what a beautiful baseball plant it is—under most inauspicious conditions. The weather would have been appropriate enough for a Hobart-Rochester football game in late November; for the beginning of the baseball season it was terrible." As bad as the weather was, it did not deter a huge crowd from showing up; 14,885 fans herded through the turnstiles, and although the turnout was less than the 20,000 some had expected, it was still the largest audience to watch a baseball game in Rochester to that point. Wrote Adams: "Politicians, policemen, city officers, leaders in business and the professionals sat elbow to elbow with office boys, delivery drivers, pool sharks and some of the rest of us."

The home team didn't give them much to cheer about. Reading's Ed Holley pitched a two-hitter as the Keystones shut out the defending International League champion Red Wings, 3–0. Rip Collins and Bob Morrow were the only Rochester players to stroke hits. Red Wings pitcher Lefty Irwin suffered the loss despite pitching a fine game, yielding only two runs in eight innings. The game was an omen for Irwin. He eventually earned the nickname "Unlucky Larry" because the Red Wings rarely scored in the games he pitched.

In flowery prose the next day, Adams was complimentary of the visiting players, the new ballpark, and Rochester's fans: "In the absence of sunshine or fair weather, Ed Holley, Reading pitcher, became the shining figure of the opening baseball contest at the new Red Wing Stadium yesterday. . . . It was well played, whether one considers the weather or not, and it was more than well played when one takes into account the fact that rain fell through most of the pastime, in drizzly form or in brisk showers. It rained hard, both before and after the contest, but no ugly weather was going to spoil the enthusiasm of the city's fandom."

The game wound up literally being a hit with the father of spectator Michael Ward. At one point, a batter lined a foul ball that ricocheted off one of the metal support beams and clocked Ward's father in the noggin. "Dad was a little groggy for awhile," Ward recalled in a 1995 interview. Ward's uncle also had an encounter with a foul ball. He attempted to catch one with his straw hat, and the ball ripped a hole through it. "It was a rough day for the family," Ward noted wryly. "They paid dearly for their efforts, and wouldn't you know it, neither one wound up getting a ball."

Mike Roman also was in the stands that day. He was a high school senior at the time and had received permission from his mother to skip school and take time off from his part-time job delivering milk by horse and buggy. "It was a legitimate excuse to miss school in those days because opening day was like a legal holiday in this town," Roman said. "It was an even bigger deal that day because of the new park. The whole town was bursting with pride." Roman sat in the bleachers just past third

There Used to Be a Ballpark

Frontier Field is the seventh ballpark in the 113-year history of professional baseball in Rochester. From 1877 to 1885, Rochester played at The Hop Bitters Grounds on North Union Street on the city's east side. In 1886, the Rochester ball club moved about a mile to the east to Culver Field at the corner of University Avenue and Culver Road. A fire destroyed that park shortly after the 1892 season, forcing the franchise to move to another city. When professional baseball returned in 1895, games were played at Riverside Park. In 1898, a new park was constructed at the corner of University and Culver, and the team played there for nine summers. Rochester laws prohibiting ballplaying on the Sabbath resulted in a number of nineteenth-century home games being played at Windsor Park, north of the city on the shores of Lake Ontario. In 1908, the club began playing its games at Baseball Park on Bay Street. That eight-thousand-seat wooden ballpark remained home to Rochester baseball until May 2, 1929, when the team moved into Red Wing Stadium. The new stadium was regarded as the "Taj Mahal of the minor leagues" when it first opened. For years, opposing players would comment to Red Wings players, coaches, and managers how much they would love to play in a place like Red Wing Stadium. The ballpark was renamed Silver Stadium on August 19, 1968, in honor of Morrie Silver, whose idea for a community stock drive in the late 1950s helped keep professional baseball in Rochester. In 1981, there was talk about building a new park, but those plans died after a messy proxy fight. Instead, the stadium underwent a $4.5 million facelift before the start of the 1987 season. A few years later, the new stadium idea was broached again, and after lengthy public debate, local and state funding was procured to build Frontier Field on a plot of land in downtown Rochester in the shadow of the world headquarters of Eastman Kodak Company.

base. In the stands beyond the left-field fence, which in those days were located nearly five hundred feet from home plate, a ragtag band played "Jingle Bells" instead of "Take Me Out to the Ballgame."

Lamented Adams in his game story: "If we only get some sun, it will be great fun to sit in those new stands with a bag of peanuts, a stub pencil and a scorecard and watch the Red Wings do their stuff. The only folks who had the breaks at yesterday's game were the newswriters. They were paid to be there." Roman, like the thousands of others who had to buy their way in, didn't allow the rain to ruin the moment. "The weather was bad, but you made the best of it," said Roman, who would spend nearly four decades working as a Rochester firefighter. "The day was oh so special, you almost didn't notice the rain. I just remember it being a lot of fun. And I remember staying until the end. We felt so much pride having a ballpark that in those days was the envy of many major-league cities. The opening of that stadium was without question the start of a special era in Rochester baseball."

4

BillyBall

*As far as I'm concerned, Billy Southworth will
always be the greatest manager of all-time. A fellow that
didn't break his neck for Billy was no good at heart.
Our gang just outdid themselves for the grandest fellow
I know.*
—former Red Wings and Cardinals great *Pepper Martin*

It became obvious during the 1929 season that the Cardinals' commitment to Rochester went well beyond the building of a new stadium. St. Louis had stocked its top farm club with several talented players who would help build a baseball dynasty in Rochester before being called up to the big leagues to join the Cardinals' infamous "Gas House Gang."

One of those hot prospects was Rip Collins, the strapping first baseman who had contributed mightily to the Wings' pennant drive during the final weeks of the previous campaign. Collins was scheduled to spend all of the '29 season in Rochester—great news for Wings fans; not so great news for International League pitchers who figured to be victimized by his slugging. Collins was joined in the infield by second baseman George "Specs" Toporcer, shortstop Heinie Sand, and third baseman Joe "Poison" Brown. During that season, the sure-handed foursome would help the Wings turn 225 double plays, breaking by thirty-two the professional baseball record established by Cincinnati.

The main beneficiaries of the airtight defense would be a pitching staff that had been strengthened by the addition of Paul Derringer and James "Tex" Carleton, two highly touted Cardinal prospects who would combine for thirty-five victories in 1929. Talent also was abundant in the outfield. It featured Ray Pepper, a three-sport star at the University of Alabama; Bob "Red" Worthington, one of the finest clutch hitters in Wings history; and George Watkins, a fierce competitor who batted .337 and kept the club loose with his bench jockeying. "Watkins," wrote McCarthy, "was an atom of energy who reckoned the season a failure because the team failed to win 162 straight games. He never wanted to lose. He possessed the vocal apparatus to keep his colleagues on edge every minute of the day." Watkins constantly rode Carleton, whom he had known for years. He admired Tex's talent and believed that if the young pitcher applied himself he would become a first-rate big leaguer. Carleton responded to Watkins's friendly barbs by winning 18 of 25 decisions to lead the league in winning percentage and earned run average (2.71). Among those wins was a no-hitter against Toronto.

Despite losing the first game in their new ballpark, the Wings got off to a strong start. Collins proved early on that his home run barrage from the previous season was no fluke. On May 4, two days after the stadium dedication, Collins ripped the first home run at 500 Norton Street as Rochester defeated Jersey City 8–3, before 15,127 fans. Besides a place in the Wings history book, the three-run blast earned Collins a pair of shoes, free dry cleaning for one suit, and a new tire and tube for his car. There would be many more long-ball gifts for Collins that summer. He would go on to hit a then-Rochester record thirty-eight homers and lead the league in runs batted in with 134.

Although things were going well for Collins and his teammates, the same could not be said for the parent club in St. Louis. The Cardinals struggled from the beginning and were stuck in fourth place on July 24 when St. Louis owner Sam Breadon decided to reverse the decision he had made in the off-season. "Deacon Bill" McKechnie, whose sin it was to allow his hurlers to pitch to Babe Ruth in the 1928 World Series, returned to his managing post in St. Louis, and Billy Southworth was sent back to Rochester. Southworth's failure in his first at-bat as a big-league skipper gnawed at his pride, but if he had to return to the minors, there was no better place to be than Rochester. Wings fans were happy to see Southworth back. They gave him a rousing ovation when he walked up to home plate with the lineup card before his first Wings home game in 1929. They remembered the masterful job he had done the previous summer when he managed a team that had no business being in a pennant race to the International League crown. It took only a couple of games for Southworth to realize that this Wings team was vastly more talented than the one he had managed before. The defense was clearly superior, as evidenced by its proclivity for turning the double

Double Trouble

According to baseball lore, double plays are a pitcher's best friend. During the summer of 1929, Rochester Red Wings hurlers had more "best friends" than a New York State Lottery winner. That season, the Wings established a professional baseball record by turning 225 double plays, surpassing by 31 the previous mark set by the Cincinnati Reds. The main initiators of the "twin killings" were shortstop Henry "Heinie" Sand and second baseman George "Specs" Toporcer. Sand started 65 double plays and was involved in a total of 154, while Toporcer was on the front end of 54 and participated in 145. Wrote Rochester baseball historian Bill McCarthy: "What a digger-up team Specs and Heinie proved to be. They saved wobbling pitchers and halted enemy rallies by the perfect—and habitual—manner in which they executed lightning double plays. One a day was a poor afternoon. On more than one occasion, they ripped off four and five of them." Although Sand and Toporcer were the focal point, this was not by any means a two-man act. In fact, twenty-two different Wings fielders contributed to the record.

The Wings' infield of first baseman James "Rip" Collins, third baseman Joseph "Poison" Brown, Sand, and Toporcer were so intent on beating the Reds record that rumors abounded that Rochester pitchers were intentionally walking hitters to set up double plays. Billy Southworth, who managed the 1929 team, said in an interview nearly twenty years later that that happened only once.

"We had made 193 double plays and the boys wanted to tie the big-time record set by Cincinnati," he recalled. "We were impatient to do it. We were way out in front this day and could afford the gamble. Along the middle of the game the boys ran into the dugout for their turn at bat. All at once, someone asked if 'Wheezer' Bell couldn't pass the first opponent to come up in the next inning. I said, 'Nothing doing.' But the rest of them had perked up and they began putting on the pressure. They were wonderful boys, were playing major-league caliber ball, and I finally agreed. Bell walked the first batter to face him and the next batter slapped a ground ball to Toporcer or Sand—I've forgotten which—and it was an easy double play.

"In the next inning, it was [center fielder George] Watkins, I believe, who made an almost impossible catch of a Texas Leaguer and doubled a runner off second. That broke the record and the boys were happy. We got 30 more of them before the finish."

For good measure, the Wings also turned two triple plays that season.

Left to right: Rip Collins, Specs Toporcer, Heinie Sand, and Joe "Poison" Brown. Courtesy of the *Democrat and Chronicle/Times-Union.*

play. And the offense was more proficient, too. There wasn't a lot of juggling to do when the heart of your batting order featured the likes of Collins, Worthington (.327 batting average, 202 hits, 113 RBI), and Watkins (.337, 110 runs scored). This time around, Southworth didn't have to sweat out a pennant race because there wasn't one; the Wings easily outdistanced second-place Toronto by eleven games.

Again, Rochester would come up on the short end in postseason play, losing the Junior World Series to Kansas City, five games to four. The championship game at Red Wing Stadium went ten innings and featured one of the most controversial rhubarbs in Rochester baseball history. With the score tied and two on in the bottom of the ninth, Specs Toporcer was called out on strikes. Toporcer, angry beyond belief, argued long and hard that he had checked his swing, but umpire John Goetz saw it differently. "Toporcer froze on the pitch, and it was good enough to be called a strike," Goetz said in an interview years later. Toporcer

was eventually tossed from the game and a report was filed with the
National Association of Baseball.

That fall, the governing body of minor-league baseball ruled that
Toporcer would be suspended for the 1930 season and fined $200. It
also slapped Southworth with a $500 fine for failing to restrain Toporcer.
Within days, Rochester newspapers were flooded with letters from angry
fans who thought the penalty was much too severe. Baseball writers
Joseph T. Adams, Jack Burgess, and Cray Remington ripped the Association for its ruling and pleaded to the executive committee to hear Toporcer's appeal. The committee finally relented and the Toporcer case became
the big story of the Association's annual meeting that December in Chat-
tanooga, Tennessee. Toporcer spoke on his own behalf, and several
prominent baseball people supported him, including Cardinals vice president Branch Rickey, who, according to *Times-Union* baseball reporter Al
C. Weber, "pulled out all oratorial stops in an impassioned 90-minute
speech." The next day the executive committee lifted the year's suspen-
sion. Toporcer's fine was increased to $500 and Southworth's was re-
duced to $250.

Of course, there was more momentous news than Toporcer's "trial"
during the fall and winter of '29. On a black Monday in October, the
stock market crashed, and thousands of Rochesterians lost their jobs and
their life savings. Many sought solace from the trauma and tribulations
of the Great Depression at Red Wing Stadium during the spring and
summer of 1930. The worst of times for the American economy just
happened to coincide with the best of times for Rochester baseball.
Southworth was back for his third season as manager, and many of the
players who had helped the Red Wings run away with the International
League pennant the year before were returning, too. The result was a
team that remains special six decades later. "You could wear your adjec-
tives thin writing of Billy Southworth's 1930 Red Wings, and not do the
club half justice," McCarthy gushed in 1950. "Those boys had spark and
spring, a wealth of class, and as they went on to capture the pennant
with 105 won and 62 lost—the Norton Street Chowder Guild saluted
them as the greatest ever assembled in in the International Wheel. They
were credited with transcending the best of Jack Dunn's seven-time winner at Baltimore. Those Wings of '30 could have zoomed into the first
division of either major loop."

It's easy to see why some would think that "Southworth's Wonder
Boys" might rank as the best minor-league club of all time. Statistically,
the '30 Wings stack up favorably with the great Baltimore clubs of the

early 1920s and the 1937 powerhouse the Yankees assembled in Newark. There were no easy outs in that Wings lineup, which featured seven .300 hitters, four players who scored more than a hundred runs and four who drove in more than a hundred. "Anyone of them," wrote an out-of-town sportswriter, "was capable of charring the stadium lawn with his pyrotechnic shenanigans at the plate." The most offensive of the bunch was Rip Collins, whose 180 RBI is a league record that probably will never be broken. With the exception of shortstop Heinie Sand, the infield that helped break the double play record the season before was back intact. The outfield was solid, too, boasting the clutch-hitting Bob Worthington, the rapidly developing Ray Pepper, and a rough-hewn Oklahoman named John Leonard "Pepper" Martin. When one of the outfielders couldn't play, Southworth didn't hesitate to write his own name on the lineup card. The codger proved he could still handle the bat, hitting a robust .370 in ninety-two games. Veteran Paul Florence started at catcher and was backed up ably by Bubber Jonnard and Earl Smith. The pitching staff was deep in talent. Six hurlers recorded ten or more victories, led by Paul Derringer, who went 23–11 with a 2.89 earned run average. Derringer would go on to win eighteen games for the Cardinals in 1931 and compile a 223–212 record in fifteen big-league seasons. Adding to the Wings best-ever claims was the quality of the competition. The International League was brimming with talent in 1930, yet Rochester still was able to capture the pennant by eight games.

Interestingly, Southworth's boys didn't start the season as if they would be rewriting the record books. Spring training had been costly for the Wings. Worthington chipped a bone in his elbow. Eddie Delker pulled his hamstring so severely he could barely walk. Even Southworth couldn't avoid the injury jinx. While checking the progress of a pitcher during practice one day, Southworth was hit on the hand by a line drive and broke his index finger in two places. The injuries had depleted the Wings, especially in the outfield, where Worthington was a starter and Southworth a key reserve. Rochester general manager Warren Giles phoned St. Louis to ask Branch Rickey for reinforcements. Rickey offered to option the young and seldom-used Pepper Martin to Rochester, but Giles balked. "He won't answer our need," he said, making a rare error in judgment. Rickey sent Martin anyway, and the hustling outfielder wound up, in the words of a sportswriter, "standing the fans on their ear."

Martin had a whale of a season for the Wings, batting .363 with 33 doubles, 18 triples, 20 homers, and 114 RBI. He would become the first player to bash a ball over the center-field wall, some 450 feet from home plate. Most important, he would invigorate his teammates and Rochester fans with his hell-bent style of play. Martin's daring baserun-

James the Ripper

Rochester has been blessed with dozens of great hitters during its 113 years of professional baseball. Players such as Stan Musial, George Sisler, Johnny Mize, Eddie Murray, and Cal Ripken, Jr., all have taken their cuts at 500 Norton Street. But none of them ever had a season in Rochester to match the one turned in by James "Rip" Collins during the summer of 1930. That year, the switch-hitting first baseman batted .376 with 40 homers, 165 runs scored, and an International League record 180 runs batted in. He also set Red Wing standards for hits (234) and total bases (436) as Rochester won the league title and the Junior World Series under manager Billy Southworth. Remarkably, despite the eye-popping statistics, Collins did not win the league's most valuable player award in 1930. Those accolades went instead to Collins's teammate, Specs Toporcer, who batted .307 with 134 runs scored, 21 stolen bases, and 61 RBI.

Collins had some memorable games during his record-setting season. One Sunday afternoon, in a game against Buffalo, more than thirteen thousand fans at Red Wing Stadium gave Collins a standing ovation after he hit for the cycle, and drove in nine runs to tie Rochester's single-game RBI record established by George "Highpockets" Kelly in 1919. He had another big day against Baltimore when he went 4-for-5 with 3 homers and 8 RBI. After the season, Collins was promoted to the St. Louis Cardinals, and he became a card-carrying member of the wild and wacky Gas House Gang. He spent nine productive seasons in the major leagues, his best year coming in 1934 when he hit a National League-leading 35 homers and drove in 128 runs while batting .333. Collins, who had christened Red Wing Stadium by hitting the first homer there in 1929, was immensely popular in Rochester. He continued to live there for seven off-seasons after he had been promoted to the majors.

ning inspired sportswriter Cray Remington to dub him the "Wild Horse of the Osage." "He never went into a bag feet first, preferring the belly slide," wrote McCarthy. "He could muss up a spotless white uniform in 20 seconds and generally needed a shave. The catapulting Pepper was amazing. It used to pull you to your feet to watch him stretch singles into doubles, doubles into triples and then end up in a cloud of dust after a swan dive." No one appreciated Martin more than Southworth, who even as an aging manager near the end of his playing days had a similar style.

Rip Collins. Courtesy of the *Democrat and Chronicle/Times-Union*.

Opponents took their caps off to the 1930 Red Wings, who rolled to a 105–62 record, with seven starters hitting above .300. Courtesy of the Rochester Red Wings.

Despite the addition of Martin, the Wings struggled badly in the early going. As June approached, they were closer to last place than first, and Southworth was growing increasingly frustrated. On May 31, Rochester lost a game to Montreal, largely because veteran center fielder Gene Bailey dropped a fly ball, misjudged another, and booted a grounder. An angry Southworth muttered to himself that he could have done better with his broken finger. On the way back to Rochester that night, Southworth had an idea. He took a catcher's mitt and cut a hole in it large enough for him to put his injured finger through. The next day before the Wings game against Toronto, Southworth went to Maple Leafs manager Steve O'Neill to see if it would be all right for him to use the altered mitt in the game. O'Neill thought Southworth shouldn't play with his finger still broken, but he eventually gave into Billy the Kid's request. "Go ahead and play then," laughed O'Neill. "You won't be able to do us any harm with that finger."

Southworth wasn't sure how he would perform, but he hoped his example of playing despite a broken finger might rouse his team from its slump. Southworth started himself in left field, and wound up leading the Wings to victory. He ripped two hits and made a diving catch to preserve an 11–8 win. O'Neill wasn't laughing after the game. He told Southworth he would not be allowed to play with the special mitt again. In the next series against Buffalo, Southworth attempted to convince Bisons manager "Derby Day" Bill Clymer to let him use it. "What?" Clymer screamed. "After what you did to O'Neill? No way."

Southworth's lesson in determination did not go unnoticed by his players. It wasn't long before the Wings had climbed out of the second division and into first place. Rochester built a six-game lead over second-place Baltimore by mid-August, but several injuries, combined with a pitching slump, enabled the Orioles to cut the lead to one and one-half games. On August 28, the Orioles visited Rochester, riding a hot streak and fully expecting to leave town in possession of first place. Baltimore had a powerful club, led by Joe Hauser, who wound up hitting sixty-three homers, a new professional record. Adding to the Wings' woes, Southworth came down with the flu before the first game of the series. Despite a 103 degree temperature, he managed to play in the first game. Worthington would help ease his pain by hitting a home run in the bottom of the ninth to send the game into extra innings, then winning it in the eleventh with a homer.

Southworth's health worsened, and he was forced to listen to the game on the radio from his bed the following afternoon. Worthington was the hero again, this time ripping a two-run triple to lead Rochester to victory. In the third game, Wings pitcher "Handsome" Johnnie Berly pitched a no-hitter for eight and one-third innings, but the Orioles tied the score to send the game into extra innings again. In the bottom of the tenth, Worthington capped his incredible series by singling home the winning run. The Wings swept the series, and for all intents and purposes the pennant race was over.

Major-league scouts who had been following the talent-rich Wings for weeks couldn't help but notice Worthington's performance. Just before the season ended, the Boston Braves purchased his contract. Berly, the pitcher who had just missed tossing a no-hitter, was signed by the New York Giants. Despite those subtractions, the Wings went on to defeat Louisville five games to three in the Junior World Series. Before the final game, Southworth told a reporter: "I am convinced that we have the best minor league ball club in the country; in fact, the best minor league team I have ever seen." It was indeed a great team, but it wouldn't stay together long.

Before the 1931 season, Branch Rickey did to the Wings what International League opponents could not—he broke up the team. Several prominent players, including Rip Collins, Paul Derringer, and Pepper

Billy's Wonder Boys: 1930 Final Statistics

Batting

Name	G	AB	Runs	Hits	HR	RBI	Avg.
George Anderson	42	92	12	27	1	14	.293
Joe Brown	162	661	153	207	10	68	.313
Rip Collins	167	623	165	234	40	180	.376
Eddie Delker	21	50	6	18	0	8	.360
Paul Florence	100	312	41	93	7	54	.298
Gordon Hinkle	10	28	3	9	0	3	.321
Pepper Martin	135	482	121	175	20	114	.363
Ray Pepper	104	412	67	143	4	78	.347
Billy Southworth	92	276	58	102	6	58	.370
Specs Toporcer	167	622	134	191	1	61	.307
Charley Wilson	142	524	82	157	8	100	.300
Red Worthington	123	467	95	175	8	113	.375

Pitching

Name	G	W	L	ERA
John Berly	30	16	8	2.49
Tex Carleton	37	13	13	5.01
Paul Derringer	41	23	11	2.89
Charles Foreman	33	10	6	3.36
George Grant	39	4	1	4.58
Larry Irvin	34	7	4	5.71
Carlisle Littlejohn	29	8	1	4.99
Bob McGraw	24	10	8	4.05
Fred Ostermueller	13	2	2	4.61
Ira Smith	35	12	7	4.27

Martin, were called up to St. Louis. Worthington and Berly had been sold to other major-league teams. Shortstop Eddie Delker was shipped to Columbus and pitcher Tex Carleton was sent to Houston, where people were going bonkers over a young pitching prima donna by the name of Dizzy Dean. Gone, too, were Specs Toporcer, a two-time league most valuable player, and Joe Brown. Both had been sold to Jersey City for a substantial amount of cash. The only holdovers from Billy's Wonder Boys were pitchers Ira Smith, Charley Foreman, and Larry Irvin; catchers Paul Florence and Bubber Jonnard; and outfielder Ray Pepper. To soften the blow, the Cardinals sent down veteran pitchers Wheezer Bell and

Carmen Hill. Wrote McCarthy: "The Wings of '30 had been plucked clean and fricasseed by Head Chef Rickey after three pennants, and the Little Skipper had to simmer a fresh kettle."

Rickey knew he had almost stripped the cupboard bare, and in an effort to soften the loss of first baseman Collins, the Cardinals vice president convinced future Hall of Famer George Sisler to sign with the Wings. Sisler was thirty-eight at the time and nearing the end of a fabulous career. Twice during his fifteen seasons in the majors "Gorgeous George" had batted over .400, including 1920, when he set a record for most hits in a season (257). When the lifetime .340 hitter reported to camp that spring, he pulled on a minor-league uniform for the first time. Most of the Wings players were in awe of Sisler, but he quickly put them at ease. He would be a calming influence throughout the difficult 1931 season. And despite his declining skills, he would play a crucial role during the pennant drive.

A minor-league record crowd of 19,006 showed up at Red Wing Stadium on May 5 for the home opener, but the fans left disappointed as the Newark Bears won, 4–1. The loss was part of an extremely poor Wings start. On Memorial Day, Rochester was mired in seventh place. It had become apparent that the Wings would not contend with the personnel they had, so Giles signed George "Showboat" Fisher, who had murdered Rochester pitching during his Buffalo Bisons days, and Swampy Wilson, a dependable third baseman. The Wings also were aided by the promotion of outfielder George Puccinelli and pitcher Ray Starr from Houston. Neither player had done much in the Texas League. "Push 'em up Pooch" was hitting only .197, and Starr had yet to pitch. Puccinelli would go on to have a solid season for the Wings with sixteen homers and a .295 average, but his best Rochester moments wouldn't come until the '32 season when he would set a Wings record with a .391 average.

The floundering Starr would wind up paying almost immediate dividends. The Cardinals' indifference toward the young pitching prospect had been perplexing. Two years before, he had hurled a perfect game for Danville, and in 1930 he had won twenty-four games for Shawnee. Starr had grown so frustrated over his situation that he contemplated quitting baseball and returning home to Oklahoma. Southworth caught wind of Starr's situation through the Cardinals grapevine, and urged Giles to sign him. "He's a big fellow, and I'd like to look him over," Southworth told the Wings president. Giles agreed. It would prove to be money well spent.

Southworth could relate to Starr's frustration. While with the New

After fifteen years as a Hall of Fame first baseman, thirty-eight-year-old George Sisler *(left)* helped Billy Southworth's 1931 club win its fourth consecutive pennant by batting .303. Courtesy of the *Democrat and Chronicle/Times-Union.*

York Giants, Billy the Kid could do nothing right in the eyes of autocratic manager John McGraw. When the Giants traded him to the Cardinals in 1926, Southworth felt as if he had found a new lease on his baseball life. He had a hunch that Starr, too, might flourish with a change of venue. The pitcher arrived in Rochester in early June, and because Starr hadn't been used by Houston, Southworth went slowly with him, using him mostly in relief. After a two-inning mop-up stint, Starr was told to get ready for his first start a few days later. "Ray made an unusual request of me," Southworth recalled years later. "He asked if I'd work him one round of batting practice the day of the game he was to start. I hesitated, but finally played a hunch and let him do it. After his first game I became a firm believer in his wish to pitch to the hitters in practice, for his control was hairline. On a couple of occasions when he didn't do it, he was wild." Starr's starting debut for the Wings was in the words of one sportswriter "a humdinger." He went the distance to beat Jersey City, then followed that with a two-hit victory against Buffalo.

Rochester's drive for four was further aided on July 19, when Giles purchased Specs Toporcer back from Jersey City. Starr celebrated the veteran's return by pitching and winning both ends of a doubleheader against Jersey City. The iron-man feat sparked a streak that would see the Wings win eight of nine. On August 9, Southworth asked Starr to work a double shift against Jersey City again, and this time the big right-hander lost a 2–1 decision in the opener, but came back to win the second game 6–1. Eleven days later, Starr made two starts in one day again, equaling the iron-man feat of former Rochester pitcher Henry Heitman. Starr won both games this time as the Wings swept Reading to stay within two games of first place Newark.

Starr wound up leading the International League with a 20–7 mark and a 2.83 earned run average. "He was a great pitcher that year," Southworth recalled. "He'd have won 30 games had he been with us all season." Starr's stamina and willingness to take on extra assignments pulled Rochester into the pennant race.

Another valuable performer was outfielder Ray Pepper. Pepper had a fine season in 1930, but was overshadowed on that star-studded club. There was no overlooking him during the summer of '31. Pepper wound up leading the league in hits (233) while batting .356. He was edged out of the batting title by Newark outfielder Ike Boone, who batted .3561 to Pepper's .3557. Pepper also drove in 121 runs and scored 123. His hitting was especially crucial down the stretch as the Wings sought to nudge out Newark for their fourth straight pennant.

On September 10, the Wings clinched the title by sweeping a doubleheader from the Royals. Carmen Hill and Wheezer Bell were the pitching stars with a pair of two-hitters, but the lasting memory from that day and that season was provided by George Sisler.

Neither team had scored when Sisler stepped to the plate at Red Wing Stadium in the bottom of the ninth of the second game. Gorgeous George had enjoyed a fine season for the Wings. He would finish with a .303 average and, remarkably, would strike out only 17 times in 613 at-bats. In all his years in baseball, he had never been on a pennant winner. That was about to change.

Jocko Conlan, a fan favorite during his Rochester days in the early 1920s, was playing in shallow left field for the Royals that day. Sisler wound up hitting a short fly ball to left, but Conlan lost it in the sun. Wrote *Times-Union* baseball reporter Al C. Weber: "The ball grazed his ear, struck him on the shoulder and bounced away. As Jocko lunged toward the left field foul line, he fell and skidded into the wire fence that fronted the bleachers. His spikes locked in the wire and before he could extricate himself, Sisler had circled the bases." Sisler couldn't stop grinning. It was cheapest homer he had ever hit and yet one of the most satisfying. Sisler would pull a muscle just before the Junior World Series against St. Paul. In a sentimental gesture, Southworth started him in the first game of the series, and Sisler singled in his first at-bat. But he reinjured the muscle, and missed the rest of the postseason. The Wings wound up winning their second straight series title, five games to three, but BillyBall and the dynasty was coming to an end.

Midway through the 1932 season, Southworth was summoned from the Wings dugout during a game. The Cardinals had made a change, transferring Billy the Kid to their other top minor-league affiliate in Columbus, Ohio. Southworth packed his belongings, bid his team farewell, and wished his replacement—Specs Toporcer—good luck.

5

The Great Depression

*Over the winter, we will all forgive and forget.
Next year, there will be a cast of new faces and perhaps,
children, Billy Southworth, the fightingest little guy to
ever step into a pair of baseball slippers, will be the
Moses to lead us out of the wilderness.*
—*Elliot Cushing,* Democrat and Chronicle *sports editor,*
following 1936 season

The immensely popular Southworth was gone, but it took a few days for reality to set in. The Red Wings won their first three games under Toporcer, and he played a big role in the first two. The day after Southworth's departure, Toporcer drove in the winning run with a seventh-inning single as the Wings beat Jersey City 3–2. The next day, the second baseman-manager went 4-for-4 in an 8–2 win over the Skeeters. That made Rochester's record an even 46–46. The Toporcer-led Wings finished a respectable 88–78 but missed the playoffs for the first time in five seasons. One of the few bright spots was Puccinelli, whose .391 average and thirty-one-game hitting streak remain Red Wings records. "Pooch" also hit 28 homers and drove in 115 runs. He was honored on Italian-American Night for his tremendous season and received an automobile from his admirers. Unhappy with the selection, he spent $175 of his own money for an upgraded car the next day, an action that left Red Wings fans simmering.

The hardship of the Great Depression had begun to show its effect at the gate. In 1932 attendance fell to 153,739—nearly half the previous

51

George "Specs" Toporcer was one of the key players in
Rochester's dynasty from 1928 to 1931, and eventually succeeded
Billy Southworth as manager in 1932. Courtesy of the
Democrat and Chronicle/Times-Union.

year's total and the lowest figure since the new ballpark was christened
in 1929. To make ends meet, the Wings' starting lineup stayed together
after the season ended and began a barnstorming tour of local villages
and towns. The first game was September 19 at Perry, with the Red
Wings winning 9–6 before fourteen hundred fans.

Rochester was scheduled to open the 1933 season on April 12 at
Albany, which had replaced Reading in the league, but it was delayed at
Hawkins Stadium by two days of snow. The wait was worth it, however;
"Silent" Jim Winford tossed a five-hitter, and the Wings whipped the
Senators 10–1. Toporcer's Wings remained in the thick of the pennant
race all summer, and the parent Cardinals did what they could to help.
On July 22, St. Louis optioned veteran outfielder Estel Crabtree to Roch-
ester to replace the injured Buster Mills in center. It was expected to be a
quick fix. Instead, the option lasted seven seasons.

Estel Crabtree provided Red Wings fans with arguably the greatest moment
in club history, a miraculous three-run homer in the 1939 playoffs.
Courtesy of the *Democrat and Chronicle/Times-Union.*

Crabtree was a fleet-footed player who batted left and threw right. Born in 1905 in Lucasville, Ohio, he weighed 170 pounds and was "6 feet from arches to hair part" according to the *Democrat and Chronicle*. Crabtree broke into baseball at Dubuque, Iowa, in 1926, hoping to become a triple threat as a pitcher, first baseman, and outfielder. He had developed into an excellent defensive player and a consistent hitter, never batting below .300 in the minor leagues, and had played for the Cincinnati Reds in 1931 and 1932. He seemed to be everything the Wings were waiting for, but it turned out they had to wait a little longer. In his first game, Crabtree suffered a broken jaw when he was hit by a ball while trying to steal second base. It would be weeks before he played again.

On July 10, 1933, the Red Wings beat the Newark Bears 6–1 at Red Wing Stadium. It would have gone down as just another game if not for one important sidelight: it was George Puccinelli's last day as a Red Wing. "Pooch," the hero of Rochester's Junior World Series win in '31, had left many fans steaming after he upgraded the car given him the previous summer. Those feelings did not improve when the outfielder engaged in a salary dispute with the Cardinals in the spring of 1933 and was kept out of big-league camp. Puccinelli sat out the July 10 win over Newark, while a Rochesterian named George Selkirk pinch-hit for Newark pitcher Al Mamaux in the eighth inning. After the game, the clubs announced that Puccinelli and Selkirk would swap teams. The deal was to be for the 1933 season only. St. Louis would retain its rights to Puccinelli and Newark, which owned Selkirk outright, would retain an option on his services. The next day, Rochester won again 6–1 behind a pair of doubles and a run batted in by Selkirk. Puccinelli pinch-hit for pitcher Jim Weaver in the eighth and flied out on the first pitch. Puccinelli was hitting .306 at the time of the trade, with Selkirk at .301.

The Wings were in the pennant race for most of the summer—they closed to a half-game of powerhouse Newark on July 28—but injuries took their toll. Toporcer tore ligaments in his left knee on July 21 and missed several games. Fritz Ostermueller, the ace of the Wings staff and the league's best-hitting pitcher, underwent an emergency appendectomy and missed the final five weeks of the season, finishing 16–7 with a league-best 2.44 ERA. Late in July, first baseman Arthur "What a Man" Shires wrenched his left knee trying to avoid crashing into teammate Charley Wilson while chasing a bloop double in the bottom of the ninth. Shires had torn up the same knee playing for the Boston Braves the season before, and a postgame examination revealed cartilage damage.

Shires had come to the Wings under unusual circumstances that summer. He began the season playing in the American Association for Columbus, one of St. Louis's eight minor-league clubs. Early in June, several club owners complained that Columbus was over the salary limit. Following a hearing, league president F. J. Hickey ordered the Cardinals to relocate several minor leaguers between Columbus and Rochester. An overnight shakeup resulted. St. Louis sent Shires, Wilson, Fred "Sheriff" Blake, and Jim Lindsey to Rochester, while Columbus received infielders Burgess Whitehead, Benny Borgmann and Mickey Heath, plus pitchers Jim Winford and Ed Heusser.

Following his injury, Shires was returned by ambulance to his Baltimore hotel, where he was to spend the night before leaving for Rochester's Highland Hospital the next day. But the injured first baseman surprised everyone the next day when he showed up at the ballpark ready to play. Toporcer put Shires into the lineup and he went 1-for-3, his leg firmly set in a brace. Shire's heroics were the only piece of good news for the Wings, who were embarrassed 18–2. Despite Shires's bravado, the Red Wings needed a new first baseman, and St. Louis called up twenty-year-old Johnny Mize from their Greensboro, North Carolina, club. Mize was a left-handed power hitter who had been optioned to Greensboro by Rochester at the beginning of the '33 season. The Georgia native had turned in a terrific season, hitting .373 with twenty-two homers, and he showed some of that power by homering in his first game for the Wings, a 7–2 win at Jersey City on August 5. He would finish the season with a .352 average, eight homers and 32 RBI in 42 games.

The Depression had hit baseball hard. There were eighteen minor leagues in the National Association in 1932 and only fourteen the following year. In a desperate effort to bring fans out, various promotions were held at ballparks throughout the nation. There was a hundred-yard dash to determine the fastest Red Wing (first prize: $20), accuracy throws from home plate to a barrel stationed at second base ($10), and a blindfolded wheel barrow-rolling contest from the pitcher's mound to home ($5).

And night baseball.

The first night game in the International League had taken place on July 3, 1930, when twelve thousand Buffalo fans watched the Bisons lose to Montreal 5–4. The Cardinals installed lights in Columbus's new Red Bird Stadium in 1932, and the first game on June 17 drew more than twenty-one thousand fans. As the 1933 season opened, plans were underway to bring night baseball to Rochester. Construction began in July, and a schedule of seven night games in August was announced, with the inaugural "owl contest" set for August 7. Each game would start at 8:15, with gates opening at 6:30. All installation contracts were awarded to local contractors. Eight towers—six around the playing field and two on the grandstand roof—were installed at a cost of $23,000, giving Rochester what club officials called the best and most expensive lighting system in the country. The towers were 102 feet high, with two hundred flood-lights furnishing 450,000-watts of power.

Rochester was the sixth International League city to try night base-ball, but the anticipation remained great. Ticket orders came in from all over western New York for the August 7 game against Newark. The excitement was similar to the opening of Red Wing Stadium in 1929, and so was the result. Reading had shut out Rochester 3–0 in the '29 opener, and Newark blanked the Wings 4–0 before more than fifteen thousand fans who paid Sunday prices to see the nocturnal event. Scores of children hung from the light poles to gain a better vantage point.

The *Democrat and Chronicle* described the scene with wonder:

> The ballpark looked like fairy lands. The players, tanned to the tint of an old and well-stained Meerschaum bowl, looked pasty white under the giant lights. Their uniforms were spotless. The green grass of the infield, clipped like a convict's head, was a delicate emerald under the flood of white light. The infield was almost a pastel. The ladies loved it. It appealed to their aestheticism.

Night baseball had indeed been an illuminating experience, and the six subsequent games at Red Wing Stadium were also well received. It would be nearly two years before the majors' first night game was played on May 24, 1935, at Cincinnati's Crosley Field.

The 1933 Red Wings clinched a playoff berth with a week left in the season, but they made a fatal mistake on the season's final day: they let Buffalo get in, too. The Bisons had been battling Toronto for the fourth and final spot under the new playoff system that had been introduced that winter for what newspapers called the Golden Jubilee Championship in celebration of the league's fiftieth anniversary. It was also a way to increase attendance—and therefore revenue—during the Depression. The first-place club would play the runner-up and the third-and fourth-place teams would do battle in a best-of-five series. By beating Rochester in the season finale, the Bisons made the playoffs by a half game over Toronto. At 83–85, Buffalo was the lone participant to play a full 168-game schedule. The second-place Wings had finished 88–77, fourteen and one-half games behind defending league champion Newark, but Rochester capitalized on its new life in the postseason. After losing the first game at Newark, the Wings won three straight to move into the Governors' Cup finals.

Their opponent would be the revitalized Bisons, who had elimi-nated Baltimore in three straight. Local sportswriters dubbed the best-of-seven showdown the "Dream of Dreams Series," but it turned into a nightmare for the favored Wings. After falling behind two games to one, Buffalo outscored Rochester 42–12 to win the series. The deciding game was played under the lights before an overflow crowd of twenty-two thousand at Bison Stadium, an 8–1 Buffalo win that featured an on-field altercation between Toporcer and Wings pitcher "Dutch" Henry. Bison Stadium's capacity was 15,022, but there was no turning away the championship-starved Buffalo fans. By game time, the crowd had so clogged the baselines that scorecard and drink vendors actually walked on the playing field to peddle their merchandise. Buffalo officials turned away another three thousand fans at the gate.

The 1934 season followed a similar pattern for the Wings. A healthier Toporcer was back as player-manager, but a thigh injury limited the up-and-coming Mize to ninety games, though he did hit .339 with 17 homers and 66 RBI. Branch Rickey was so impressed by the numbers Rip Collins had put up with the Cardinals in 1934 that he was willing to part with his rising star in Rochester. Following the '34 season, Rickey purchased Mize's contract from the Wings. And on Christmas Eve, he sold the first baseman to the Cincinnati Reds for $55,000. Fortunately for St. Louis, Cincinnati's judgment was as bad as Rickey's. Despite a terrific spring, Mize was sent back to St. Louis on April 22, 1935, the Reds claiming his thigh injury had not sufficiently healed to risk gambling $55,000. The Cardinals then sent him to Rochester, and Giles pronounced Mize "in perfect physical shape." Reds manager Charlie Dressen was near tears when his front office decided to pass on the youngster, calling Mize the greatest first base rookie he had ever seen.

In the end, Dressen's vision proved 20/20. Mize hit .317 with 12 homers in just 65 games with the '35 Wings. He would go on to play fifteen years in the majors—a career interrupted by three years in the service during World War II—and finish with a .312 batting average and 359 home runs with the Cardinals, Giants, and New York Yankees. After years of being ignored by voters, the "Big Cat" finally was inducted into the Baseball Hall of Fame in 1981.

The Red Wings achieved some measure of revenge by eliminating Buffalo from the 1934 playoff race and once again finished second to Newark at 88–63. Rochester rolled past Albany four games to one in the first round of the playoffs but was again denied a Governors' Cup championship, this time losing in five games to the Toronto Maple Leafs. After Toronto took the first three games, the *Democrat and Chronicle* opined that the Wings had "their backs to the wall, so tight that the mortar marks of the bricks are raising welts."

That December, the Red Wings sold Fritz Ostermueller to the Bos-

ton Red Sox. A Red Wing for four seasons, the chicken farmer from
Quincy, Illinois, had never mastered his control enough to suit team
officials. The months preceding the 1935 season were unlike any that
Red Wings fans had experienced. The club normally named the next
year's manager in December or January, but Toporcer's fate remained in
the air through New Year's Day. There was no lack of support in the
press; the *Democrat and Chronicle* called Toporcer "the outstanding
candidate for the job."

Word finally came on January 4. Toporcer was leaving the Wings.
The bespectacled manager had met with Wings president Warren Giles
twice in December and both times had refused to accept a pay cut from
the $7,100 he made in 1934. Giles also would not budge, saying in a
statement to the press that Toporcer "is not the player he was." Toporcer
was adamant about his stance.

"I feel I am entitled to the same salary which I received for managing the club in 1934," he said, "and I will not accept a penny less."

Toporcer had lived in Rochester since 1923 and had become connected with a local insurance firm. The first infielder to wear glasses in
the majors, he had been in the Cardinals organization for fourteen years.
Still, he took the divorce in stride. "Baseball idols are soon forgotten,"
he said. "Perhaps the time is ripe to plan for a permanent livelihood."

The time apparently was not ripe enough. Toporcer soon landed
with the Syracuse Chiefs, where he became the full-time second baseman.
He remained so popular in Rochester that on April 27, 1935, two hundred Red Wings fans traveled to Syracuse with police inspector James
Collins to present a check to their idol on "Toporcer Day."

Three managerial candidates surfaced immediately in Rochester:
Pat Crawford, a utility infielder with the Cardinals; Burt Shotton, who
had managed the Philadelphia Phillies from 1928 to 1933 (never finishing higher than fourth); and Ray Blades, a former Red Wings and
Cardinals outfielder now managing in Columbus. Some fans had their
own ideas and began circulating a petition around town to bring back
Billy Southworth. The highly successful manager had finished the 1932
season at Columbus after leaving Rochester, then left for a coaching job
with the New York Giants but was now out of baseball.

As the days rolled by and no replacement manager was named, the
press began to ride Giles. "The first impression was that the Wings were
seeking a high-class manager to succeed Toporcer," the *Democrat and
Chronicle* wrote. "Now it seems to have developed into another free-for-
all, with Lefty the bat boy likely to bob up as a serious contender any
day."

Giles thought he had ended the suspense on January 25, when he named Crawford to head the '35 club. Instead, his problems were just beginning. The same day newspapers were trumpeting Crawford's appointment, the thirty-three-year-old infielder was being rushed to Kinston (North Carolina) Memorial Hospital with septicemia, an infection in his blood stream that had localized in his liver.

The news shocked everyone. Estel Crabtree mailed his 1935 contract back to Rochester the day of Crawford's appointment and included a note: "Just heard of your choice for manager, and believe me, you named the right man. Pat Crawford is a splendid fellow and a great leader."

Crawford had developed the infection following a hemorrhoid operation weeks before, and it had grown progressively worse. His temperature had risen to 105 and his doctor said he had a "slight chance" of recovering. Amazingly, he did. Following six blood transfusions, Crawford made steady progress, though his wife said he still had not been informed of his new job in Rochester. Crawford eventually made a full recovery, but he never managed the Wings. On February 16, 1935, Giles named Eddie Dyer, a minor-league manager with the Cardinals for seven years, as Rochester's "assistant manager." Dyer would take over the club until Crawford returned.

He would not be there for long.

The 1935 Wings had been widely considered a pennant contender but they fell apart under Dyer. Blown leads became as common as called strikes, and the new manager was fired on June 1 with the club mired in seventh place at 17–25. The easygoing Dyer, a loyal member of the Cardinals organization for years, had been chosen by Branch Rickey to guide the Wings. Giles had wanted Burt Shotton, a stern, no-nonsense baseball man who had managed Giles's Syracuse Stars in 1927.

This time, Giles got his man.

Dyer accepted his firing with class, even staying in Rochester an extra day to watch from the grandstand as his former club, guided by interim manager Tony Kaufmann, split a doubleheader with Buffalo.

"I don't blame anybody," Dyer said. "If I didn't get the most out of the boys or used bad judgment at times, there's nobody to blame but myself."

Dyer would have better days. In 1946, he was named manager of the St. Louis Cardinals and led the club to a seven-game World Series triumph over the Boston Red Sox. He would manage the Cards for four more seasons, with three second-place finishes and a career winning percentage of .578.

The fifty-one-year-old Shotton arrived five days later from Florida. Tanned and rested after a year away from the game, the former Phillies manager was optimistic he could turn the Wings around. "If you are as glad to get me back as I am to be back, I'm sure we're going to have a pleasant summer," he told Giles upon arriving at the train station.

Pleasant it was not. The Wings continued to flounder, going 43–64 under Shotton to finish in seventh place at 61–91. It was their worst record since Arthur Irwin's 1920 team finished 45–106. Turned off by the underachieving Wings, the fans stayed away. Rochester drew only 94,358 in 1935, by far its worst total since Red Wing Stadium had opened six years earlier.

One player who could have improved the Wings' chances was having the season of his life in Baltimore. George Puccinelli, cut loose by the Cardinals before the season, tore up the International League in 1935. Motivated by his motto that "a homer a day earns any guy's pay," Puccinelli led the eight-team circuit in seven offensive categories, including homers (52), RBI (172), and average (.359), to easily win league MVP honors.

Giles cleaned house in 1936, replacing his entire starting infield and switching minor-league managers, with Shotton going to Columbus and Ray Blades taking over the Wings. Blades had been a player-coach with the 1929 Red Wings championship team, then went on to manage the Columbus Red Birds to Junior World Series titles in 1933 and 1934.

The 1936 team started out strong, challenging for the pennant through the heat of July. But this was a team with nineteen former or future big-leaguers. Egos ran high, and the hunger was not what it would have been on a team of youngsters trying to prove themselves. The "Bladesmen," as the press had begun calling them, edged out Newark for second place and finished 89–66, six games behind league champion Buffalo. In the playoffs, Rochester fell apart and lost to fourth-place Baltimore in six games, losing the finale 13–2 after committing seven errors.

The press was not kind. The game story in the *Democrat and Chronicle* began: "Folding up like a Hawaiian hut in a hurricane, a blundering, fumbling Red Wing team last night passed out of the International League playoffs by booting the Baltimore Orioles into a 13–2 victory before 5,000 disgusted fans at the Stadium."

More bad news followed one week after the '36 season when Giles, the Wings president since 1928, left to become general manager and vice president of the Cincinnati Reds. Giles had been a fixture in Rochester since Branch Rickey commissioned him to move the Cardinals' top farm team from Syracuse to Rochester in 1928. Offered a $12,000 contract by the Reds, he resigned on September 19 and took club secretary Gabe Paul—whose career began as the Red Wings mascot—with him.

Giles would go on to a distinguished career as one of baseball's top executives, serving as Reds president from 1946 to 1951 and then taking over as National League president until 1969. He was elected to the Baseball Hall of Fame in 1979. Paul would also move on to better things, as president of the Cleveland Indians (1961–71) and the New York Yankees (1973–77).

The Cardinals moved quickly to replace Giles, naming Oliver B. French as the Wings' new president two days after Giles's resignation. French, a native of Charleston, Missouri, had been part of the Cardinals organization since 1929, most recently as president of the Asheville, North Carolina, club in the Piedmont League.

If 1936 was full of great expectations, the following season was filled only with question marks. The '37 Wings featured rookies who had played primarily in classes C and D, and they were given little chance to compete for a pennant. "Rochester has lost all its class," wrote the *Newark Star-Eagle* on the eve of the opener.

The Red Wings christened $1 million Roosevelt Stadium in Jersey City with a dramatic opening day win on April 23. Playing before 31,234 —the largest crowd in minor-league history at that time—Rochester beat the Skeeters 4–3 in twelve innings when a rookie first baseman named Walter Alston drove in Estel Crabtree from second on a single to left. It was Alston's fourth hit of the day, and speculation began that this new ballplayer would one day find himself in the Baseball Hall of Fame. Alston would indeed land in Cooperstown, but not as a player. Working under the pressure of twenty-three one-year contracts beginning in 1954, Alston managed the Brooklyn–Los Angeles Dodgers to four World Series titles.

The prized Red Wings rookie was speedy center fielder Johnny Hopp, who had hit the first home run at Roosevelt Stadium in the opener. The next day, Hopp was presented with a three-foot bronze key to the city. The opening day win was not the sign of things to come, however. The green Red Wings struggled under Blades and were virtually eliminated from the playoffs on September 3, losing 19–0 to Montreal at Royal Stadium. A former University of Rochester ace named Gerry Zornow made his International League debut that day, pitching to five Royals in the fifth inning. He retired only one, allowing three hits and a walk. Zornow would never pitch for the Wings again, but he would experience great success in Rochester as president and chairman of Eastman Kodak Company.

Norbert "Nubs" Kleinke gave fans something to cheer about, winning eleven consecutive games en route to a 19–8 record and a league-high 150 strikeouts. But the '37 Wings landed in sixth place at 74–80, a

Slingin' Sammy Gives Baseball a Fling

When Sammy Baugh was a young boy growing up in Temple, Texas, in the 1920s, he and his friends would spend lazy summer afternoons at a filling station, listening to Yankees games on one of the few radios in town. Announcers would paint colorful word pictures of Babe Ruth and Lou Gehrig in action, and Baugh would fantasize about playing ball for the Bronx Bombers. "I'd always wanted to be a big-league ballplayer," he recalled in 1995 in a Texas accent as thick as an armadillo's shell. "Of course things don't always turn out as planned, now do they?"

No, they don't. Baugh wound up making a name for himself slinging pigskin rather than horsehide. A star quarterback with the Washington Redskins from 1937 to 1952, Slingin' Sammy was named to the National Football League's seventy-fifth anniversary team. That's not to say he didn't give professional baseball a shot, because he did. In fact, he spent part of the 1938 season playing shortstop for the Rochester Red Wings, the St. Louis Cardinals' top farm team at the time. As his statistics attest, Baugh was hardly the most productive player to perform at 500 Norton Street. In thirty-seven games, he batted just .183 with a triple, a home run, and eleven runs batted in. "I didn't exactly set the damn league on fire," he said.

Baseball Hall of Famer Rogers Hornsby took notice of Baugh during a national baseball tournament in the summer of '37. He told Baugh that Cardinals farm director Branch Rickey would be interested in talking to him about signing a professional baseball contract. Rickey was aware that Baugh, a football All-American at Texas Christian University, was already committed to play for the NFL's Redskins, so he signed him to a baseball contract for the following year. The agreement included a clause that enabled Baugh to leave baseball in late August so he could attend football training camp. Baugh wound up leading Washington to the 1937 NFL title during his rookie season, but in a football exhibition a month after the championship game, he injured his sternum. A few weeks later, he reported to the Cardinals' spring training camp in Florida, but was in such pain he could barely swing a bat. St. Louis assigned him to Columbus, Ohio, and midway through the summer promoted him to Rochester.

Although he struggled during games, Baugh was a fan favorite. To take advantage of his marquee value as a football star, the Red Wings occasionally staged pregame throwing contests involving Baugh and several of his teammates. A barrel was placed at second base, and Baugh would attempt to throw a football into it from behind home plate. His fellow Wings tried the same thing, using baseballs. Baugh, to the delight of the fans and the chagrin of his teammates, usually won.

After the 1938 season, Rickey attempted to sign Baugh to another baseball contract. "This time, Mr. Rickey didn't put in a clause for me to leave early for football," he said. "It didn't take no damn genius to make up my mind about which road I should travel." That road eventually took him to the Pro Football Hall of Fame in Canton, Ohio.

distant thirty-six games behind the incredible Newark Bears, a collection of future New York Yankees who finished 109–43. Blades, playing under a one-year contract, blamed himself for the Red Wings' failures. "I made more mistakes than all the other guys on the club put together," he said.

◇

The '38 Wings fared better under Blades, finishing third at 80–74. Hopes were high when the Wings won the first two games of their playoff series at Newark and a huge crowd, complete with a band and radio crew, greeted the club upon their return to Lehigh Valley Station. There would be little to cheer about in the next several days; Newark rallied from a three games to one deficit to win the series. It was the Red Wings' bats that went into hibernation early against the Bears, managing only one run in the final twenty-eight innings. When the Wings returned from Newark after game seven, they were met at the train station only by their wives.

Despite the disappointing finish, Blades had impressed St. Louis brass and the club named him to run the Cardinals in 1939. Almost immediately, the name of Billy Southworth began to reverberate throughout Rochester as fans clamored for "The Kid" to replace Blades. This time their prayers were answered: Oliver French brought Southworth back to Rochester after a seven-year absence.

Southworth had endured a roller-coaster ride through baseball since leaving as Red Wings manager during the 1932 season. He caught on as coach and right-hand man under New York Giants manager Bill Terry, his good friend, in 1933, but the two fiery personalities clashed and Southworth left the Giants at the end of the season. He went back to Columbus and worked as a salesman, but his heart remained in baseball. He tried to convince Branch Rickey that he had mellowed, but it wasn't until 1935 that the Cardinals boss gave Southworth a second chance, naming him manager of the Class B Asheville Tourists in the Piedmont League. The president of the Tourists was Oliver French, and the two hit it off from the start. Southworth led Asheville to the Piedmont League's first-half title but dropped the playoff finals to the Richmond Colts four games to two.

During the '36 season, Southworth made one of his trademark diving catches and injured ligaments of all the ribs on his right side. It was the end of his playing career, but his managerial rebirth was just taking off. Southworth's talents were noticed by Memphis Chicks owner Tom Watkins, and when his club fell to last place in August 1936, Watkins asked Rickey if Southworth could take over his team. The Chicks were not affiliated with the Cardinals, but Rickey agreed on the condition that St. Louis could have Southworth back at any time. Memphis was a Class A team, and Rickey felt Southworth had earned the chance to move up to a higher level.

In 1937, Southworth rebuilt the Chicks into a second-place club. One of his players was nineteen-game winner Del Wetherell, a Rochester winter resident who had pitched for Southworth's 1932 Red Wings club. "It's a pleasure to pitch for Billy," Wetherell said. "If things don't go well, he comes out and asks you how you feel. If you feel all right, he just gives you a pat on the back, says something encouraging and you'd be surprised how much it helps."

When Blades left Rochester to run the Cardinals after the '38 season, French jumped at the chance to promote his old friend from Asheville. And Southworth, who was only forty-four, was delighted to be back. "In Rochester, we were given Red Wing tags to put on the handles of our suitcases," Southworth recalled. "And after I left, I kept that tag on my grip, feeling that it would somehow help to get me back. Last year, however, I sort of lost hope of ever returning so I took it off. Now I'd like to have another one to put on there for good."

Southworth's first impression of his new club was not a favorable one. "The International League will have to be a lot weaker than when I saw it last if we are going to get by with this ball club," he said from the Wings' spring training complex in Winter Garden, Florida. One week later, after the Red Wings had destroyed a pair of semipro teams by scores of 24–2 and 23–1, Southworth was singing a different tune. "This is going to be the hustlingest club I've ever sent on a field," he said. "The spirit is terrific. We're not gonna let up. We'll win 'em when those other playboy teams are out seeing the sights."

Southworth's pitching staff was solid, led by right-handed ace Si Johnson, and the lineup included Crabtree, back for a seventh season, catcher "Sad" Sam Narron, and shortstop Marty Marion, beginning his third season with the Wings at age twenty-one. Rochester won its season opener, beating Newark 1–0 on Johnson's two-hitter and a tenth-inning single by "L'il" Danny Murtaugh, a scrappy second baseman. The ever-popular Crabtree, now thirty-four, put together his finest season yet, hitting .337 with 14 home runs and 94 RBI. He was named Most Popular Red Wing in a fan poll and was a nearly unanimous media selection as team MVP.

The Red Wings finished the season in second place at 84–67 and beat Buffalo four games to one in the first round of the International League playoffs. Newark—which needed a one-game playoff to edge Syracuse for the final spot—stunned first-place Jersey City in six games to set up an unlikely Governors' Cup final. Southworth chose an inconsistent rookie left-hander named Elwin "Preacher" Roe as his surprise starter in game one at Red Wing Stadium. Roe, who would go on to great success with the legendary Brooklyn Dodgers teams of the 1950s, lasted less than two innings. Fortunately for the Wings, Mike Ryba pitched brilliantly in relief and Rochester rolled 8–1.

The next night, Si Johnson tossed a four-hitter and the Wings won 2–0 to take a commanding lead in the best-of-seven series. The finals shifted to Newark, and so did the momentum. The Bears won three straight at home to send the Wings staggering back to Rochester on the verge of elimination, the ghosts of their 1938 collapse haunting them.

Game six was set for 8:30 P.M. on Saturday, September 24. Johnson started for Rochester against George Washburn, a rematch of the pitchers' duel in game two. Rochester struck first, scoring two runs in the second. Newark roared back to take a 6–2 lead into the ninth. Bears reliever Hank Borowy quickly set down the first two Red Wings he faced, and the crowd of 4,202 began dispersing through the exits. But Dusty Cooke pinch-hit for pitcher Ken Raffensberger and drew a walk. With the game seemingly in hand, Borowy allowed Cooke to take second and then third uncontested. Whitey Kurowski lined a single off second baseman Ham Schulte's glove to score Cooke and make it 6–3. "We still thought the game was over," said Harold "Tiny" Zwetsch, a stadium ticket taker who had found a seat down the right-field line for the final few innings. "We were afraid to start hoping."

Harry Davis was next, and he, too, waited out Borowy for a walk. That was enough for Bears manager Johnny Neun, who summoned Norman Branch in to pitch to Crabtree. "I went up there just trying to meet the ball square," Crabtree said. "I was looking for the first one to be in there, and when I saw it I teed off." The ball finally landed over the right-field fence, sending what was left of the crowd into hysterics.

"Everyone was halfway out the stadium," recalled longtime stadium usher Alex Turchetti. "And then everyone started running back in when they realized what had happened."

Zwetsch, whose career with the Wings spanned sixty-five years, said bedlam fell upon the ballpark. "The people really went wild," he said. "We really thought we were done, but Crabby saved it. And you know what? It couldn't have happened to a nicer guy." Crabtree, ironically, was one of the last to realize what he had done, telling reporters, "I was almost to third base before I realized it was a homer." The press box turned into a madhouse as writers ditched their stories and their nearly completed box scores. The Bears were so certain of victory that they had cabs waiting outside to rush them to the train station for a midnight ride to Newark.

The crowd remained in a frenzy as Crabtree was mobbed by his teammates at home plate. Wrote McCarthy: "Men, deliriously daffy over the wallop, transformed from tenors to baritones—permanently."

Branch regained his composure long enough to retire Jack Sturdy for the final out. The game remained scoreless through the tenth. Then the eleventh. Then the top of the twelfth. Branch had stayed in the game to shut down the rejuvenated Wings. Preacher Roe had come in to pitch scoreless ball for three innings. In the bottom of the twelfth, Davis hit a slow grounder that Ham Schulte threw away, sending Davis to second. Crabtree's bouncer to first moved the runner to third. Neun ordered Sturdy walked intentionally and the Bears infield moved in to cut off the run at the plate. Branch got two strikes on Jim Asbell, but the outfielder whacked a single to left and scored Davis with the winning run. The series, miraculously, was tied.

Afterward, the fiery Southworth refused to acknowledge surprise at Crabtree's heroics. "I never blinked an eye when ol' Crabby put the wood to that ball," he said. "That guy [Branch] was staggering around like a punch-drunk fighter."

> One thousand dollars reward will be paid by the baseball fans of Newark, N.J., for the "arrest" . . . of Estel Crayton Crabtree, who "killed" the Bears with a four-ply shell in Red Wing Stadium about 11:02 P.M., Saturday, September 24, 1939.
> —Democrat and Chronicle, Sept. 25, 1939.

Everybody was talking about Crabtree's homer the next day as the clubs met to decide the International League champion and Louisville's opponent in the Junior World Series. "I was beginning to smell that fragrant bluegrass of Kentucky," longtime Newark sportswriter Mike

Gaven said before the game, "but there is an awful odor to it now." Ray Kennedy, the Bears' devoted secretary, stared out at the field from the press box and bemoaned the playoff money that had been snatched away. "A $15,000 home run," he said. "That's what it was any way you try to figure it. When is Crabtree going to run for mayor in this town? He'd be a cinch—even on the Socialist ticket."

The disheartened Bears took another bitter loss in game seven. As 15,500 delirious fans watched, Harry Davis lined a bases-loaded single with one out in the bottom of the ninth to score Carden Gillenwater and give Rochester a 2–1 win and its first Governors' Cup title. The Wings ran out of miracles in the Junior World Series, losing in seven games to a Louisville Colonels team that was 75–78 in the regular season. The Colonels didn't have a .300 hitter in their lineup but were led by a young shortstop named PeeWee Reese, who led the league with 18 triples and 35 steals. Louisville won game seven 7–3, scoring four runs in the eleventh inning at Red Wing Stadium.

It was a disappointing end to the season, but nothing could really take away from the thrill of Crabtree's miraculous home run and another championship under Southworth.

6

The Wings of War

Abner Doubleday would have committed hari-kari managing this club.
—*unidentified sportswriter,* describing 1945 Red Wings

There was nothing more for Billy Southworth to prove as a minor-league manager. In his five seasons in Rochester, the Red Wings had not missed the playoffs, and they won four pennants and two Junior World Series titles. He had helped talented teams and not-so-talented teams realize their potential and, in the process had become immensely popular with his players and the fans. He had served his apprenticeship well and was more than ready for another shot at a major-league managing job. But when the 1940 season began, Southworth found himself back in Rochester, wondering if another big-league opportunity would ever come. Elliot Cushing, the longtime sports editor of the Rochester *Democrat and Chronicle,* could sense Southworth's frustration. He thought that Southworth had developed into an even better manager than he had been during the Red Wings' glory years of the late 1920s and early 1930s. Like many knowledgeable baseball observers, Cushing believed Southworth was miscast in the minors. He thought Billy the Kid should be in St. Louis, managing a Cardinals team that was far removed from the glory of its Gas House Gang days, a team in desperate need of a dynamic leader.

In an effort to help his friend, Cushing wrote an impassioned letter to Cardinals owner Sam Breadon. He told Breadon he would be acting against his own best interests if he bypassed Billy Southworth. The sports editor concluded his letter by advising Breadon not to "lose this one in the sun." Breadon never responded to Cushing's correspondence, but it must have had some influence because roughly a week later, Wings president Oliver French was notified by Breadon that Southworth was being promoted to manage St. Louis. McCarthy surmised that one of the factors in Southworth's promotion was Cushing's assurance that there would be no outcry by the Rochester media or fans if the manager was called up during the season. On June 7, 1940, the *Democrat and Chronicle* carried Cushing's national scoop announcing Southworth's promotion. The sports editor wound up being right about the reaction of the Rochester fans. Although sorry to see such a beloved figure depart, they were happy that Southworth finally would be getting a legitimate opportunity to prove he could manage in the big leagues. Cushing's assessment of Southworth's managing skills also were on target. Billy the Kid wound up reviving a moribund Cardinals team, guiding it to a third-place finish in 1940. Under his leadership, St. Louis would win three National League pennants, and two World Series. In 1941 and 1942, Southworth would be named manager of the year by *The Sporting News,* at that time the nation's most authoritative sports publication.

The disappointment his departure caused in Rochester was softened somewhat by the announcement that center fielder Estel Crabtree would be taking over as player-manager. The popular Crabtree, fresh off his dramatic homer the postseason before, was excited about the prospect of guiding the Wings. It didn't hurt that he had been left with a club that was in first place with a 32–15 record, three games in front of Jersey City. Crabtree had aspirations of leading the Red Wings to the International League pennant, but roughly a week into the job, he fell ill with a kidney ailment. He underwent surgery at Rochester's Genesee Hospital. Veteran pitcher Mike Ryba managed the team in his absence. When doctors told Crabtree he couldn't manage for the rest of the season, he resigned, and the Cardinals replaced him with Tony Kaufmann, who was brought in from Decatur of the Three-I League. The choice was well received by Rochester fans, who recalled Kaufmann's playing days with the Wings. They remembered how he had played a key role in Rochester's 1928 pennant drive, and how he had returned to the Red Wings in 1933 and pitched parts of five more seasons with them.

Kaufmann inherited a lineup that was solid, but not spectacular. Shortstop Frankie Crespi and second baseman George Fallon developed into an outstanding double-play combination; catcher Ray Mueller was superb defensively and did a great job handling the pitchers; and first baseman Harry Davis, third baseman Whitey Kurowski, and outfielders Harold Epps and Augie Bergamo provided much of the offense. But

Four men managed the Wings to the 1940 pennant, including *(left to right)* Billy Southworth, Tony Kaufmann, and Estel Crabtree. Pitcher Mike Ryba, not pictured, managed the club for a week. Courtesy of the *Democrat and Chronicle/Times-Union.*

pitching is what carried Rochester to its tenth International League pennant. The rotation of Mike Ryba, Hank Gornicki, Charley Brumbeloe, and Hersh Lyons ranks as one of the finest in Rochester baseball history. The Fabulous Foursome, as they came to be known, accounted for 80 of the Red Wings' 96 victories. The bullpen wasn't too shabby either. It featured Johnnie Berly, who had pitched for Rochester in the 1920s and 1930s, and would go on to set league records for most appearances in a season.

"Old Folks" Ryba was the ace of the staff, winning 24 of 32 decisions while pitching a league-high twenty-five complete games. His heroics earned him International League MVP honors, and after the season he was sold to the Boston Red Sox. He had been assigned to Rochester in 1939 to assist Southworth as a coach and backup pitcher and catcher. But he threw the ball so well during spring training that Southworth

decided to put him in the rotation, where he remained until joining the
Red Sox. Ryba's maturity set a positive example for the other pitchers.
One day, he was the victim of three errors by substitute shortstop Lynn
Myers. Most pitchers would have lost their temper, but Ryba calmly
shook off the mistakes and went on to beat Buffalo that day, 4–3, in
thirteen innings. Gornicki went 19–10, Lyons 19–12, and Brumbeloe
18–11. Brumbeloe topped the staff with a 2.58 earned run average in
230 innings. He may have had the most natural ability of the foursome.
Wrote McCarthy: "Young Brumbeloe was a rugged individualist and a
hurler with witch-craft. He probably [walked] more men than any curver
in the loop, but was just wild enough to be effective." Despite his talent,
his career would not go far, and he would retire from baseball to become
a preacher. The Wings wound up winning the title by two and one-half
games over Newark. The feeling was that nobody would be able to stop
them in the playoffs, but fourth place Baltimore pulled off the upset after
falling behind two games to none in the series.

It would be ten years before the Wings won another pennant, and
that decade-long drought would feature some of the worst baseball ever
played at 500 Norton Street. Kaufmann returned in 1941, but, unfortunately, most of his pitching staff did not. Hank Gornicki was back, and
although he led the team with a 2.83 earned run average, he wasn't quite
the pitcher he had been the year before. Clem Dreisewerd emerged as the
ace with a 15–6 record, and young Max Surkont, whose fastball had
been compared to Bob Feller's, excited the fans with his hard throwing.
Ray Mueller continued to be superb behind the plate. He led the International League by throwing out forty-six would-be base stealers. Davis
drove in eighty-eight runs and Kurowski hit thirteen homers, but beyond
their performances, there wasn't a lot to get excited about offensively.

One of the few memorable performers from that team was a young
kid by the name of Stan Musial. He had been signed a few years earlier
by the Cardinals as a pitcher, and had led the Florida State League with
an 18–5 record, but a shoulder injury suffered while making a diving
catch in the outfield ended Musial's pitching career. The injury wound
up being a godsend. It forced Musial to make a full-time conversion to
the outfield, and the result was a Hall of Fame career. "I remember the
day he arrived in Rochester. He showed up at the bullpen carrying his
clothes in a paper bag," said Tiny Zwetsch. "He couldn't afford a real
suit." Musial was with the Wings for only fifty-four games, but he left an
indelible impression. He ripped four hits, including a homer, in his Red
Wing Stadium debut and wound up batting .326 before being called up
by the Cardinals for good.

Musial's hitting helped drive the Wings to a fourth-place finish,

Stan the (Young) Man Musial

After watching the young hitter with the unorthodox stance take batting practice at Red Wing Stadium one day during the summer of 1941, a major-league baseball scout turned to Rochester manager Tony Kaufmann and shook his head disapprovingly. "He'll never make it up there," the scout told Kaufmann. "Not with that stance, he won't."

Kaufmann couldn't believe his ears. Sure, Stan Musial's stance was ugly. ("He looks like a kid peeking around the corner to see if the cops are coming," was the way one player described it.) But the line drives the stance produced were a thing of beauty, and were enough to convince Kaufmann that Musial not only would make it "up there," but become The Man among boys.

After battering pitching in the Class C Western Association for two months, Musial was promoted to Rochester in July of '41. The pitcher-turned-outfielder arrived at the same time as Erv Dusak, a raw-boned slugger who was one of the most highly regarded prospects in the Cardinals chain. Dusak debuted with three hits to Musial's one, and also made a spectacular catch. But when the Wings returned to Rochester, Musial made an indelible impression, and Dusak eventually faded from the scene. Musial ripped four hits, including a homer, in his first game at 500 Norton Street, and kept up the torrid pace for the remainder of his stay in the International League. He finished with 10 doubles, 4 triples, 3 homers, 21 runs batted in, and a .326 average in 54 games.

"I remember one of the guys who had been sent down from the Cardinals telling me that I would be in St. Louis the following season," Musial recalled in a 1987 interview. "I figured I would be back in Rochester for another year of seasoning. But the Cardinals had a couple of injuries [toward the end of the 1941 campaign], and they called me up the day after our playoff series with Newark ended." Musial seized the opportunity by hitting .426 in twelve games with St. Louis that summer. He would never play in the minor leagues again.

The player with the corkscrew stance wound up earning seven National League batting titles, three Most Valuable Player awards, and a bronze plaque that hangs in the Baseball Hall of Fame at Cooperstown.

good enough for a postseason berth. The battle for that final playoff spot became so intense that during a late-season game, Kaufmann got into a scuffle with Buffalo Bisons manager Al Vincent. The argument reportedly was provoked by Kaufmann's incessant razzing of Bisons pitcher Virgil

Stan Musial. Courtesy of the Rochester Red Wings.

Trucks. Vincent gave Kaufmann a black eye, but the Wings manager was hurting even more during the playoffs as Newark disposed of Rochester in just five games.

◇

By the spring of '42, a goodly number of major-and minor-league players were off fighting in World War II. Without enough skilled players to stock the teams, several minor leagues decided to suspend operations or disband. Several baseball officials wondered if it was prudent to be playing ball games during a war and had considered shutting down the sport altogether. But President Franklin Roosevelt advised them against taking such drastic measures. He said the playing of the games boosted morale here and abroad and he praised the sport for its role "in the war-time program."

And so in places like Rochester, the show went on. But it wasn't a very good show. *Times-Union* sports editor Matt Jackson reported from spring training that the team was "all chaff, no wheat." He couldn't have been more right. For the first time in thirty-four years, Rochester finished in last place. Attendance was less than half what it had been the year before, declining from 148,694 to 72,891. Those who stayed away didn't miss much. Three managers took their lumps as Rochester went 59–93. Kaufmann started the season managing the club but was replaced by Estel Crabtree, who had been demoted by St. Louis. Crabby lasted just one week on the job before being replaced by Ray Hayworth. Wings president Oliver French had no comment on Crabtree's short stay. "I didn't resign at Rochester," was Crabtree's only comment to reporters. Perhaps no one symbolized the team's futility more than Dreisewerd, who set a Wings record with fourteen consecutive losses. His only win came during the final week of the season.

Pepper Martin, the Gas House Gang star who had entertained Wings fans thirteen years earlier with his hustle and head-first slides, returned to manage Rochester in 1943. Although the team would win fifteen more games than it had the season before, the experience would prove to be a bad one for Martin. Many Wings fans turned on him, and at one point Martin became so fed up with the criticism that he quit. The players persuaded him to return, but Martin clearly had been hurt by the incessant booing and second-guessing.

There were some noteworthy performances that season. Pitchers Ira Hutchinson and Sylvester "Blix" Donnelly each won seventeen games and Walter Alston, who would go on to become a Hall of Fame manager with the Dodgers, returned to the Wings after a six-year absence and batted .240. The top Wing that season was shortstop Al "Red" Schoendienst. He won the International League MVP award after leading the league in hitting with a .337 average. He was so good that sportswriter Al Weber nicknamed him "The Team."

Ken Penner replaced Martin as manager in 1944, and the team finished seventh in the eight-team league. Highlights were in short supply.

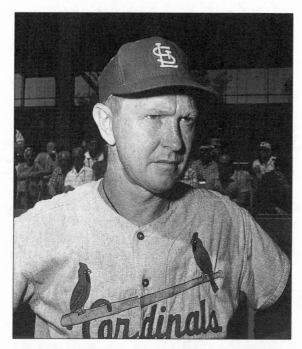

Nicknamed "The Team" by sportswriter A. C. Weber,
Wings shortstop Red Schoendienst won the batting title
and was named International League MVP in 1943.
Courtesy of the *Democrat and Chronicle/Times-Union.*

Ora Burnett and Maurice Sturdy combined for eighty stolen bases, and
Glen Gardner showed his moxie, pitching and winning both games of a
doubleheader against Syracuse. Alston moved a little closer to the end of
his playing career and the start of his managing career by batting a paltry
.158. Perhaps the most emotional moment of the season came in June
when Red Schoendienst played in his final game before heading off to
war. The shortstop was batting .372 through twenty-five games and
appeared to be on his way to winning his second consecutive batting
title and MVP award before Uncle Sam came calling. To show their
appreciation, the fans took up a collection during his final game and
presented him with several caps filled with coins and bills totaling nearly
$500. The young redhead had to fight back tears in the clubhouse after
the game.

Three years to the day after the Japanese bombing of Pearl Harbor,
the *Democrat and Chronicle* reported that Burleigh Grimes, a former

pitching great and one of baseball's most colorful figures, had been hired to replace Penner. Elliot Cushing gushed over the move. "The fact that [St. Louis owner] Sam Breadon was willing to go outside the Cardinal chain to obtain a manager is indicative of his determination to put his house in order in Rochester, where a long series of managerial flops by the Cardinal organization has rubbed much of the lustre off one of the best minor league franchises in the country," wrote Cushing. "It is doubtful that Breadon would sign a man of Grimes's ability without intending to give him the necessary tools to work with."

Grimes, the last of baseball's legal spitball pitchers, was an intensely competitive man who would attempt to intimidate hitters by throwing at their heads. Known as "Ol' Stubblebeard" because he would refrain from shaving two days before each pitching start, Grimes remained every bit as cantankerous as a manager. He came to the Wings after a successful stint with their International League rivals, the Toronto Maple Leafs. He had guided the Leafs to the pennant in 1943 and had done an even better job the following summer when he managed a mediocre club to a third-place finish. Cushing and many others believed that the forceful Grimes would revive the Wings. What they had not taken into account was how dreadful the team's personnel was. Grimes went through fifty-one players during the summer of '45. Some arrived and left so fast that they never learned the first names of their teammates. The "Dead Wings," as some took to calling them, led the league in errors and wound up finishing dead last with a 64–90 record. Pitcher Frank Radler suffered most, losing 23 of 29 decisions. Kemp Wicker pitched a nineteen-inning gem against Toronto, but all he had to show for it was a 2–1 loss. One sportswriter summed it up best when he quipped: "Abner Doubleday would have committed hari-kari managing this club." Given Grimes's personality, he probably felt more homicidal than suicidal.

Things did not get any better for Ol' Stubblebeard and his Dead Wings in 1946. Joseph Ziegler had taken over as the club's general manager, and he and Grimes got along about as well as two kids fighting over a toy. The personality conflict, coupled with the losing, prompted Ziegler to fire Grimes on June 14. Said Ziegler in his statement: "I have been of the opinion that this team has been poorly handled all season. I believe we have a much better ballclub than our present league standing indicates. I don't think Grimes has gotten the most out of the players we have. It is my belief that a managerial change will benefit the club." Grimes stormed out of town, but before he left, he made sure he was paid in full for the rest of the season. Benny Borgmann, a one-time basketball star, replaced Grimes, but there wasn't much improvement. The Wings finished one spot better than they had the year before. Interestingly, Danny Murtaugh, a Wings second baseman, originally was scheduled to replace Grimes, but he was bypassed because the Cardinals thought he still had a future as a player despite the fact that he was twenty-nine. Murtaugh had batted .332 that season with 11 stolen bases and 62 RBI before being called up to St. Louis. He was traded to the Boston Braves after the 1946 season, and later wound up with Pittsburgh. He batted .254 in parts of nine seasons in the big leagues, but would achieve lasting fame as the manager of two Pittsburgh World Series championship teams, including 1960, when the Pirates upset the heavily favored New York Yankees of Mickey Mantle and Roger Maris.

One of the few stars on that 1946 team was Vernal "Nippy" Jones, who batted .344, but lost the league batting title to Montreal's Jackie Robinson. Branch Rickey, the former Cardinals personnel whiz, had taken the first step toward integrating professional baseball by signing Robinson, a black, to a Brooklyn Dodgers contract. Rickey felt the experience in the International League would help prepare Robinson for the racial taunts and threats he would face a year later in the major leagues. Robinson endured tough times in many of the cities, especially Syracuse, where the players threw a black cat onto the field when Jackie came to bat. But there were no such incidents documented in Rochester, where Robinson and his Royals became a huge draw.

Although 1946 had been a disaster for Rochester baseball, attendance more than doubled at Red Wing Stadium, starting a postwar boom that would continue for several seasons in ballparks across America. Borgmann returned to the Cardinals scouting department after the season, and was replaced by Cedric Durst, who had been a reserve outfielder on the great Yankee teams of the late 1920s. Injuries prevented the Wings from improving much in the standings. John Mikan, Ray Yochim, and Max Surkont combined for forty-five wins, but Wings pitchers spent so much time in the trainer's room that a writer dubbed them "The Sore Arms." Any hopes of finishing in fourth place and capturing a playoff spot were dashed during a dreadful midseason road trip in which Rochester lost nineteen of twenty-one games. The top performance of the season was turned in by Hal Rice, who drove in nine runs in a game against Baltimore. Rice's feat equaled the Rochester RBI record shared by Rip Collins and George Kelly. Sweet-swinging Nippy Jones and long-ball-swatting Russ Derry were the main hitting stars. Although the Red Wings were out of the pennant picture early, Jones managed to hold fans' interest with his quest for the International League batting title. The 1947 race came down to the final day of the season, and Nippy batted .337 to nip Syracuse's Hank Sauer (.336) and Newark's Allie Clark (.334) for the title.

The off-season was a time of momentous change for the Cardinals organization. Former postmaster general Robert Hannegan and Fred Saigh, Jr., purchased the team from long-time owner Sam Breadon for just over $4 million. Shortly after buying the club, they visited Rochester and promised the fans a first-division team. The words did not ring hollow. For the first time in seven years, the Wings finished above .500 and returned to the playoffs, where they lost to eventual champion Montreal in seven games. More than three hundred thousand fans walked through the turnstiles at Red Wing Stadium during the 1948 season, second only to the attendance mark established during the 1930 championship season. Rice led the team in hitting, but it was Frankie Gravino, from nearby Newark who captured the fancy of the fans. The powerfully built Gravino muscled three homers over the Red Wing Stadium center-field fence, the first to do it that many times. He would finish with eighteen homers in just 321 at-bats and would go on to compile impressive power stats for a number of minor-league clubs.

The biggest news, though, would involve Durst, who was demoted to Omaha after the season. The Red Wings featured several party animals, who were labeled "The Play Boys" by sports editor Matt Jackson. Durst, in an attempt to bring the carousers in line, fined three players $250 apiece, and two others $100 each. The actions came too late in the eyes of the Cardinals owners, who had read the press criticism that Durst wasn't tough enough on his players.

The 1949 season would mark the arrival of two men who would become extremely popular in Rochester and play important roles in the history of both the Red Wings and the Cardinals. Vaughan "Bing" Devine took over as general manager after the popular Joe Ziegler left to take a similar position with Toronto, and Johnny Keane was hired to manage the team.

Devine was born in St. Louis and practically raised at Sportsman's Park, where he saw several games for free as a member of the Cardinals' Knothole Gang. While attending Washington University in St. Louis, he landed a job compiling stats in the Cardinals office, which led to various positions in the team's minor-league system. After serving in the Navy Fleet Airborne from 1943 to 1945, he became the assistant to general manager Frankie Lane. Devine took over as general manager two years later and turned the club into a perennial contender. Devine acquired Curt Flood, Lou Brock, Dick Groat, Bill White, and Julian Javier through trades, forming the nucleus of the Cardinal teams that would win World Series in 1964 and 1967.

Like Devine, Keane was a native of St. Louis and grew up a devout Cardinals fan. As a teenager he saved up enough money to pay his way

Russ Derry set the Red Wings standard for home
runs, hitting 42 in 1949 and 134 in six seasons.
Courtesy of the *Democrat and Chronicle/Times-Union*.

into the World Series game between the Cardinals and Yankees in which Babe Ruth hit three home runs. Keane's biggest thrill came when the Cardinals signed him out of high school to a minor-league contract. He spent three games at the start of the 1935 season with the Wings before being reassigned to Houston. While there, he was struck in the head with a pitch and spent six weeks in a coma. He recovered and returned as a player-coach. In 1938, he began his managerial career in the Cardinals chain. Twenty-one years later, he was named a coach in St. Louis, and a year after that, he took over as manager of the club. He led the Cardinals to the National League pennant and a World Series title victory against the New York Yankees in 1964, then stunned the baseball world by resigning the following day and taking over for Yankees manager Yogi Berra.

At the fall 1948 press conference introducing him as the new Red Wings manager, the cigar-smoking Keane told reporters: "Johnny Keane is not going to win you any pennant. Johnny Keane can't do it. The job is to get ballplayers. Then we get the pennant." Keane would get the ballplayers, and his three seasons in Rochester would be fruitful ones, with a first-place finish and two seconds.

After a decade of dull, often uninspired baseball, a new era was dawning at 500 Norton Street. The summer of '49 would be a record-setting one for the Wings, on and off the field. A crowd of 18,681, the second largest in team history, showed up on opening day. It was an indication of things to come. By season's end, the Wings had drawn a minor-league best 443,536 fans, and had established a team attendance record that still stands. The postwar boom as well as the boom provided by the bats of Russ Derry and Steve Bilko were among the big reasons spectators were coming to Red Wing Stadium in droves. Many showed up just to watch the two take batting practice. Derry owned the town in '49, slugging forty-two homers, still the most in Wings history. During his six years in Rochester, Derry would hit a team-record 134 homers. No one else in franchise history has ever reached 100.

Bilko, though, may have been even more popular than Derry among Red Wing fans because his homers were usually of the tape-measure variety. He hit thirty-four in 1949, including several over the center-field scoreboard at Red Wing Stadium. He became the only player to hit one over the even more distant center-field wall at Delormier Downs in Montreal. Recalled former Wings road secretary Mike Carpenter: "The Montreal players were aghast." At six-foot-one, 230 pounds, Bilko was a huge man who would be plagued by weight problems throughout his life. His stellar seasons at Rochester earned him promotions to St. Louis, but his major-league career never lived up to expecta-

Slugging first baseman Steve Bilko's best years were
spent in the Pacific Coast League, but he slammed 34
homers and drove in 125 runs for the 1949 Wings.
Courtesy of the *Democrat and Chronicle/Times-Union*.

tions. In parts of ten big-league seasons, he hit just 76 homers and struck
out 395 times in 1,738 at-bats. "He was one of the best right-handed
hitters I ever played with—or ever saw," Derry said. "I never thought he
got the chance he should have in the big leagues. Too many baseball men
looked at him as too big and too fat, and then they'd put him on reducing
diets and he'd get weak. If they had just turned him loose, he would have
made a real name for himself." As it turned out, Bilko's greatest years
would come with the old Los Angeles Angels of the Pacific Coast League.
He won league MVP honors in 1955, 1956, and 1957—hitting 56, 55,
and 37 homers in those years. He ended his playing days in Rochester in
1963, sharing first base with Luke Easter and Joe Altobelli. Even though
his skills had eroded considerably by that time, he remained a fan favor-

Pitching Goose Eggs

On August 13, 1950, Rochester Red Wings pitcher Tom Poholsky and his Jersey City counterpart Andy Tomasic went the distance—long distance. For twenty-two innings at Red Wing Stadium, they matched fastballs and curves and goose eggs. Finally, five hours and fifteen minutes after the first pitch had been delivered, Rochester third baseman Don Richmond smashed a run-scoring single down the right-field line to give Rochester a 3–2 victory and end one of the most remarkable pitching duels in baseball history. "The funny thing about that day was that it was one of the few Sundays that season when we weren't scheduled to play a doubleheader," Poholsky recalled in a June 1995 interview. "Of course, as things turned out, we wound up playing the equivalent of a doubleheader and then some."

There was no indication early on that this was going to be a day when pitching would dominate. The score was tied at two after two innings. But then the youthful Poholsky and the veteran Tomasic got into a groove. Three up, three down. Three up, three down. Before they knew it, the game was fourteen, fifteen innings old. "Andy and I struggled a bit early on, and then we found our control," Poholsky said. "Both of us were getting ahead on the counts, and you saw a lot of guys coming up there and swinging at the first or second pitches. The game really zipped along."

The six-foot-three Poholsky was twenty years old at the time, and one of the most highly regarded pitchers in the St. Louis Cardinals chain, which is why Red Wings manager Johnny Keane called the Cardinals front office several times during the game to make sure it was O.K. to keep pitching him. "I didn't know about the phone calls until afterward," said Poholsky. "Johnny would ask me each inning how I felt, and I told him I felt fine, which I did. I really don't recall being tired. I think my conditioning and the weather had a lot to do with that. It was about 74 degrees with no humidity. If it had been a humid day there's no way either of us would have been able to go that long."

By the twenty-second inning, each man was pitching on guile and adrenaline. Wings shortstop Dick Cole led off the bottom of the inning with a single, his fourth of the game. Tomasic, anxious to keep Cole close to the base, was called for a balk for the first time that season. That brought up Richmond, a dangerous hitter who was on his way to winning his first of two consecutive International League batting titles. Tomasic tossed a knuckleball and Richmond drilled it into the right-field corner. Few among the 5,863 spectators on hand for the opening pitch had left. They stomped their feet and cheered lustily as Cole touched home plate with the winning run, ending what was at the time the longest game in league history. Keane rushed out to the mound to congratulate Tomasic for his game performance in a losing effort. As Tomasic made the long walk to the clubhouse, Wings fans gave him a standing ovation. Poholsky, too, had hoped to shake hands with his comrade in arms, but by the time the Wings ace had completed all his interviews and had finished his postpitching treatments with trainer Danny Whelan, the Little Giants had departed.

Poholsky wound up having his best season in pro ball. He led the league in wins (18) and earned run average (2.17) and was named the International League most valuable player as the Wings won the pennant by seven games. He would never come close to matching those figures during his five seasons with the Cardinals, going 31–52 with a 3.93 earned run average.

ite. Recalled one longtime Wing follower: "Bilko playing first base looked like a circus elephant standing on a drum. But, man, nobody hit a baseball like that guy did."

Led by the slugging of Derry and Bilko and the pitching of Cloyd Boyer (15–10) and Tom Poholsky (14–10), Rochester finished the 1949 season with an 85–67 record, good for second place behind Buffalo. Montreal, which featured an aspiring thespian named Chuck Connors at first base, swept the Wings in four games in the first round of the playoffs. Connors also played forward on Rochester's National Basketball Association team in the winter months and was a fan favorite at 500 Norton Street even though he suited up for the opposition. Connors, who would gain fame as the star of the popular 1950s television series *The Rifleman*, loved to play up to the crowd at Red Wing Stadium. One longtime Wings ticket holder recalls a game where Connors smacked a home run and ran around the bases backwards.

Rochester's decade-long pennant drought came to an end in 1950, when the Red Wings easily outdistanced second-place Montreal by seven games. Keane said he needed players to win, and the Cardinals provided him with an abundance of good ones that summer. The Red Wings were an International League pitcher's nightmare. They led the league in team batting, triples, and home runs. Rochester's dominance was underscored in the individual statistics. Third baseman Don Richmond scored a league-high 126 runs and won the first of two consecutive batting titles with a .333 average. Derry topped the league in homers (30) and RBI (102). And pitcher Tom Poholsky won IL most valuable player honors after leading the league in victories (18), earned run average (2.17), and complete games (21 in 25 starts, including one that lasted an incredible twenty-two innings). Spot starter-reliever Ken Wild was virtually unbeatable, with a 12–1 record. Most expected a Montreal-Rochester final, but the Royals, who featured a left-handed pitcher named Tommy Lasorda, failed to hold up their end of the deal when they lost to Baltimore in the opening round. Keane's Wings disposed of Jersey City but lost to the Orioles in the final series.

Keane would field another competitive team in 1951. Led by Richmond, who batted .350 to become Rochester's only two-time batting champion, the Wings finished second with an 83–69 record. Syracuse eliminated them in the first round of the playoffs, four games to one. Montreal clearly was the class of the league. Managed by former Rochester first baseman Walter Alston and paced by Dodger prospects such as Junior Gilliam and Tommy Lasorda, the Royals finished eleven games in front of Rochester and breezed to another playoff title before losing to Milwaukee in the Junior World Series.

Longtime Wings fans were saddened by news out of Buffalo. Former Rochester captain and manager Specs Toporcer suffered such a rapid deterioration of his eyesight that he was forced to resign as manager of the Buffalo Bisons. Despite three eye operations, Toporcer was blind by 1952. He wound up writing an autobiography, *Baseball from Backlots to Big League,* and became a popular inspirational speaker until his death in 1989 at the age of ninety.

Keane's reign as one of the finest managers in Rochester baseball history ended following the 1951 season, when he was reassigned to the Cardinals' other Triple-A team in Columbus, Ohio. But Wings fans wouldn't be singing the blues for long. Colorful Harry "The Hat" Walker was coming to town. Winning baseball would continue on Norton Street.

7

Top Hat

I've got a feeling that if we can get lucky or get hot, we can go all the way.
        —Harry Walker, 1952

Harry "The Hat" Walker was a speedy, left-handed hitting outfielder from Mississippi and the younger brother of Brooklyn Dodgers outfielder Fred "Dixie" Walker. Harry got his nickname from major-league sportswriters because of the way he continually fussed with his baseball cap at the plate. "Mostly I bother the pitcher," he said in explaining his hat habit. "I guess it bothers other people, too. Everyone but me. Larry Goetz, the umpire, once got a little hot and told me: 'Harry, why don't you leave the damned thing in the dugout or stick it in your pocket?' I just can't do it. Couldn't do it for money."

Walker came up through the St. Louis Cardinals organization, and went 3-for-10 in three games for the 1940 Red Wings. He earned lasting fame during game seven of the 1946 World Series. With two outs in the eighth and the Cardinals and Boston Red Sox tied 3–3, Walker lined a double to left-center off Bob Klinger. The hit sent Enos Slaughter all the way home from first on a play that became more famous for Red Sox shortstop Johnny Pesky holding the ball too long. Walker was traded to the Philadelphia Phillies early in the 1947 season and won the National League batting title with a .363 average that year. After brief stints with the Chicago Cubs and Cincinnati Reds, he was traded back to St. Louis in 1950 and played sparingly for the Cardinals the next two seasons.

When St. Louis offered the thirty-three-year-old Walker the chance

Former National League batting champ Harry "The Hat" Walker guided
the Wings to an upset win in the 1952 Governors' Cup finals.
Courtesy of the *Democrat and Chronicle/Times-Union.*

to be a player-manager with their minor-league club in Columbus in 1951, he accepted. Walker won the American Association batting title, hitting .393, but flopped in his managerial debut as the Red Birds finished eighth. Despite his poor finish, Cardinals executives believed Walker had done a commendable job. Feeling a change of scenery might be helpful, the Cardinals gave Walker the Wings job when they transferred Keane to Columbus. A player's manager who did not drink or smoke, Walker believed a loose club was a happy club. "When you put ballplayers under a severe set of rules and regulations off the field, you only force them to hide out on you in the places you want them to stay away from," he said prior to the 1952 season. "I believe in making the boys govern themselves."

Walker inherited a veteran Red Wings team in 1952, with third baseman Don Richmond, second baseman Lou Ortiz, catcher Johnny Bucha, and outfielders Russ Derry and Larry Ciaffone returning. Also back was Ellis "Cot" Deal, who had moved to the outfield in 1951 when his pitching arm failed him. Determined to get back on the mound, Deal pitched in the Puerto Rican winter league following the '51 season and asked Walker for another shot in spring training. "I love to play baseball and I don't care where I play," Deal said. "But there's more money in pitching, and that's why I'm determined to make it as a starting pitcher." Deal won four games in spring training and earned an opening day start against the Springfield Cubs on April 16. That night in Chicago, Sugar Ray Robinson knocked out Rocky Graziano in the third round to retain his middleweight boxing title. The Cubs did likewise to Deal, winning 10–1. Walker hit leadoff, played center field, and banged out three hits. By May 3, he was batting .469. Unfortunately, his team was winning at a similar level, falling to 11–14 on May 12. That day, the Cardinals returned first baseman Steve Bilko, though the slugger wouldn't be able to play for six more weeks because of a broken arm.

By the time Bilko returned, the Wings—sportswriters called them the "Hatters"—had saved their sinking ship. Still, there appeared to be no stopping the Montreal Royals, the top affiliate of the Brooklyn Dodgers.

The Royals were led by second baseman Junior Gilliam, the eventual league MVP, third baseman Don Hoak, and a lefty-lefty pitching combination that ranked among the league's best. The ace was Johnny Podres, who would go on to become one of the greatest pitchers in Dodgers history. He was joined by Tommy Lasorda, who would enjoy his greatest success as longtime manager of the Los Angeles Dodgers.

On September 5, Wings left-hander Jackie Collum threw a no-hitter against Ottawa in his final regular-season start, the first by a Wing since Blix Donnelly in 1943. Collum finished the year 9–10, but would heat up in the postseason. With Walker hitting .365, the Wings finished third at 80–74, sixteen and one half games behind the Royals and eight in back of second-place Syracuse. But Rochester stunned its Thruway rival in the first round of the playoffs with a four-game sweep. The Wings' pitching was the story, with Collum, "Preacher" Jack Faszholz, and Al Papai tossing complete games. "I've got a feeling," Walker said in the exuberant Wings clubhouse, "that if we can get lucky or get hot, we can go all the way."

The Red Wings waited five days for Montreal to finally eliminate Toronto in seven games, then waited another two days as rain postponed game one of the Governors' Cup championship. Finally, on September 20, the Wings won their fifth straight playoff game by downing the Royals 5–3. Lasorda celebrated his twenty-fifth birthday the next day with a three-hit shutout, but the Wings won the next two games to take a three games to one lead. Montreal pulled out game five on Walt Moryn's three-run homer in the eighth, winning 6–5, and the Royals sent Lasorda out for game six.

The future Dodgers manager and Slim-Fast pitchman would last only two batters. Lasorda gave up a double to Walker and a single to Don Richmond, then uncorked a wild pitch. Lasorda raced to guard home plate and was steamrolled by Walker. He left the field on a stretcher and his team never recovered, losing 3–2 to give Rochester its second Governors' Cup championship.

The third chapter in this improbable run came against the Kansas City Blues, champions of the American Association, in the Junior World Series. The Blues were coached by former Red Wing George "Twinkletoes" Selkirk, a graduate of Rochester's Edison Tech High School, and were a power-hitting club led by Bob Cerv and Bill "Moose" Skowron. Kansas City won two of the three games played at Blues Stadium to open the series. The Red Wings Cinderella story appeared over when Kansas City blasted Rochester 9–0 in game four at Red Wing Stadium, taking a commanding three games to one edge. Right-hander Ed Erautt threw a two-hitter in that game, improving to 27–5. The Wings took the next two games but were huge underdogs in game seven, with Jackie Collum facing the nearly invincible Erautt, who had recorded the best record in the minors after spending six years with the Cincinnati Reds. But on this day, in this season of Norton Street miracles, Erautt proved very mortal. He gave up one run in the first and five in the second, leaving before retiring the side. "I had good stuff all the way, as good as I've ever had," Erautt said afterward. "I just couldn't get the ball over the plate."

The Blues hit Collum for four runs in the sixth, but right-hander Jack Crimian shut the door on Kansas City with three and two-thirds innings of scoreless relief, giving Rochester an 8–4 win and its first Junior World Series title since 1931. Crimian had pitched six no-hit innings of relief in games five and six, but he saved the best for last in his sixty-sixth appearance of the season. "I wouldn't trade this for anything," said an elated Walker, who had accomplished the rare feat of going from worst to first in one season. "Not for a goose that is guaranteed to lay a little ol' golden egg everyday and twice on Sunday."

Despite Rochester's improbable climb to the top of the Triple-A mountain, Montreal was the overwhelming choice to win the International League pennant the following spring. Even Walker acknowledged that the Royals, led by Cuban outfielder Sandy Amoros, would be the team to beat. The Wings manager was even more convinced after Montreal rocked his club 17–4 in the season opener, as Amoros tied an International League record by going 6-for-6. That gave Walter Alston an incredible 14–0 mark on opening day and handed the Wings their first season-opening loss in seven years.

The '53 Wings were loaded offensively. Eight players would finish the year above .300, including Tom Burgess (.346), rookie outfielder Wally Moon (.307), and Walker (.303). Cot Deal was double trouble for opponents, winning sixteen games on the mound and hitting .279 as a part-time outfielder. With so much depth and firepower, a long winning streak could develop at any time, and late in the season Rochester began one the greatest stretches in franchise history. On August 14, the Wings trailed Buffalo by five games and Montreal by four. Then they swept both front-runners in four-game series to move to the top spot for the first time all season. Amazingly, the Wings dropped out of first while stretching their streak to ten as Buffalo won more games over the same period.

On August 23, Toronto snapped Rochester's ten-game winning streak with a 6–2 victory and Buffalo swept Syracuse. That left the Red Wings 76–54, one and a half games out of first. The Wings and Maple Leafs split the next two games. What followed drew the attention of the entire baseball world. The Red Wings simply forgot to lose. They beat Toronto twice, Ottawa four times, Springfield four times, Baltimore twice, and Syracuse four times, including a 6–1 triumph on September 9 that clinched the league pennant. Then they ripped Baltimore three straight times, bringing their amazing record-setting winning streak to nineteen games. During that stretch, the Wings had outscored opponents

The Streak

From August 26 through September 12, 1953, the Rochester Red Wings won a club record nineteen straight games. Here are the results:

Rochester 8, Toronto 5
Rochester 5, Toronto 0
Rochester 5, Ottawa 2   Rochester 10, Baltimore 7
Rochester 8, Ottawa 5   Rochester 11, Baltimore 2
Rochester 2, Ottawa 0   Rochester 12, Syracuse 5
Rochester 11, Ottawa 4   Rochester 9, Syracuse 4
Rochester 9, Springfield 8   Rochester 11, Syracuse 7
Rochester 9, Springfield 7   Rochester 6, Syracuse 1
Rochester 9, Springfield 5   Rochester 9, Baltimore 2
Rochester 10, Springfield 0   Rochester 3, Baltimore 0
                                Rochester 5, Baltimore 1

152–65. In wins six through fifteen, they had scored at least nine runs in every game. The winning streak finally ended in the second game of a doubleheader on September 12, when Baltimore edged Rochester 5–4 on Joe Lonnett's home run in the tenth inning. The Wings had won an amazing thirty of thirty-two games, and their nineteen-game streak was five more than the club record. They finished the season 97–57, seven games in front of the once-invincible Montreal Royals.

Many Wings worried that the extended streak had taken too much out of the team, and their fears seemed justified when Baltimore, which had finished a distant fifteen games out, took them to a seven-game playoff series before losing the finale 8–1 in front of a crowd of 11,532 at Red Wing Stadium. That would mark Baltimore's last game as a minor-league team. Rumors already were circulating that Bill Veeck's St. Louis Browns were headed to Baltimore, and the move became official in the off-season. The Baltimore Orioles became a major-league team in 1954, and they would soon be reunited with the Red Wings.

Montreal had waited one year to avenge its stunning loss to Rochester in the 1952 Governors' Cup finals, and the Royals showed no mercy this time, sweeping the Wings in four straight. "The champs are dead," the *Democrat and Chronicle* blared the next day. "Long live the champs." Like the Orioles, Walter Alston's last minor-league game came against the Red Wings. On November 24, 1953, the Royals manager was named skipper of the Brooklyn Dodgers, replacing Charlie Dressen. Alston would go on to become one of the most successful managers in baseball history, winning Brooklyn's only world championship in 1955 and add-

Harry Walker's 1953 team won a club record nineteen straight games but fizzled in the playoffs. Courtesy of the *Democrat and Chronicle/Times-Union*.

ing three more titles with the Los Angeles Dodgers. Alston worked with one-year contracts throughout his twenty-three years as manager before retiring after the 1976 season. His old Montreal pitcher, Tommy Lasorda, took over and managed Los Angeles for the next two decades, winning world championships in 1981 and 1988.

The International League truly lived up to its name in 1954, with the addition of the Havana, Cuba, Sugar Kings, which gave the league representatives from three nations. Richmond also returned to the league after a thirty-six-year hiatus. The hot new star in Rochester was a bespectacled outfielder named Bill Virdon, who had been acquired from the New York Yankees along with pitcher Vic Raschi for Cardinals outfielder Enos Slaughter. Virdon hit .333 to win the IL batting title, but the loss of Wally Moon, Tom Burgess, and first baseman Joe Cunningham to St.

The Buck Stopped Here

The gravelly voice that would become familiar to millions of American sports fans spent a season in Rochester describing the exploits of the Red Wings before heading to the big time. Jack Buck, the longtime St. Louis Cardinals play-by-play man and network broadcaster, spent the summer of 1953 at 500 Norton Street. He has fond memories of that summer. He had come here from a Columbus, Ohio, television station, where he did weather and sports on the same newscast as budding comedian Jonathan Winters. Buck had broadcast Columbus Redbirds baseball during 1950 and 1951, but when his station stopped broadcasting games in '52, Buck became an announcer without a team. Baseball was in his blood, so when he heard about the opening in Rochester, he jumped at the opportunity.

In those days, announcers normally didn't travel to road games. They did re-creation broadcasts based on ticker-tape reports. "You were at the total mercy of the teletype operators, and sometimes you'd receive some awfully strange information," he said. "There would be times when the message from the ballpark would be garbled and you had to stall for time while waiting for the information to be corrected. I remember broadcasting a lot of fictitious foul balls in those days." Buck also remembers postgame visits to watering holes near Red Wing Stadium, and the city's vast expanse of lilac bushes. "I also recall," he deadpanned, "the strange weather. Rochester was a surprising city. You'd go to bed at night in the spring and the ground would be bare. You'd wake up and it would be blanketed with snow." After the 1953 season, Buck was promoted by the Cardinals, and shared the broadcast booth with the inimitable Harry Caray.

Buck is the most famous alumnus of Red Wings broadcasts. The club has been blessed with numerous gifted announcers through the years, including Gunnar Wiig (the original Voice of the Wings), Joe Cullinane, Josh Lewin, and Tom Decker.

Louis cut the heart out of the Red Wings offense. Rochester finished third at 86–68, then lost a six-game playoff series to Montreal.

The '54 season marked a dramatic social moment in Red Wings history, as Thomas Edison Alston, a six-foot-five first baseman, became the first black player in club history. The news was trumpeted on the front page of the *Democract and Chronicle*. Alston came down from St. Louis on June 30 along with Tom Burgess.

Alston hit a two-run triple and finished 1-for-4 in his Red Wings debut, a 5–4 win over Havana, but his appearance attracted only 1,905 fans to Red Wing Stadium. That same day, popular third baseman Don Richmond was traded to Syracuse for pitcher Duke Markell, who worked as a Brooklyn policeman in the off-season. Richmond joined the Wings in June 1949 and won back-to-back International League batting titles in 1950 (.333) and 1951 (.350). He was inducted into the Red Wings Hall of Fame in 1990.

Change was the big theme in 1955 as well. On May 27, Walker left the field during the sixth inning of Rochester's game against Toronto. It would be the last time he wore a Red Wings uniform. The St. Louis Cardinals were preparing to dismiss manager Eddie Stanky, whose underachieving club was mired in sixth place in the National League at 17–19. Walker was their choice to replace Stanky, and the Cardinals ordered him off the field.

Democrat and Chronicle beat writer George Beahon was all over the breaking story. Beahon strongly suspected that Walker was getting the call to St. Louis, but the manager was coy with Beahon when confronted, so Beahon chose an alternate route. He befriended Wings coach Lou Kahn, and Kahn telegraphed the decisive clue. Watch the early innings of tonight's game, Kahn advised Beahon. While Walker was ejected on a seemingly innocuous call in the sixth, Beahon had his story. The firing of Stanky and the hiring of Walker were announced simultaneously the next day at a press conference in St. Louis, and Walker's replacement in Rochester also was selected.

It was a familiar name. Fred "Dixie" Walker was Harry's older brother and one of three coaches under Stanky in St. Louis. Dixie Walker had spent nineteen years as a major-league outfielder, compiling a lifetime batting average of .306. Like Harry, Dixie was a former National League batting champ, winning the 1944 crown with a .357 average for Brooklyn. Dixie Walker had served more than four seasons as manager at Double-A Atlanta and Houston. He took over Houston on August 1, 1954, and led the Buffs to the Texas League title.

The "New Walkermen," as the papers dubbed them, were 23–18 when Dixie arrived on May 30. They would finish the season 76–77—the Wings' first losing season since 1946—and attendance would fall to a nine-year low of 153,498. The Wings squeezed into the playoffs in the fourth spot, then stunned pennant-winning Montreal in five games and swept Toronto to win another Governors' Cup title. Their luck ran out

The Unhappy Life of Thomas Edison Alston

Jackie Robinson broke the International League color barrier with the Montreal Royals in 1946, but the Rochester Red Wings would remain as white as an unused baseball for eight more years. The Wings finally were integrated on June 30, 1954, when Thomas Edison Alston, the first black to play for the St. Louis Cardinals, was sent down to Rochester. Alston, a six-foot-five, two-hundred-pound first baseman, had gotten off to an auspicious start with the Cardinals that season, hitting home runs in the third and fourth games of his major-league career. But the hot spell didn't last long, and St. Louis demoted him to Rochester in hopes he would rediscover his stroke.

Alston wound up hitting .297 with seven homers and 42 RBI in 79 games with the Wings. He said in an interview nearly forty years later that he didn't remember being subjected to any of the racial hatred that Robinson endured while playing in the IL. Wings manager Harry "The Hat" Walker, though, recalled one incident when an opposing player peppered him and Alston with epithets. "I told the guy to shut up, and he said, 'You wanna make something of it?' and the next thing you know he and I are wrestling like two alligators in the dugout," Walker said.

Alston was recalled by the Cardinals late that summer and spent the rest of the season in a reserve role. During the next three summers, he would yo-yo between the majors and minors before being released.

Alston's life after leaving baseball was a sad one. The man with the sweet swing but troubled soul returned to Greensboro, North Carolina, and tried to slit his wrists. Not long after that unsuccessful suicide attempt, he went to a church in the middle of the night, poured kerosene on the pews, and lit a match. The building burned to the ground. The police took Alston away.

He spent parts of the next ten years in two different mental institutions in North Carolina. After his release in 1969, he lived in a small apartment in Greensboro. He pretty much kept to himself, living off disability benefits and taking medicine for his depression and arthritis. Occasionally, he would journey to War Memorial Stadium, home of Greensboro's Class A team, to watch a game and someone would recognize him as a former major leaguer. And occasionally someone would mail him a picture to autograph. "When someone remembers, that makes me feel good," he said three years before his death in the winter of 1994. "Real good."

Thomas Edison Alston with August Busch.
Courtesy of the *Democrat and Chronicle/Times-Union.*

in the Junior World Series, as Bill Rigney's Minneapolis Millers won a seven-game series to capture the Triple-A crown.

Harry Walker's venture in St. Louis was ill fated. Unable to jump-start the Cardinals, "The Hat" was dropped by impatient general manager Frankie Lane following the '55 season as St. Louis finished seventh at 68–86 (51–67 under Walker). Walker was reassigned to manage Double-A Houston—Dixie's old job—and it would be ten years before he landed another big-league position. As for Dixie, he returned in 1956 and led the Wings to a second-place finish at 83–67. Again, Rochester rolled through the International League playoffs, beating Miami in five games behind Cot Deal and then stunning Toronto in seven, winning the final two games at Maple Leaf Stadium.

For the first time since the Shaughnessy playoffs were created in 1933, the Red Wings had won consecutive Governors' Cup titles. The Junior World Series remained elusive. American Association champ Indianapolis, managed by former Red Wing George Selkirk, swept the first three games in Rochester, then finished the Wings off with a 6–0 win at the appropriately-named Victory Field in Indianapolis.

The headline in the *Democrat and Chronicle* following game two —a 12–4 Indians win—was YOUNG DAKOTAN WRECKS WINGS and detailed the power surge of a young Indianapolis outfielder who had driven in seven runs on two homers and a single.

The player's name was Roger Maris.

"The kid's got a lot of power," Indians manager Kerby Farrell said. "Only 22 years old, too. He's got quite a future." In 1961, Roger Maris set a major-league record by hitting sixty-one homers for the New York Yankees. No one has approached the mark since.

Another Indianapolis player made an impression on Red Wings fans as well. Joe Altobelli, a power-hitting first baseman from Detroit, finished the series 6-for-13 with a homer in the game four clincher. The Junior World Series offered Altobelli his first trip to Rochester. It would not be his last.

Despite the loss to Indianapolis, the '56 season had been a success. The Red Wings had won their third Governors' Cup title in five seasons and appeared ready to contend for more championships in the second half of the decade. It wouldn't work out that way. Change was in the air, and the Red Wings' toughest battle was about to begin.

8

Flying the Coop

*I believe baseball can break even and make a buck
or two in Rochester. Meanwhile, time runs out for us.*
—Cardinals GM *Frank Lane*, 1956

For twenty-eight years, the St. Louis Cardinals and Rochester Red Wings had enjoyed a mutually satisfying relationship. During the period from 1928 to 1956, the Red Wings won seven International League pennants, four Governors' Cups, and three Junior World Series. The Cardinals captured eight National League pennants and five World Series behind former Red Wings such as Johnny Mize, Stan Musial, and Red Schoendienst.

Under Branch Rickey, the Cardinals had been the undisputed architects of the minor-league system. By 1940, the Cardinals owned thirty-two minor-league teams and had working agreements with eight others. But in the mid-1950s, many baseball teams began experiencing economic difficulties as more fans left the city for the suburbs. The Brooklyn Dodgers and New York Giants headed to the West Coast. The Boston Braves ventured to Milwaukee. And the St. Louis Browns became the Baltimore Orioles. The Cardinals had no desire to leave St. Louis, but they were intent on increasing their profit margin. They began downsizing their minor-league farm system, going from twenty-two affiliates in 1954 to eighteen in 1955 and then fifteen in 1956.

Following the 1956 season, the Cardinals dropped an additional four affiliates. One of the victims was the Red Wings.

The rumors began a week after the 1956 season ended. They be-

Former music-store owner Morrie Silver was instrumental
in securing the sale of the Red Wings from the
Cardinals to Rochester Community Baseball, Inc.
Courtesy of the *Democrat and Chronicle/Times-Union.*

came official on October 30: the Cardinals were pulling out of Rochester.
The news shocked the city. Red Wings director Carl Hallauer received
official confirmation via telegram, signed by Cardinals assistant GM Bing
Devine. "I called Bing and asked if we could get a crack at buying the
franchise first," Hallauer recalled years later. "He said he would give
us [three or four days]." The asking price for the team, stadium, and
surrounding real estate was set at $500,000. Hallauer was still trying to
figure out how to raise half a million dollars when he arrived at the
Rochester Club that evening. One of the first persons he met was his
friend, local businessman Morrie Silver.

"What would you think of Rochester without the Red Wings?"
Hallauer asked as he handed Silver the telegram. Silver read it, then

began peppering Hallauer with questions. Within minutes, he decided to organize a pledge drive to secure a community buyout of the Cardinals. Quietly, he began to work behind the scenes.

Community ownership was a risky business. Buffalo had drawn two hundred thousand fans in its first civic venture in 1955 despite an eighth-place club, but only after relentless promotions and a late-season plea for support. Columbus, Ohio, had taken over its club from the Cardinals two years before, and Richmond, Virginia, and Indianapolis, Indiana, had become community-owned the previous season. Despite Silver's enthusiasm, there was little hope of a successful community take-over in Rochester. "It is my thinking," Hallauer said, "that no individual or small group in this community will put up enough money to take the club over."

The Cardinals also were dropping three other clubs: Class C Fresno, Class B Peoria, and Class A Allentown. They were keeping their American Association team in Omaha and their Double-A Texas League club in Houston. "It is no longer practical from a player-development standpoint for the St. Louis club to maintain three top clubs," Cardinals GM Frank Lane said in making the stunning announcement. "The Rochester club has operated at a great deficit for the past several years despite teams which consistently finished in the first division. We hope local Rochester interests will acquire the franchise and be able to operate it successfully. Should some group take over the operation, it can be assured full cooperation of the St. Louis Cardinals, including some sort of working agreement if desired."

The Red Wings board of directors held an exploratory meeting one day after the shocking announcement. Community ownership remained the only realistic solution, but no person or group had stepped forward with a viable plan.

> *Call this bitter if you like, but it becomes a little annoying when the St. Louis Cardinals repeatedly point out the red ink in the Red Wings books as the sole reason for their withdrawal of baseball sponsorship here. That's not the whole story. What general manager Frank Lane of the parent Cards didn't tell Rochesterians is far more significant than what he said in announcing the heave-ho. Spokesmen for the industry which owns the Cardinal system time and again have said that the company would be much more interested in the setup if it were permitted to sell its product [beer] in Red Wing Stadium.*
> *Give the Cardinals an opportunity to sell their*

suds in Red Wing Stadium, as they have been permitted
to do in Omaha's park, and then ask them to choose
between the two cities.
    Betcha they'd take Rochester.
—*Paul Pinckney, Democrat and Chronicle, Nov. 2, 1956*

Bitterness was growing in Rochester, but survival dictated a more open-minded attitude. By mid-November, with baseball's winter meetings in Jacksonville, Florida, just three weeks away, the Red Wings' future remained in limbo, but officials were talking with St. Louis about continuing a working relationship in 1957. There would be little time to find another parent club, and it would be nearly impossible to coax a major-league team into joining with such a vulnerable franchise.

Lane stressed the urgency of the situation. "We have heard offers from at least two other cities eager to acquire an International League franchise," the Cardinals GM said. "We are doing everything we can to give Rochester an opportunity to retain the franchise. The last thing we want is to sound as though we are delivering a threat. We merely want something to happen. The moment we hear something from Rochester, we are ready to send Bing Devine and [real estate specialist] Al Banister into your city to talk with these people."

FOR SALE: One International League ballpark,
beautifully conditioned, well-appointed, one IL fran-
chise, "some" players outright and others via working
agreement with St. Louis Cardinals.
MINIMUM DOWN PAYMENT: $75,000.
PROSPECTIVE PURCHASERS: None.
—*George Beahon, Democrat and Chronicle, Nov. 16, 1956*

Devine and Banister did travel to Rochester a few days later at the request of the Red Wings board of directors, though no offer had been tendered to the Cardinals. The meeting lasted three hours, and Devine was asked if he was discouraged about Rochester's prospects for retaining baseball. "Let's say I'm not encouraged," the former Wings GM replied. Devine and Banister returned to St. Louis by train after a ten-hour stay in Rochester, promising to prepare and submit a proposal for any prospective purchasing group.

The offer came November 24, one week before the winter meetings. If Rochesterians could raise $200,000—$75,000 for a down payment and $125,000 working capital—in a stock sale over the next five days, the Cardinals pledged to field a "home-owned," high-caliber Triple-A team in the city. The proposal was a generous, if unprecedented, one. It included the right of "first refusal" of specific ex-Rochester players who might be optioned out of St. Louis, the privilege of arranging the working agreement to any length desired by Rochester and access to any of the players currently on the Red Wings roster.

The Cardinals set their asking price at $550,000 for the stadium, surrounding real estate, park equipment, and franchise. The Wings board of directors seized the opportunity, setting up two "polling places." One would be manned by general manager George Sisler, Jr., at Red Wing Stadium, the other at the Little White House by Bill Gannett of the Rochester Convention and Publicity Bureau.

> *I'm prejudiced, but this is how I think:*
> *That baseball is the bread-and-butter sport, and summertime without it would be awful.*
> *That if baseball goes, pro basketball will go too.*
> *That Rochester could become a ghost town, sportswise, in two years.*
> *That Atlanta interests are hovering like scavenger birds, waiting for Rochester's civic efforts to crack.*
> *That once baseball leaves, it doesn't come back.*
> —George Beahon, Democrat and Chronicle, Nov. 26, 1956

With Morrie Silver spearheading the drive, public response was swift: $55,220 was pledged the first day and $98,150 by the second. The figure hit $138,420 on day three and $194,750 the following day, though unofficial totals placed it over the necessary $200,000. Support came from the famous and not-so-famous. Sisler pledged to buy stock and to stay on as Red Wings general manager. Mrs. Betty McGinnis of nearby LeRoy, the daughter of baseball star Rabbit Maranville, pledged in memory of her father. Members of the Rochester Royals professional basketball team pitched in $100 and made their Powers Building office available for additional pledges. The Rochester Americans hockey team threw its support behind the Wings, pledging to buy $500 worth of stock and giving away two free game tickets to the first five hundred people making pledges of any amount. Genesee Bowl sponsored a Save the Wings bowling tournament.

Most of the pledges came through telephone calls in which the caller announced his pledge amount and gave his name and address. The average pledge was $111, but the amounts varied. A twelve-year-old boy in Irondequoit named Billy Cooper pledged his "life" savings of $100;

Athletic Supporters

Of the millions of spectators who have passed through the turnstiles at the old ballpark at 500 Norton Street, two stand out. Leather-lunged Red Smith qualifies as the most vociferous Red Wings supporter of all time. Bill Nill may have been the most devoted. In some respects, the two are as much a part of Silver Stadium lore as any of the players who performed there since its opening in the spring of 1929.

Smith, whose stentorian voice and unbridled enthusiasm made him the team's unofficial cheerleader for several decades, was so popular among management, players, and fans that the Red Wings honored him with special nights during the 1957 and 1965 seasons. He was born Victor Joseph Smith in Utica, New York, in 1885, and according to late *Times-Union* sports editor Matt Jackson "the nurses on hand [for the delivery] claimed no child in maternity ward history was ever gifted with such lungs and tonsils as the carrot-topped Smith."

The Old Redhead, as he came to be known, was raised in an orphanage, and later earned money outrunning competitors on the professional track and field circuit. But it was his vocal cords rather than his feet that earned him lasting fame. Shortly after Smith arrived in Rochester in 1915, local boxing promoters Sam and Elmer Weidrick signed him to perform introductions on fight cards in Rochester and Buffalo. These were the days before microphones and public address systems, so it was imperative to get someone with a voice loud enough to be heard over the din of the crowd. Smith fit the bill. He was as entertaining as he was loud. The frustrated thespian exhibited an ability to rouse fight fans into a frenzy long before modern-day ring announcer Michael Buffer evoked similar emotions with his oft-imitated "Let's get ready to rumble" signature phrase. It wasn't long before Smith was introducing world boxing champions such as Jack Dempsey, Carmen Basilio, and Sonny Liston.

With the introduction of the public address systems, sports "barkers" like Smith became obsolete. But that didn't stop the Old Redhead from entertaining folks at Rochester Americans hockey games and Rochester Royals basketball games. His voice, however, was most prominent at Silver Stadium where, even into his eighties, the cigar-chomping Smith could be seen roaming the stands with the aid of a cane, leading various sections in cheers. A friend of Smith's once told a reporter: "Believe me, Red would sleep in the locker room, if the Wings would let him."

Bill Nill was less visible and vocal, but no less passionate. He always claimed that the true baseball fans sat in the bleachers. The Red

Wings were such a big part of the locksmith's life that when he died in August 1978, his widow, Peg, buried his ashes beneath the bleachers down the left-field line. "About a week after the funeral, she showed up at the game," recalled Keith Meyers, a longtime Red Wings fan who often sat near the Nills. "She said, 'He's here,' and my wife and I nodded, thinking she meant in spirit. And Mrs. Nill said, 'No, he's really here,' and she pointed to a mound of dirt beneath the bleachers. It was an appropriate burial place because the two of them were there all the time, and they always seemed to enjoy the socializing that took place. By burying him there, it was like Bill still could be close to the action and still be amongst friends."

Nill attended his first game in 1909 at the old Baseball Park on Bay Street, and he became a fixture at Rochester games. The only three home openers he missed in sixty-nine years were the ones staged while he was off fighting in World War II. Nill died while preparing to attend a Red Wings game.

Newark businessman John Bilotta promised to raise $5,000 from his area; an elevator operator asked where he could send his $10; and the Italian Civic League pledged a staggering $20,000. Local businesses also rallied around the Wings as Bausch and Lomb, Haloid, and Rochester Gas and Electric set up pledge booths at their offices.

With the money secure, the Red Wings' new community sponsors needed a name and a leader. A mayor's committee chose Rochester Community Baseball, Inc., for the name and unanimously selected Morrie Silver to run it as chairman.

The forty-six-year-old Silver had, as the *Democrat and Chronicle* noted, "a Horatio Alger" background. A native of Rochester and a graduate of East High School, Silver's plans to attend Cornell University were shelved when his father, Charles, fell ill. Morrie and his three brothers and sister found jobs to help support the family, with Morrie selling the *Times-Union* on downtown street corners. He was so successful that the newspaper soon hired him for their circulation department.

After twelve years, Silver left to open the Columbia Institute of Music in 1937. Membership eventually peaked at five hundred students, and when Silver opened a music store on Clinton Avenue he soon led the country in the sale of records, increasing revenues from $25,000 to the millions in the postwar boom of the late 1940s. Silver eventually sold the store and created the M. E. Silver Corp., a distributor of appliances.

"You want to know why I do so well?" he once said in answering a reporter's question. "Because I like people and value friendship, and I try to live by the Golden Rule. Maybe that's corny, but it's true."

A modest man with a generous heart, Silver had quietly pledged a sizable amount toward the pledge drive. Now, with his business talents too valuable for the home-owned Red Wings to pass up, he became the key figure in Rochester's independent baseball operation.

> JACKSONVILLE, Fla.—Rochester has landed the popular, enormously capable Morrie Silver as "executive chairman." No better businessman could grace the chair. His present plans do not include a visit to this convention city. But the official designation of a general manager and then a field manager are first on the operating agenda—after completion of the stock-selling drive.
> —George Beahon, Democrat and Chronicle, Dec. 2, 1956

Silver's task was to raise more than $300,000 to meet the Cardinals' asking price of $550,000, although many felt that this could be reduced through negotiations.

"If it were my money only, I would spend more recklessly than I would the public's," Silver said. "The citizen who has invested $10 and $20 and up must be fully protected here. By investing myself, I am responsible to the public and myself."

One day after forming their new board, the Red Wings lost their manager. Dixie Walker, wary of the Wings' uncertain future, had been lured to Toronto by Maple Leafs owner Jack Kent Cooke. The choice could not have been more surprising. Fifteen months before, Cooke had lambasted Walker for using second-line pitchers in a doubleheader loss to Montreal that cost Toronto the 1954 pennant by a half-game. Walker had defended his decision, saying he was resting his top pitchers with the playoffs only two days away, and then had added insult to injury by sweeping Cooke's club in the postseason.

The Red Wings would field a team in 1957, and they would continue their working agreement with St. Louis. That was cause for celebration, but not everyone had forgiven the Cardinals' abandonment of Rochester. One major stockholder in the new baseball corporation suggested dropping the nickname "Red Wings" as a sign of independence. The name had been adopted in 1928, when the Cardinals moved the Syracuse franchise to Rochester, and was considered an offshoot of the nickname "Cardinals." Most fans questioned rejected the idea, feeling

Morrie Silver *(left)* and Cardinals assistant GM Bing Devine complete sale
of Red Wings from St. Louis to Rochester Community Baseball, Inc., in 1957.
Courtesy of the *Democrat and Chronicle/Times-Union.*

that "Red Wings" had become part of the community's consciousness. One, however, suggested renaming the club the "Silver Streaks" in honor of the club's new leader.

"And a hi-ho from Silver to that gentleman," Morrie Silver replied. "He was very kind. But I'm not looking for any personal publicity in this job. My aim is a sound club that will produce top entertainment and dividends for all of us."

On December 11, Rochester Community Baseball, Inc., named a complete board of directors and officers. The list included: president, Morrie Silver; vice presidents, Frank Horton and Fred Weismuller; treasurer, Warren Allen; and secretary, Bill Gannett. Pledges had continued to pour in even after the $200,000 deadline and now topped $325,000, with 7,258 Rochesterians making pledges. The remaining piece of the puzzle was securing the package deal (stadium, franchise, etc.) from the Cardinals, and Silver had remained in negotiations with St. Louis officials throughout the week. The deal was finalized on December 12 at the

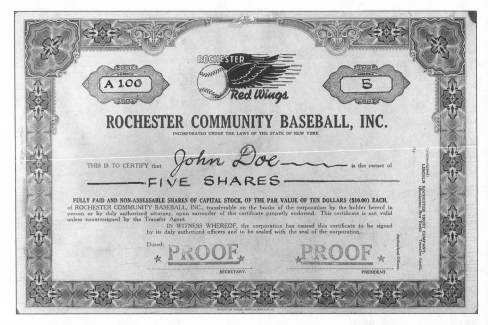

A sample copy of the stock certificate purchased by 8,222 shareholders.
Shares were $10 each. Courtesy of the *Democrat and Chronicle/Times-Union*.

Rochester Club, with the Cardinals lowering their price to $525,000. Rochester Community Baseball, Inc., acquired ownership of Red Wing Stadium, the International League franchise, and twelve acres of surrounding real estate.

Silver also announced several benefits not in the original proposal:

1. Outright ownership acquisition of twelve Red Wings players, identity to be announced later

2. One-sixth equity in the International League, which had estimated assets of $250,000 (Richmond and Havana were excluded)

3. Annual payment from St. Louis to Rochester of $10,000 in consideration of a working agreement up to five years at Rochester's option

4. Agreement of St. Louis to pay all amounts in excess of the $750 monthly salaries of any players optioned to Rochester under major-league contracts

5. Agreement by St. Louis to pay the Rochester manager's salary in excess of $9,000 per year.

In addition, the Cardinals would provide the Red Wings' spring training site (Daytona Beach) and assume the transportation costs of any players going to or from the Cardinals.

Not wanting a mortgage payment hanging over the team's head, Silver set a deadline of January 15, 1957, for raising an additional $300,000—through the sale of public stock—to purchase the club outright from the Cardinals. That deadline was extended when the fundraiser fell $39,200 short, but by late January Rochester Community Baseball had its money courtesy of 8,222 stockholders buying 42,297 shares at $10 per share. Things began moving swiftly from there. On January 26, George Sisler, Jr., kept his promise and announced he was leaving the Cardinals after sixteen years to remain with the Wings as general manager.

"It is not without some feeling of nostalgia that I leave the Cardinals," Sisler said. "However, I am completely sold on Rochester and its baseball picture and I am glad to make the change."

Four days later, Cot Deal was named to replace Dixie Walker as the first manager of the community-owned Red Wings. Deal had been an outfielder, pitcher, pinch hitter, and coach with the Wings. Now he was their field boss. "It is my firm conviction that Deal will be one of the finest managers ever to wear a Red Wing uniform," Sisler said.

Deal did whatever he could to help the team—starting, relieving, playing outfield on occasion, and even catching, when his regulars were injured—but he was saddled with mediocre talent. The Cardinals had begun stocking the Red Wings' roster with rookies, making it difficult for Rochester to compete in the International League. The Wings finished 74–80 in Deal's first season and 77–75 in his second, losing to Toronto four games to one in the playoffs.

On August 1, 1959, Deal decided he had had enough. The Wings fell to Columbus 8–7 that night. It was their twentieth loss in twenty-five games and kept them in last place at 53–59. Minutes before midnight, after his club had left the ballpark, a tired and frustrated Deal resigned "for the best interest of the club, the franchise and myself."

Deal had tried to resign five days earlier, but Sisler had talked him into staying. This time, Sisler accepted Deal's resignation and named veteran pitcher Bob Keegan, a Rochester native who had pitched a no-hitter for the Chicago White Sox in 1957, as interim manager. Sisler hand-picked Deal's replacement a few days later. He was Clyde King, a thirty-four-year-old former major-league pitcher who had guided Colum-

Shots Heard 'Round the Besibol World

At the stroke of midnight on July 26, 1959, Cubans took to the streets of Havana to celebrate the first anniversary of Fidel Castro's ascent to power. The rum flowed freely, as did shots of a different sort. Nowhere was the party more raucous or scary than at Gran Stadium, where thousands of fans were watching the second game of an International League doubleheader between the Rochester Red Wings and the Havana Sugar Kings. Moments after Havana had tied the score at three with a two-run homer in the bottom of the ninth inning, a new Cuban flag was carried into the center-field bleachers by several machete-wielding sugar-cane cutters who had come into town to take part in the festivities honoring Cuba's new premier. As the colors were unfurled, fans and soldiers fired pistols, rifles, and machine guns into the air. Even veteran Red Wing players who had witnessed similar volatile behavior during previous visits to the Havana ballpark couldn't help but become as skittish as first-time passengers in a Manhattan rush-hour taxi.

The haphazard shooting gradually subsided, and play resumed. Billy Harrell homered to put Rochester ahead in the top of the eleventh, but the lead and the stadium's relative calm would be shortlived. In the bottom of the inning, Jesse Gonder led off with a bloop double over third. Red Wings manager Cot Deal noticed that Gonder had not touched first base on his way to second. Deal trotted out to discuss the matter with base umpire Frank Guzzetta. "There was only a three-man umpiring crew and Frank didn't see it because he was hustling down to second to get into position for a possible play there," Deal recalled in a June 1994 interview. "But the plate umpire saw Gonder miss the bag at first, and I asked Frank to appeal to him for help, Guzzetta notified me that there was no way he was going to ask for help to make a questionable call against the Sugar Kings with all those gun-toting fans in the stands. He told me we'd have a riot."

Deal was too engrossed in the game to think about the larger ramifications of calling Gonder out. The manager put his hands around his own neck, indicating to Guzzetta that he had choked on the call. The umpire tossed Deal out of the game. On his way to the clubhouse, Deal told utility infielder Frank Verdi to take over for him as manager. The Sugar Kings tied the score, and in the top of twelfth Verdi took his spot in the third-base coaching box. After the Wings leadoff hitter Dick Rand grounded out, more shots rang out in the stands. Verdi hit the dirt like a tree that had just been chopped in two.

"I'm lying on the ground thinking the first baseman threw the ball and missed the third baseman and hit me in the head," Verdi recalled. "Ed Vargo, the umpire, is yelling, 'Frank are you all right? They almost got me.' I'm thinking, 'What do you mean they almost got you?' Then I saw the blood on my hand. My ear was bleeding. There was a hole in my cap. It took a little chunk out of my ear and (the bullet) landed on my shoulder. It was a .45. I wanted to keep it, but some private-eye type wouldn't let me."

The umpires immediately called the game, and Verdi and the rest of the players hightailed it into the clubhouse. Wrote George Beahon in the *Democrat and Chronicle:* "The chariot scenes from Ben Hur would have suffered in comparison to the sight of players from both dugouts and bullpens exercising the grand old military maneuver of getting the hell out of there."

Verdi was all right, his life saved by the batting helmet liner he normally wore under his baseball cap. Deal and general manager George Sisler called club president Frank Horton and IL president Frank Shaughnessy and were told to get out of Cuba, ASAP. The Sunday doubleheader was not played despite threats from some of Castro's heavy-hitting "advisors." After long, ominous talks, the bearded, machine gun-carrying Cuban *soldados* allowed Sisler and the Wings to board a plane for Miami. On the flight to the States, Verdi went over to Deal and said: "I thought of something. You don't wear an insert in your cap and if you had been in the coaching box instead of me, do you realize that getting that thumb might have saved your life?" Deal smiled and nodded. "Umpires aren't such bad people after all," the manager replied.

American teams became increasingly reluctant to play road games in Havana after the incident. The following summer, Castro, a one-time professional pitching prospect, declared himself a Communist and commenced seizure of all U.S.-owned property, including oil refineries, sugar mills, ranches, and banks. On July 13, 1960, the Havana franchise was transferred to Jersey City.

bus to a fourth-place finish in 1958 and was now the pitching coach in Cincinnati. Convinced that he could better pave his way to a major-league managerial position by running a minor-league team—a blueprint that Frank Robinson would follow with the Red Wings nineteen years later—King quit the Reds and accepted Sisler's offer. The '59 Wings finished 74–80, but King turned things around in his first full season.

Gibson's Final Audition

The last superstar to emerge from the Red Wings-Cardinals marriage was an intimidating right-hander from Omaha, Nebraska. His name was Bob Gibson, and he would go on to become one of the greatest pitchers of the modern era.

Gibson pitched in 20 games for the Red Wings in 1958, going 5–5 with a 2.45 ERA. After a 3–5 season with St. Louis in 1959, he made six more appearances with Rochester in 1960 and went 2–3 with a 2.85 ERA. Gibson went on to win 251 games in his seventeen-year career, winning two Cy Young Awards and earning induction into the Hall of Fame in 1981. He completed arguably the greatest season ever by a major-league pitcher in 1968, going 22–9 with a 1.12 ERA. Gibson made 34 starts that season and turned in an incredible 28 complete games, with 13 shutouts.

"Bob Gibson is the luckiest pitcher I ever saw," said his longtime batterymate in St. Louis, Tim McCarver, who hit .357 in 17 games for the 1959 Wings. "He always pitches when the other team doesn't score any runs."

The Red Wings finished third at 81–73 in 1960 and beat Richmond in the first round of the playoffs before losing the Governors' Cup finals to Toronto in five games.

As a hand-picked selection of Sisler's, King felt little allegiance to the increasing demands of the Cardinals brass. The manager defied their orders to play marginal prospects ahead of proven veterans, and during the playoffs, exasperated Cardinals farm director Walter Shannon, Jr., finally laid down the law: in 1961, King would be replaced by a St. Louis organization man who would focus on developing players for the Cardinals.

The major-league club further infuriated Red Wings fans and executives by trading five popular stars, Jim Frey—the 1960 batting champion—Billy Harrell, Dick Ricketts, Wally Shannon, and Bob Sadowski, to Buffalo for outfielder Don Landrum. That proved to be the final Cardinal sin in a relationship that had been deteriorating for four years. On October 1, 1960, the board of directors of Rochester Community Baseball hastily called a news conference at the Sheraton Hotel. Despite having two years left on their working agreement with St. Louis, the Red Wings announced they were ending their affiliation after thirty-two years. They would not be single for long.

9

Birds of a Feather

*I don't know what the future has in store. We
have to give the Baltimore organization a chance to see
what they can do for us before we pass judgment.*
—Red Wings general manager *George Sisler, Jr.*,
on the team's shift in affiliation
from the St. Louis Cardinals to the Baltimore Orioles

Timing is everything in baseball,
and it just so happened that at the
time the Red Wings and Cardinals were filing for divorce in the fall of
1960, the Baltimore Orioles began searching for a new partner. The
Orioles had grown disenchanted with their International League arrange-
ment in Miami. They wanted to affiliate with a city that supported minor-
league ball, a city with a rich baseball tradition. When Orioles general
manager Lee MacPhail heard that Rochester was a free agent, he contacted the Red Wings. A relationship that would last even longer than
the one Rochester had with St. Louis was formed. Rochester sportswriters called it "Operation Big Switch," and it was hailed by people throughout baseball. Even the Cardinals felt the Red Wings had made a wise
move. "You will be with one of the greatest organizations in baseball,"
Cardinals general manager Bing Devine told the Rochester *Times-Union*.
"We have found the Baltimore Orioles the most competitive team in
baseball when it comes to signing young prospects."

In an effort to ensure that the relationship got off on the right foot,
the Orioles announced that King had been rehired to manage the Wings.
Rochester would win just one pennant and one Governors' Cup during

The first big star of the Orioles-Red Wings merger was Boog
Powell, who slammed a league-high thirty-two homers in 1961.
Courtesy of the *Democrat and Chronicle/Times-Union*.

its first decade with the Orioles, but they would be exciting seasons, as a
busload of talented players who would go on to contribute to Baltimore's
World Series championships in 1966 and 1970 wound up refining their
skills at 500 Norton Street.

The first big star of the new affiliation was a mountainous first
baseman named John "Boog" Powell. His father used to call him "Little
Booger," but the nickname was shortened to "Boog" after the little boy
grew up to be a six-foot-four, 230-pound man. Powell had helped lead
his high school football and baseball teams to Florida state championships. The University of Florida offered the two-way tackle a football
scholarship, but he turned it down to sign a bonus contract with the
Orioles for $25,000 or $50,000, depending on which newspaper report

you believed. After two highly productive years in the lower minors, the Orioles promoted him to Rochester, and his booming home runs conjured memories of past Red Wing sluggers Russ Derry, Johnny Mize, and Steve Bilko. Powell proved he belonged in their long-ball company by hitting .321, driving in ninety-two runs and leading the International League in homers with thirty-two. Early in the season, Howie Haak, the former Wings trainer-turned-major-league baseball scout, visited Rochester and announced: "Powell is the best prospect in all of baseball."

Years later, when Powell was inducted into the Red Wings Hall of Fame, he recalled with fondness his year in Rochester. It was a memorable season, on and off the field. At a teammate's birthday party during the summer of '61, Powell met a Rochester woman named Janet Swinton, and the two were married a year later. Powell's long homers and pitcher Art Quirk's seven-inning no-hitter against Syracuse on the Fourth of July were among the high points of the season. But they couldn't compare to what happened one day after the regular season concluded.

The Wings and Toronto Maple Leafs had finished the regular season tied for fourth place with 76–78 records. A one-game playoff was scheduled to determine who would advance to the Governors' Cup series. A coin flip was held to decide if the game would be played in Rochester or Toronto. Maple Leafs general manager Frank Pollock called tails and the coin landed on heads. Much to the delight of Wings general manager George Sisler, Jr., the game would be played at Red Wing Stadium.

Just over seven thousand spectators showed up for the game on September 11, 1961, and they witnessed one of the most bizarre and dramatic baseball contests in the 113-year history of professional baseball in Rochester. Herb Moford, the ace of the Wings pitching staff with fifteen victories, started, and after just seven pitches, the Leafs led 4–0. When they added three more in the second, the fans began booing Rochester manager Clyde King. With Toronto up 8–3 entering the bottom of the seventh, it appeared as if the Leafs would be going to the playoffs and the Wings would be going home. But Jim "Mugsy" Finigan, a light-hitting second baseman who entered the game batting only .224 with two home runs, ripped a two-run single and Rochester rallied for six runs to take a 9–8 lead.

The euphoria was short-lived. Toronto regained the lead with two runs in the eighth and one in the ninth. More boos rained down from the stands. With one out in the bottom of the ninth, Fred Valentine singled. That brought up Finigan again, and he stunned everyone by depositing a fastball 360 feet into the left field bullpen. The two-run homer, known in Red Wings lore as "Finigan's Rainbow," a takeoff on

The Legend of Luke Easter

The Buffalo Bisons had decided to go with younger players, so early in the 1959 season they sold veteran slugger Luke Easter to the Red Wings for $100. No one knew Easter's age for sure, though some believed he was forty-five when he first pulled on his Rochester flannels.

The mountainous 6-foot-4½, 240-pound first baseman's legend was firmly established by the time he joined the Wings. He had slugged numerous tape-measure home runs for the Homestead Grays of the Negro League, and some believe Easter would have established all sorts of slugging records in the major leagues had the color barrier not existed during the prime years of his career. He spent parts of six seasons with the Cleveland Indians after Jackie Robinson integrated the game in 1947, and in his three full seasons, Big Luke smacked 86 homers and drove in 307 runs.

The Indians demoted him early in the 1954 season and he never played another game in the major leagues. But his mystique grew in minor league cities throughout America where his tape measure homers and infectious smile made indelible impressions. During his first season with the Wings, he wound up batting .262 with 22 home runs and 76 RBI. He would spend five more seasons in Rochester as a player and coach, and not come close to matching those numbers, but it wouldn't matter. Easter's unforgettable home runs and engaging personality would make him perhaps the most popular player in the history of Rochester baseball. Wrote *Democrat and Chronicle* sports columnist George Beahon: "Foul weather or fair, he never denied an autograph. During those years, after I filed stories from the press box to the morning paper, I would see Luke still around the clubhouse or parking lot, signing his name and making friends for the franchise."

"Luke Easter Nights" became an annual affair at 500 Norton Street. The one the Wings staged on August 17, 1963, prompted Big Luke to finally come clean with his age. Club President Morrie Silver had offered to give Easter $10 for every year of his age, and $520 was enough to get him to spill the beans. "My baseball age is 42," he said, smiling, "but my real age is 52."

Easter played his final game during the 1964 season, and stayed on as a coach. Boog Powell and Curt Blefary were among the sluggers who credited Easter with helping them achieve success in the major leagues. Luke returned to Cleveland in 1969 as a coach with the Indians. He stayed in the area until his death on March 29, 1979. He was a union steward at the time, and was carrying money from checks he had cashed for his fellow workers when he was accosted by two men, who shot and killed him.

Luke Easter. Courtesy of the *Democrat and Chronicle/Times-Union.*

the Broadway musical, *Finian's Rainbow,* sent the game into extra innings. Toronto failed to score in their half of the tenth, setting the stage for more Wings drama. Barry Shetrone led off by beating out an infield hit. Harry Chiti sacrificed him to second and Powell, the International League's home run leader, was intentionally walked. Shetrone and Powell advanced on a wild pitch, and Joe Durham was then walked intentionally to load the bases. Valentine struck out on a 3–2 pitch, and Finigan stepped into the box with two outs. Leafs pitcher Cal Browning delivered a fastball, and Finigan slapped it into right field to score Shetrone with the winning run.

A total of forty-two players, including seventeen pitchers, saw action in the four-hour marathon. None of them stood out like Finigan. He had four hits and six RBI in six at-bats. "Never in my baseball managing career did I ever have a team with more guts, more spirit, more fight than this year's Rochester Red Wings," said King, who was so emotionally spent that sportswriter Matt Jackson described him as being "as limp as a rag doll and as happy as a June bride." The Maple Leafs locker room was as quiet as a funeral home. Outside it, Pollock, the Toronto general manager, leaned against a wall and muttered to himself: "I don't believe it. I have never seen a crazier game in all my life. I just don't believe it." Leaf owner Jack Kent Cooke, who would win three Super Bowls after purchasing the Washington Redskins years later, was not pleased with the outcome.

More than one hundred fans waited outside the Wings clubhouse for Finigan to appear. A longtime Wings season-ticket holder said the home run reminded him of the dramatic blast Estel Crabtree hit in 1939. A young man next to the old-timer, replied: "Who's Crabtree anyway? We want Finigan." Their new hero emerged from the clubhouse after about an hour. A young man ran up to him, grabbed his hand, and thrust it skyward. The crowd went wild. The following day, the *Democrat and Chronicle* carried a huge headline on page one that read: WINGS DO IT! MAKE LEAGUE PLAYOFFS. Sparky Anderson, a coach for Toronto, predicted Rochester would go on to win it all. But the man who would become the third winningest manager in major-league history would be off-base with his prediction. The Wings wound up losing to Buffalo in the Governors' Cup finals.

Not that it mattered. Finigan's homer had been so dramatic that everything after it became anticlimactic. Little did anyone know at the time, but that big day would also be the second baseman's last hurrah. That winter, Sisler, somewhat reluctantly, mailed Finigan a contract for the 1962 season. It called for him to receive the same salary as he had the year before. Finigan sent the contract back unsigned and reminded Sisler of "Finigan's Rainbow." Said Sisler: "He wanted a raise on the basis of that one game. I told him that if he had performed the way we expected him to during the regular season, we wouldn't have had to play that extra game against Toronto." Sisler stood firm on his offer, and Finigan didn't budge either. He refused to sign and never played another game of professional baseball.

Powell was promoted to Baltimore after the season, and went on to establish himself as one of the Orioles all-time greats. Prospect Pete Ward took his spot as the Red Wings first baseman and nearly matched

Powell's numbers with 22 homers, 90 RBI, and a .328 average. Buster Narum paced the pitching staff with twelve victories, but the Wings could do no better than fourth again. They lost in the first round of the Governors' Cup playoffs to Jacksonville, and King wound up leaving after the season to take a job as the Cardinals roving minor-league pitching coach. The St. Louis officials who did not want his managerial contract renewed with the Red Wings two years earlier were long gone, victims of a Cardinals housecleaning effort. King would go on to manage several major-league teams and would briefly serve as general manager of the New York Yankees.

He was replaced in Rochester by Darrell Johnson, who guided the Wings to a seventh-place finish in 1963. One of the few highlights occurred on June 9 when Nat Martinez threw a seven-inning no-hitter against Jacksonville. The team was mediocre to be sure, but the fans were too busy embracing aging minor-league sluggers Steve Bilko, Luke Easter, and Joe Altobelli to notice the shortcomings. The three players were past their primes, but they had managed to strike a chord with Rochesterians. Bilko had endeared himself to Red Wings followers who remembered his frequent tape-measure shots of the late '40s and early '50s. Easter was quite possibly the most beloved Red Wing of all time, a gentle giant of a man who was entertaining to watch even when he was striking out, which he did often. Altobelli would become even more revered as a Wings manager in the 1970s, but he was pretty popular as a player, too. He had been one of the International League's top players for years, and his heritage made him a big draw in Rochester's large Italian-American community. He was so popular that before he left to start his minor-league managing career early in the 1966 season, Morrie Silver held a day for him at the stadium and presented Alto with a car.

Bilko was gone in 1964, and the aging, often injured Easter appeared in just ten games. Altobelli returned and had a fairly productive season with 11 homers and 52 RBI while playing parts of 122 games. Other Triple-A veterans included Steve Demeter and Lou Jackson. The roster also featured former major-leaguers Gino Cimoli, Joe Pignatano, and Mike McCormick. Of those three, McCormick would be the only one to return to the big leagues with any degree of success. That's not to say the team was devoid of youth; Baltimore had assigned several prospects to Rochester, including first baseman Curt Blefary, pitcher Darold Knowles, and second baseman Davey Johnson, who would become the only player ever to be a teammate of both home run hitting legends Hank Aaron and Sadaharu Oh. Johnson wound up having the most successful major-league career of that crop of Orioles prospects, but Blefary was

Another Silver Save

As the major stockholder in Rochester Community Baseball, Morrie Silver had remained deeply involved with the Red Wings. He stepped down as president in October 1957, ten months after securing the community takeover of the Wings from the St. Louis Cardinals, but remained on the board's executive committee. Vice president Frank Horton replaced him, but when Horton left for Washington, D.C., as a U.S. congressman in 1962, Silver returned until Joseph T. Adams assumed the presidency the following year.

When Adams departed, Silver was renamed president of the Red Wings on November 18, 1964. And when George Sisler, Jr., left as general manager to become president of the International League in July 1965, Silver filled that role as well.

By the mid-1960s, overspending had resulted in a $12,286 deficit for Rochester Community Baseball. "We are," Silver said, "on the verge of bankruptcy."

So the former music-store owner went to work, inaugurating a sweeping austerity campaign to cut costs and reduce the deficit. By the end of the '65 season, the deficit was down to $1,713. Silver suffered a near-fatal heart attack on Thanksgiving Day, but he recovered over the winter and returned as general manager in 1966.

This time, he turned the club's financial structure completely around, building a $161,472 profit, more money than all twenty-three of the other Triple-A teams had made combined. For the second time in nine years, Morrie Silver had saved baseball in Rochester.

"It is a superb tribute to Silver, the Wings and Rochester fans," said former Wings GM Bing Devine, president and general manager of the New York Mets at the time. "I suppose my board of directors will be on the phone wondering how they can get Silver down here to New York."

Silver worked for a token $1 salary, often saying, "the Rochester fans and their love of baseball is my pay."

the dominant Wing that season. Following in Rochester's rich tradition of power-hungry first basemen, Blefary hit 31 homers, drove in 80 runs, batted .287, and was just edged out for league rookie-of-the-year honors by future Detroit Tigers standout Jim Northrup.

Rochester began the last day of the 1964 season in fifth place, one percentage point behind Toronto. In order to make the playoffs, the

Wings would have to beat the Bisons in Buffalo and Toronto would have to lose to the Chiefs in Syracuse. Mike McCormick, who would have major-league success with the San Francisco Giants, hit a solo homer and shut out the Bisons 1–0 on a five-hitter. "We finished before Syracuse and Toronto did, and I remember George Sisler got on the phone with someone in the Syracuse press box, and kept giving us updates until it was over," Altobelli recalled. "We went wild when we heard the final verdict." The final verdict was a Syracuse victory, which meant the Wings had clinched fourth place and a playoff spot. Jacksonville won the pennant, and was expected to have an easy time with the Wings, but Hurricane Dora knocked down the Suns scoreboard, and the first two games of the series were switched to Rochester. The Wings stunned Jacksonville by winning both games, then two more in Florida for the sweep. Rochester won the Governors' Cup finals in six games over Syracuse as Herm Starette pitched sensationally out of the bullpen. He saved game two with three and two-thirds innings of sparkling relief, then followed that by allowing only three hits in five and two-thirds innings in game six as the Wings won their first Cup since 1956.

There would be no repeat of those heroics in 1965. The veteran Wings finished a game under .500 and out of the playoffs. In his last full season as a professional baseball player, Joe Altobelli thrilled Rochester fans by clubbing a team-leading 20 homers and batting .295. Third baseman Steve Demeter also had a solid year with 88 runs batted in and a .299 average. Pitcher Bill Short led the league in winning percentage (13–4, .765), and hard-throwing Frank Bertaina was the pacesetter in strikeouts (188).

Wings president Morrie Silver was disappointed in the club's performance in the standings and the stands. Attendance had declined by more than sixty thousand from the previous season, and Silver believed that a more dynamic manager than the bland Johnson might help revive interest in Rochester baseball. The Orioles suggested Earl Weaver, who had interviewed for the job three years earlier after Clyde King's departure. Silver thought Weaver deserved a shot the second time around, and he would not regret the move. Though only thirty-four, Weaver already had ten years of minor-league managing experience by the time he arrived in Rochester. His first opportunity to manage came in 1956 when he was still playing for Knoxville, an independent team in the Class A Sally League. Late in the season, Dick Bartel was fired and Weaver was asked to take over. He guided the team to a 10–24 record and was hired the following season to manage one of the Orioles' Class A teams. He suffered through another losing season, but he would not finish under .500 again until 1986 in his second tour of duty managing the Orioles.

A Man Named Alto

As an opposing player, Joe Altobelli made numerous visits to Rochester during the late 1950s and early 1960s. But it wasn't until 1963 that he had an opportunity to pull on the Red Wing flannels. Wings general manager George Sisler, Jr., needed a first baseman, and he convinced his friend, Buzzie Bavasi of the Los Angeles Dodgers, to loan him Altobelli for the entire season. It would be the start of a long and wonderful relationship between player, team, and town. "I never realized what a huge favor George, Buzzie and Morrie [Silver] had done for me until years later," Altobelli said. "Coming to Rochester was one of the best things to ever happen to me."

The left-handed slugging Altobelli became such a hit with the fans, including many from Rochester's large Italian-American community, that Sisler purchased his contract from the Dodgers at the end of the 1963 season. In parts of four years, Altobelli clubbed forty-seven home runs, including one torrid stretch in 1965 when he hit eight in eight games. After that season, the Detroit native decided to move his family permanently to Rochester. He has been there ever since.

Silver, the Wings president, was so fond of Altobelli that he held a night at the ballpark in his honor and presented him with a new car. Silver also was instrumental in getting Altobelli's managerial career launched in the Baltimore Orioles farm system in 1966. Five years later, Alto returned and guided the Red Wings to four pennants and two league championships in six years. His 1971 team is regarded as among the best in minor-league baseball history.

Altobelli won two major league manager of the year awards and led the 1983 Baltimore Orioles to a World Series title. In November 1991, he returned to his adopted home town to become general manager of the Red Wings, a position he held until early 1995, when he became a special assistant to Rochester Community Baseball president Elliot Curwin. Altobelli, who came to be known as Mr. Baseball in Rochester, was instrumental in the drive that resulted in the building of a new stadium to replace Silver. His number twenty-six jersey is the only uniform retired in Red Wings history.

Joe Altobelli. Courtesy of the *Democrat and Chronicle/Times-Union*.

If Silver was looking for a colorful skipper, he could find none more colorful than Weaver. A notorious umpire baiter, Weaver had been thrown out of numerous games during his career. Perhaps his most famous ejection occurred during a 1963 game in Charleston, West Virginia, when he became so incensed with an umpire's call that he yanked third base from its moorings and carried it into the clubhouse and locked the door. The Charleston team had only one set of bases, so the game couldn't resume until a clubhouse boy talked Weaver into giving back the base.

That hot temper would be on display often during his two seasons managing the Red Wings. One newspaper report said that Weaver was ejected twenty-one times while with Rochester. "Kenny Rowe and I would sit in the bullpen and wager a dinner or a beer on the inning we thought Earl would get tossed," said Rochester reliever Paul Knechtges. "Sometimes we felt sorry for the umpire because we knew what it was like to have Earl get in your face. Believe me, it wasn't a pleasant experience." If Weaver was especially irritated, he would kick dirt on the umpire and pepper him with expletives. "There was a method to Earl's madness," Knechtges said. "He wasn't just putting on a show. He saw his arguments with the umpires as a way to fire up the players and the fans. And he really believed that by blowing up he could intimidate the umps and get more calls to go his way in the long run. That was Earl. Always looking for any edge he could find. It was all part of his competitiveness. I don't care if it was baseball, golf or cards, I never met anyone who wanted to win as fiercely as Earl did." That competitiveness and managerial skill clearly were evident in Rochester, where Weaver led the Wings to a pennant in 1966 and a second-place finish the following summer.

The first-place finish caught virtually everyone by surprise. Veteran International League reporters predicted the inexperienced Wings would finish in the second division in 1966. Weaver clearly did not share their pessimism. "We thought he was crazy because Earl was opening the season with an incredibly green club," longtime Red Wings announcer Joe Cullinane recalled. "Earl had only two guys [third baseman Steve Demeter and second baseman Mickey McGuire] with any significant Triple-A experience. But he was confident in the young players he had. Most of all, he was confident in himself."

After the Wings got off to a slow start in 1966, a worried Silver called Weaver into his office. The team president wanted to do something to help Weaver. "He showed me this list with the International League's top hitters on it and told me he would go out and purchase the contracts of any two I wanted," Weaver recalled in a 1995 interview. "I said,

First baseman Mike Epstein was the power behind
the '66 International League champs, slamming
29 homers and driving in 102 runs. Courtesy
of the *Democrat and Chronicle/Times-Union.*

'Morrie, I really appreciate your offer, but just give us some time. We
have some great young talent on this club. Things will jell.' The Wings
roster stayed put, and, in time, youngsters such as slugging first baseman
Mike Epstein and slick-fielding shortstop Mark Belanger helped Rochester make a pennant drive.

Epstein proved to be another in a long line of powerfully built
Red Wings first basemen. The six-foot-three, 230-pounder had played
fullback at the University of California under Buffalo Bills coach Marv
Levy. But like Boog Powell before him, Epstein decided that baseball was
where his future lay. After watching Epstein hit several batting practice
offerings out of sight, former major leaguer Rocky Bridges called him

A Double No-No

Hundreds of pitchers have played for the Red Wings. Hundreds have pitched against them. But no one has ever duplicated Dave Vineyard's accomplishment in the mid-1960s. In one nine-month span, the right-hander tossed no-hitters both for and against the Wings.

Vineyard pitched for Rochester from 1962 to 1966, compiling a 31–25 record. He also made nineteen appearances with the Baltimore Orioles in 1964 and finished 2–5. On July 28, 1966, Vineyard entered his start at Toledo with a 5–6 record and a 4.04 ERA. He was wild that night, walking six batters, but he was also unhittable as the Wings beat the Mud Hens 1–0. It was Rochester's first nine-inning no-hitter since Duke Markell's gem against Columbus on April 9, 1955. It would also turn out to be Vineyard's last victory as a Red Wing.

The twenty-five-year-old from West Virginia developed arm trouble after his no-hitter and finished the '66 season 6–9. He had suffered arm problems in winter ball two years earlier and had pitched only twenty-five innings in '65. But there were no sour grapes from this Vineyard. He kept the injury to himself and pitched through the pain.

"I couldn't hardly complain about my arm being bad. Not again," he said. "Not after Baltimore and Rochester kept me through all the other trouble."

The Orioles didn't keep Vineyard much longer. Following the 1966 season, he was traded to the Toronto Maple Leafs. In his first start against his old team, Vineyard pitched a six-hitter as Toronto won 4–2. One week later, on May 23, 1967, he no-hit the Wings in a 2–1 win at Toronto, with Rochester's run the result of an error by third baseman Johnny Ryan.

Only 262 fans attended the game.

"Super Jew," and the nickname stuck. "I took no offense," said Epstein, who had the moniker sewn onto his practice shirts. "In fact, I rather like it. It's a takeoff on Superman." Epstein's season wound up being nothing short of super. He hit 29 homers, drove in 102 runs, and batted .309, and was named International League Most Valuable Player and Rookie of the Year, as well as Minor League Player of the Year by *The Sporting News*. Epstein was extraordinary off the field as well. It was not uncommon for him to quote Greek philosophers in postgame interviews or discuss the moves of Russian chess masters. "Mike would have all these books in his locker, and Earl would just shake his head as if Mike were strange," broadcaster Joe Cullinane recalled. "But Earl didn't think Mike was strange at the plate."

Weaver was right in urging Silver to be patient. He also knew what he was talking about when he predicted a pennant back in spring training. The '66 Wings blossomed into a solid club. The infield of Epstein, second baseman Mickey McGuire, shortstop Belanger, and third baseman Steve Demeter was among the best in Rochester history. The pitching was strong, too. Ed Barnowski won seventeen games, Dave Vineyard and Tom Phoebus tossed no-hitters, and Frank Bertaina struck out seventeen Toledo Mud Hens in one game, breaking by one the record shared by Will Calihan (1888), Walter Beall (1924), and Phoebus (1966).

The race came down to the final game of the season. A Wings victory over Syracuse at 500 Norton Street would clinch Rochester's first pennant in thirteen years. The Wings controlled the game from the start and were cruising along with a 10–2 lead heading into the ninth inning. After the Wings had batted in the eighth, Weaver trotted from the third base coaching box toward the dugout, and the fans gave him a standing ovation. "Before you knew it the score was 10–6, and the Chiefs have two or three runners on base," Cullinane recalled. "I really believed deep down, we weren't going to be able to put out the fire even though we had two outs." As he had done often that summer, Weaver summoned Knechtges from the bullpen. Arturo Lopez, a contact hitter, stepped to the plate. "I threw this hanging slider that Lopez creamed," Knechtges said. "I mean, the minute he hit it, I'm going, 'Oh no. Oh no.' I turned around and our center fielder, John Scruggs, makes this incredible leaping catch to save the day. Earl shot out of that dugout, and the crowd went wild." The Wings had won the pennant with an 83–64 record, and the frenzied fans refused to let Weaver and his players go to the clubhouse for their celebration. Silver called it the proudest moment of his life. The playoffs were anticlimatic for the Wings, who lost in the first round to Richmond, three games to one.

A month into the 1967 season, it appeared as if Epstein would be returning to the Wings. He had seen little playing time in Baltimore, and the Orioles figured he would be better off if he were in the lineup every day in Rochester. Epstein thought otherwise. The most heralded rookie since Mickey Mantle felt he had nothing left to prove at the Triple-A level and that his only hope was to be traded to a big-league team that needed a first baseman. "The Orioles have Boog Powell, an All-Star, at first base, and he's relatively young, so where am I going?," Epstein told a reporter. His refusal to report to Rochester became national news.

He announced he would retire if the Orioles didn't trade him. There

A Feud Takes Root

It was one of the most publicized and longest running feuds in sports. For nearly two decades, Jim Palmer, the know-it-all pitcher, and Earl Weaver, the know-it-all manager, staged an ego battle the equivalent of two sumo wrestlers bumping bellies. Theirs was a classic power struggle between strong-willed individuals, and it had its genesis in Rochester, long before Palmer became a Hall of Fame pitcher, and long before the Earl of Baltimore guided the Orioles to four American League pennants and a world championship. The tempestuous relationship began while the two were wearing the red and white flannels of the Red Wings in 1967. Weaver was in his second year as Rochester manager and Palmer had been sent down to rehabilitate his ailing right arm and back. In his first start against the Buffalo Bisons, Palmer was cruising along with a 6–0 shutout before running into trouble in the fourth inning. He loaded the bases, then delivered two balls to a player he was told by Earl was a punch-and-judy hitter. Weaver, angry over the wild streak, shot out of the dugout and stormed to the mound.

"Throw the ball over the middle of the plate," barked Weaver. "This guy is nothing." Palmer didn't appreciate Weaver's tirade, but he grudgingly followed orders. He threw the next pitch over the middle, and "the nothing"—who went by the name of Johnny Bench—hit the ball over the fence for a grand slam. It would be the only grand slam Palmer would allow in his illustrious professional baseball career. "At that point," the pitcher said years later. "Earl Weaver lost all credibility with me. I never listened to him again." The man who would go on to become a household name modeling Jockey underwear was undressed for twelve hits and nine earned runs in his two brief appearances with the Red Wings in 1967. Still beset by arm problems, Palmer returned briefly to Rochester the following season and was shelled both times, leaving town with an obscenely high 13.50 ERA. Palmer had been a good hitter in high school, and he contemplated making the conversion to the outfield. But the Orioles felt his future lay in his pitching, and they encouraged him to continue rehabbing his shoulder and arm. Their patience was rewarded, and he returned to the big leagues and finished with a 268–152 record and a 2.86 earned run average. While compiling those impressive statistics, Palmer continued having run-ins with Weaver, who was promoted to Baltimore in 1968. They settled their differences after retiring from baseball. Said Weaver: "Jim was a big part of my bread and butter. Anybody would've handled him the same way—send him out there every fourth or fifth day. I think we excelled together for so many years. I don't think it could've been any better. I couldn't have asked for anything more." Said Palmer: "Earl and I actually were similar in many ways. He wanted to be the best manager in baseball and I wanted to be the best pitcher in baseball. Sometimes we got in each other's way, but I'll say this, when Earl managed, I can never think of a time when we went into the season and we weren't one of the favorites to win."

was even a report out of New York that a World Wrestling Federation promoter was offering Big Mike nearly $50,000 to take part in an exhibition match. After the stalemate dragged into its second week, the Orioles grudgingly capitulated and dealt Epstein and pitcher Frank Bertaina to the Washington Senators in exchange for veteran pitcher Pete Richert. The following season, Epstein was demoted to the Senators farm team in Buffalo, and wound up returning to Rochester as a visiting player. When the Bisons came to town, Epstein was booed lustily by the same fans who had once cheered his baseball heroics. Years later, all would be forgotten; in 1985, Epstein attended a Red Wings Oldtimers' Game at Silver Stadium and received loud applause.

The Epstein sideshow did not distract Weaver. His 1967 Wings finished second in the IL, thanks in large part to the exploits of Dave Leonhard and Curt Motton. Leonhard topped the International League in victories (15) and winning percentage (.833), and Motton led the league in runs batted in (70) while hitting .323 with 19 homers. Rochester lost to Columbus in the opening round of the Governors' Cup finals, and shortly after the series ended Weaver was promoted to the Orioles coaching staff. In 1968, Hank Bauer was fired as the Orioles manager and replaced by 1996 Hall of Fame inductee Weaver, who would establish himself as the winningest manager in team history.

Weaver's departure opened the door for Billy DeMars to take over the Wings. DeMars certainly had paid his dues, having spent twenty-five years in baseball as a player and manager. His mentors had included baseball legends Connie Mack and Walter Alston. Many of the players who had gone on to star for the Red Wings and Orioles had worked under DeMars in the lower minors. One of those prospects was Merv Rettenmund, who would play a key role in Rochester's third-place finish in 1968. The powerful outfielder wound up with twenty-two homers and led the International League in hitting with a .331 batting average. Like

Earl Weaver.
Courtesy of the *Democrat and Chronicle/Times-Union.*

Epstein two years before, Rettenmund was named league MVP and rookie of the year as well as Minor League Player of the Year.

Perhaps the highlight of the season occurred on August 19 when Rochester honored Morrie Silver, the man who had twice saved baseball from extinction in the Flower City. In a ceremony before a game against Jacksonville, the Red Wings officially renamed the ballpark Silver Stadium. Bing Devine, the former Wings and Cardinals general manager, thought the honor was richly deserved. "He was a sports fan and was interested in protecting the community," Devine said. "If the team was being disposed of, he wanted to make sure Rochester got it. . . . Morrie Silver was only interested in helping the community. . . . Anything he wanted to get done, he accomplished." Silver told the crowd that night that he had a simple reason for devoting himself to saving the franchise. "I just couldn't imagine youngsters growing up in years to come not being able to see professional baseball in Rochester."

Shortly after Rochester was bumped from the 1968 playoffs by Columbus, DeMars left to take a coaching job with the Philadelphia Phillies. There was a movement afoot by some Wings fans to have the popular Altobelli return to Rochester to manage the team, but the Orioles instead suggested promoting Cal Ripken, Sr., and Silver approved. At thirty-two, Ripken became the youngest manager in the history of Rochester professional baseball. He also became the fifth Wings manager in eight years. Ripken had been a reserve catcher with the 1961 Wings, batting .083 in eleven games. Although many considered him young to be managing a Triple-A team, Ripken came to the Rochester job with eight years of minor-league managing experience.

There were few stars on that 1969 club, which finished fifth and out of the playoffs for the first time in four years. The main batting threats were Terry Crowley (28 homers, 83 RBI) and Elijah Johnson (.301 batting average). Little Freddie Beene, five-foot-eight, 140 pounds soaking wet, led the league in wins (15), and Mike Adamson set the pace in strikeouts with 133. Marcelino Lopez provided a highlight on May 4 when he tossed a seven-inning no-hitter in a 5–1 victory against Richmond.

Ripken's 1970 club was loaded with talent. It included three of the most coveted prospects in baseball: Bobby Grich, Don Baylor, and Roger Freed. Grich, a shortstop, was around for just sixty-three games that season, but that stretch was long enough for him to make an indelible impression. During that span, he drilled 9 homers, stole 10 bases, drove in 42 runs, and batted .383 before being called up by the Orioles. Baylor had spent fifteen games with the Wings in 1968, but he batted only .217 and was clearly overmatched. By 1970, it was the International League pitchers who were overmatched attempting to stop Baylor. The powerful and quick outfielder hit 22 homers, stole 26 bases, drove in 107 runs, and batted .327. As talented as Grich and Baylor were, neither was regarded as the top prospect in the Orioles chain. That distinction belonged to Freed, who compiled some eye-popping statistics himself during his summer in Rochester. The big outfielder reminded some of former

A Near-Death Experience

Chico Fernandez searched frantically, but to no avail. His batting helmet —the one with the protective ear flap—was nowhere to be found. The Rochester Red Wings player-coach was due up, so there was no time to continue the search. He grabbed a flapless helmet and headed to the plate. As Fernandez dug in during the sixth inning of that August 3, 1969 game against Tidewater at Silver Stadium, he couldn't get comfortable. It was the helmet. Without the flap, it just didn't feel right. Tides pitcher Larry Bearnarth, who was cruising along with a seven-run lead, threw two quick strikes, then delivered a side-arm fastball that got away from him. It sailed inside—way inside—and head high. Fernandez froze like a deer transfixed by headlights. The ball crashed against his left temple, an area that would have been protected by his normal helmet, and Fernandez went down as if shot. "It made a sickening sound," recalled Joe Seil, a fan at the game. "And then the crowd went strangely silent. The only sounds you heard were Fernandez screaming. You started to wonder if he was going to die right there." Fernandez, who was filling in for injured Wings second baseman Art Miranda, squirmed in the dirt and occasionally kicked the air as the trainers attended to him. They managed to place him on a stretcher, and on his way to the ambulance he called out in Spanish for his wife and kids. At Rochester General Hospital, doctors discovered that the impact of the pitch had caused a two-and-one-half inch long crack in Fernandez's skull. Fragments of the bone were pushing against his brain. Surgery was performed immediately to save his life. Afterward, one of the neurosurgeons said: "He would have died [without the surgery]. If you don't do anything, these things are fatal." The shaken-up Bearnarth left the game moments after the ambulance did and headed to the hospital to visit Fernandez. Wings manager Cal Ripken, Sr., absolved Bearnarth of any guilt. "He just tried a waste pitch and it got away inside," Ripken said. "You don't try to hit people when you're leading by that margin and you're up 0–2 in the count." In the days and weeks that followed, Fernandez was deluged with letters from well-wishers throughout the country. A moment of silent prayer was held in for him before the next game at Silver. Fernandez eventually came out of his coma and made a full recovery. He never played another game, but he did land a job as a minor-league instructor with the Los Angeles Dodgers. Bearnarth became a successful major-league pitcher and pitching coach. Strangely, the scariest moment in each of their careers probably would not have happened had Fernandez walked up to the plate with his own helmet—the one with the protective ear flap.

Chico Fernandez, writhing in pain, after 1969 beaning.
Courtesy of the *Democrat and Chronicle/Times-Union.*

Wings legend Steve Bilko. In 1970, he put up Bilko-like numbers, hitting .334 with 24 homers and 130 RBI to sweep league MVP and rookie of the year honors along with the Minor League Player of the Year Award. He would be traded to the Philadelphia Phillies in the off-season, but his major-league career would never amount to much. He spent parts of 8 seasons in the big leagues, hitting .245 with 22 homers in 344 games.

The powerful triumvirate of Freed, Baylor, and Grich led the 1970 Wings to a third-place finish. Columbus eliminated Rochester in the first round of the playoffs, and the team underwent its sixth managerial change in a decade. But this change was welcomed. Joe Altobelli, the man who had made his off-season home in Rochester since 1965, was returning to manage in his adopted hometown.

10

Dream Team

*I managed some great teams in Rochester, but
none of them compare to the '71 team. It was one of a
kind.*

—Joe Altobelli, March 1995

When the Orioles decided to reassign Red Wings manager Cal
Ripken, Sr., to Double-A Dallas–Fort Worth in 1971, they didn't look
far for his replacement. Joe Altobelli had played for the Wings from
1963 to 1966 and had moved to Rochester in 1965. Always popular
with the Rochester fans—Morrie Silver had organized a Joe Altobelli
Night in 1966—the Detroit native had spent the past five years managing
the Orioles' lower minor-league teams, advancing to Dallas–Fort Worth
in 1970.

"When I learned I was going to Rochester, I was excited," Altobelli
said. "I'd waited five years to manage in the place where I lived. But I
said to myself, 'Boy-oh-boy, Joe, you'd better win. You're from there.
You're going to have to live there not only during the summer but the
winter as well.' "

Altobelli had reason to be optimistic heading into the season. Shortstop Bobby Grich and left fielder Don Baylor had put up incredible
numbers with Rochester the year before, but neither could crack the
Orioles' star-studded lineup in '71. Three-time International League all-
star Mike Ferraro was returning at third base and first baseman Terry
Crowley was back after spending the 1970 season with Baltimore.

But not everyone was returning. Roger Freed, the International

1971 Red Wings
courtesy of

CENTRAL TRUST COMPANY
ⓒ A Charter New York Bank   Member F.D.I.C.

First Row (l. to r.): Greg Weston, (Visiting Bat Boy), George Farson, Bob Grich, Don Fazio, Mickey Scott, Sam Parrilla, Fred Beene, Jim Knipper (Bat Boy).

Middle Row (l. to r.): Jim Hutto, Mike Ferraro, Terry Crowley, Pete Ward (Coach), Joe Cullinane (Announcer), Joe Altobelli (Manager), Rich Coggins, Orlando Pena, Bill Kirkpatrick, John Datch.

Back Row (l. to r.): Rudy Owen (Trainer), Don Baylor, George Manz, John Montague, Ray Miller, Larry Johnson, Rick Delgado, Roric Harrison, Bill Burbach, Ron Shelton, Herman Schneider (Ass't. Trainer).

Greatest Red Wings team ever? The 1971 team could lay claim to the title after winning the Junior World Series in Joe Altobelli's rookie season as manager. Courtesy of the Rochester Red Wings.

League's MVP in 1970, had been traded to Philadelphia in December for pitcher Grant Jackson, a National League all-star in 1969, plus minor leaguers Sam Parrilla and Jim Hutto.

The pitching was a question mark. John Montague (6–9) and Bill Kirkpatrick (7–8) were back, but the club's two best pitchers from 1970, Fred Beene (9–3) and Frank Bertaina (12–3), had been traded. Filling those spots would be George Manz, who had gone 7–4 with a 1.99 ERA at Dallas-Fort Worth, and Roric Harrison, a dismal 6–11, 5.57 at Triple-A Portland. Harrison had been acquired from the Milwaukee Brewers and didn't join the Wings until the final day of spring training. Reliever Mickey Scott, the lone left-hander, was coming off a 6–3 season.

"I had us up the ladder," Altobelli said. "It wasn't hard for anybody who knows baseball to know that Bobby Grich and Don Baylor were going to become major leaguers. The easy ones stuck out like sore thumbs."

Altobelli was the first to speak to Grich and Baylor when they were demoted in spring training. "They came down on the same day," Altobelli said. "The thing I remember telling them is, 'I know you feel like you're going to miss a World Series, and I know you think you deserve to be up there. I also know that if you play the way you know you're capable of playing, you'll more than make up for the money you think you're losing.' Both of them became millionares about four years later."

The media seemed to sense something special was brewing on 500 Norton Street. "Local fans are in for a treat this year," *Democrat and Chronicle* beat writer Jim Castor wrote on the eve of the season opener. "Rochester boasts a new manager, a few new players and enough talent to capture the Governors' Cup."

Despite the optimism, the Wings didn't play like champions in the early going. On April 16, they opened with a 12–3 loss to the Louisville Colonels on a chilly night at Fairgrounds Stadium. The defeat was truly a team effort: Rochester was held to six hits by Jim Lonborg, the 1967 American League Cy Young Award winner who was trying to jumpstart his career, and five Red Wings pitchers were rocked for sixteen hits, including two by a young catcher named Carlton Fisk.

The defense was strictly patchwork. Grich was serving military duty in California and second baseman Ron Shelton, who would gain fame as a filmmaker, was suffering from a bladder infection. So Altobelli improvised: he shifted Ferraro to second, started utility man Art Miranda at short and moved Hutto to third. The result was four errors by the Wings. "It wasn't the start we expected," Altobelli said. "It was the opener and everyone was excited. We thought we had a heck of a team, but we were pretty embarrassed."

It got worse. The Red Wings were 0–5 going into the April 22 home opener, and opponents were averaging nine runs and twelve hits. The Wings were getting roasted by opponents. Now they had to dine with fans at the annual American Legion Welcome Home dinner the night before the home opener. "I felt embarrassed," Altobelli said. "The big thing was to get home, get back on the field and get a win as quick as possible. Instead, we were going to this banquet."

Hungry for a winner, the fans nonetheless gave the winless club a rousing ovation. The next day, the Wings gave a chilled crowd of 7,275 something to cheer about. With temperatures hovering in the forties and winds swirling all afternoon, pinch hitter Larry Johnson drilled a game-winning double in the eighth as Rochester beat Richmond 4–3 and

From Silver Stadium to the Silver Screen

Bobby Grich doesn't remember where the bus was headed. It could have been chugging east along the New York State Thruway toward Syracuse or perhaps south to Louisville or Richmond or points beyond. What Grich does remember is that while he and several of his Red Wings teammates were nursing some cold beers in the back of the Greyhound, Ron Shelton, the college guy, was sitting by himself near the front, scribbling furiously in his notebook again.

"I plopped myself next to him and said, 'Shelly, what are you doing? Writing a book?' " Grich recalled of that 1971 road trip. "And Shelly says, 'Bobby, I'm gonna write a movie about our minor-league experiences, and I'm going to invite you to the party when it debuts.' Well, 16 years later, I get this envelope, and in it are two tickets for a screening in L.A. for a new movie by Ron Shelton called *Bull Durham*. So I went and I watched, and afterward I told Shelly, 'You took damn good notes.' "

When Grich's anecdote was recounted for Shelton during the spring of 1995, the man who made the successful transition from Silver Stadium to the silver screen chuckled. It seems that Shelton's former Red Wings teammate may have taken some literary license and stretched the truth a tad. "Great story by Bobby, but I honestly don't remember the incident," Shelton said.

Whether Grich's tale is apocryphal or true is subject for debate. What isn't debatable is that Shelton's reel life has been profoundly influenced by his real life, including the parts of two seasons he spent playing infield for the Red Wings. Shelton's quest to make the big leagues was winding down by the time he reported to Rochester near the end of the summer of 1970. He was with the Wings for the entire 1971 season and batted .260 with one home run, nine runs batted in, and two stolen bases in sixty-six games. He was traded to the Detroit Tigers organization and assigned to their Triple-A affiliate, but he declined to report. He had spent five years in the minors. He and his wife had just had their second child. He figured it was time to move on.

While studying for his masters degree in fine arts at the University of Arizona, Shelton worked a procession of dreary jobs that included driving trucks, cleaning bars, and digging ditches. At night, he would paint and sculpt, and although that provided a creative outlet and he was good at it, he still hadn't found what he was looking for. A movie buff during his playing days, Shelton decided to give screen writing a try.

He took a match to the first two scripts he wrote, but he didn't give up. In 1982, nearly nine years after he started, one of his scripts was filmed. The movie was called *Under Fire*, and starred Nick Nolte. Shelton followed that with *The Best of Times*.

It wasn't until *Bull Durham* was released in 1988, however, that the former Red Wing second baseman became one of Hollywood's heavy hitters. The film, starring Kevin Costner and Susan Sarandon, was a hilarious portrayal of life in the minors, told by someone who had been there and had paid rapt attention. *Bull Durham* became a box office smash, grossing more than $50 million, and earned Shelton an Oscar nomination for best screenplay.

The idea for the movie's plot was inspired by Shelton's old Rochester manager, Joe Altobelli, and a baseball cult figure named Steve Dalkowski. "I played in the Orioles system about five years after Dalkowski, and everywhere I went I heard stories about this pitcher who was the hardest and wildest thrower in baseball history," Shelton explained. "Alto used to always tell stories about him. Dalkowski was a big drinker, and in an effort to keep him under control, the Orioles decided to room him with Alto, a veteran minor-leaguer who was nearing the end of his career. Alto said he wound up rooming with Dalkowski's suitcase. The pitcher was out drinking the whole season. So when I began toying with an idea for a movie about life in the minors, I thought about building a plot around a mature, aging minor-leaguer [named Crash Davis] and a wild-throwing, immature pitcher [named Nuke Laloosh]."

After *Bull Durham*, Shelton enhanced his filmmaking reputation with *White Men Can't Jump,* an homage to trash-talking hoop hustlers that starred Woody Harrelson and Wesley Snipes, and *Blaze,* which starred Paul Newman as Earl Long, the zany former governor of Louisiana who had an affair with a stripper. He also wrote and directed *Cobb,* a 1995 film about the dark side of Baseball Hall of Famer Ty Cobb. "I use sports the same as other directors use the Old West," he said. "In the Old West and in sports, you have a belief system in place. What I do is take that belief system and twist it, turn it and light it from an unusual angle."

finally entered the win column. "It was a tremendous relief," Altobelli recalled. "We didn't want to lose the home opener and Larry really picked us up."

Although he was a reserve, Johnson was one of Altobelli's favorite

Ron Shelton.
Courtesy of the *Democrat and Chronicle/Times-Union.*

players, an overachieving first baseman who had stuck around in baseball simply because of his bat. Nicknamed "the Sea Lion" for his oddly
shaped body, Johnson had broken his legs as a youngster growing up in

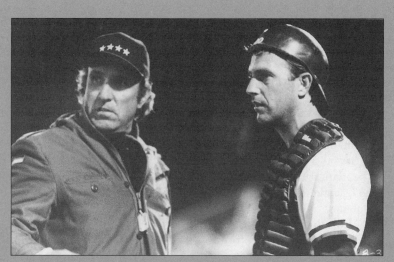

Ron Shelton and Kevin Costner.
Courtesy of the *Democrat and Chronicle/Times-Union*.

Virginia. In high school, his coach would make the players run sprints to the right-field fence and back to the dugout if they struck out. To save himself the embarrassment, Johnson concentrated on making contact. In 1971, he would strike out just eight times in 251 at-bats for the Wings.

The drive toward .500 continued, and it took some strange turns. On May 15, with Rochester ahead 7–6, fifty-mile-per-hour winds in Winnipeg, Manitoba, knocked down parts of the center-and right-field fences and forced umpires to call league president George Sisler, Jr. The weather cleared before Sisler issued a ruling, and the Wings edged the Whips 8–7. Four Red Wings hit homers—including winning pitcher Roric Harrison—as Rochester won its fourth straight to improve to 9–12. Four days later, the streak hit eight when Crowley drove in five runs in an 8–4 home win over Toledo. That pushed the Wings' record to 13–12, the first time they'd been over .500, but the day was most notable for two off-field incidents: the arrival of second baseman Don Fazio and the departure of general manager Bob Turner.

Fazio had retired from baseball after failing to make the Boston Red Sox roster in 1970. He had settled in Rochester and was looking forward to his job as a physical education teacher at Roth Junior High School in Henrietta. "I was 28 with a wife and two kids," he said. "I figured it was time to move on." The Wings had other ideas. Hoping to solidify their defense, they made Fazio a unique offer: play only home games until school let out, then join the club full-time. "It was an offer I couldn't refuse," Fazio said. "I still loved the game and now I had a chance to play in the town where I lived. I was thrilled."

Turner, the club's GM since 1968, resigned in a dispute with board members over promotional ideas and was replaced by the team's assistant general manager. Carl C. Steinfeldt had spent sixteen years with the Wings, first as a grounds crew attendant, then as a concessionaire, press box attendant, clubhouse boy, and assistant ticket manager. At thirty-one, he became the youngest GM in Wings history, a record that lasted until January 10, 1995, when twenty-seven-year-old Dan Mason replaced Altobelli.

The Wings continued to flirt with .500 and swept the Charleston Charlies on May 28 to improve to 18–17. But the big story in Charleston that night was right-hander Greg Arnold, who pitched Rochester's first no-hitter since Tom Phoebus in 1966. Arnold beat the Charlies 6–0 in the first game of a double-header. He struck out nine in the seven-inning game but also allowed nine baserunners—five on walks, three on errors, and one on a fielder's choice. Arnold was hardly overwhelmed by his feat, telling a reporter after the game, "Heck it was just a no-hitter." The usual superstitions were in force throughout the game, with teammates leaving the right-hander to sit by himself on the bench, and no one daring to mention the "N" word for fear of breaking the spell. The fun-loving Arnold, a pop singer in the off-season, finally broke the silence midway through the game. "I said, 'Hey fellas, I know I've got a no-hitter going. Relax.' "

After the no-hitter, it was all downhill for the free-spirited pitcher. On June 27, he lasted just one and one-third innings against Tidewater, giving up three runs and five walks. The *Democrat and Chronicle* wryly noted that Arnold "had a no-hitter going when Joe Altobelli pulled him after he walked the bases loaded." Four days later, after being banished to the bullpen for the first time in his career, Arnold was shelled. He gave up four hits in two innings—including a game-winning double to Jim Campanis—as Charleston edged the Wings 10–9 at Silver. Harry Dalton, the Orioles' vice president and director of player personnel, witnessed the barrage and took immediate action. The next day, Arnold was ordered to Raleigh-Durham, an unaffiliated team in the Class A Carolina League. True to his pitching form, Arnold balked at the demotion and threw one final curve by quitting baseball to pursue his singing career. His final line with the Wings was a 2–7 record, a 4.78 ERA and 55 walks in $63\frac{2}{3}$ innings.

In mid-June, the hitters took center stage in a 15–4 romp at Winnipeg Stadium. That wouldn't have been notable except that they did it in ten innings. Fifteen batters went to the plate in the eleven-run outburst, which came a week after a nine-run inning against Louisville. Shelton had his first four-hit night of the season, and winning pitcher Bill Burbach got into the act with a three-run triple in the tenth.

Burbach's offensive showing may have been pure luck, but there was nothing fluky about the the the hitting displayed by another Red Wings pitcher. Roric Harrison had begun his career in 1965 as an outfielder with Salisbury (Maryland) of the Carolina League, but in reverse Babe Ruth fashion he was converted into a pitcher the same year. Control problems had kept Harrison in the minors, but the twenty-four-year-old right-hander never lost his hitting touch. While pitching for Portland in 1970, he hit five home runs. He added four more in '71, hitting .273 (18-for-66) with six doubles and 15 RBI. "Roric could just hit the ball, plain and simple," longtime Wings broadcaster Joe Cullinane said. "Every time he came up, he was a threat to do something special."

Cullinane's fondest Harrison memory was a June 12 game in Toledo, when the right-hander belted a grand slam and pitched a two-hit shutout over the Mud Hens. He also doubled and scored on Baylor's grand slam in the ninth as the Wings rolled 11–0 before 4,407 fans at Lucas County Recreation Center. "I was broadcasting the game high above the third-base side," Cullinane recalled. "The crowd was really quiet, and after the game, Roric told me that he could hear every word I said from the mound. He was listening to the broadcast while he pitched! I told him he should listen to me more often."

Harrison wasn't through with Toledo. On July 12, he set a Red Wings franchise record by striking out eighteen Mud Hens, breaking by one the mark set by Frank Bertaina (also against Toledo) five years earlier. Harrison fanned at least one Mud Hen in every inning and struck out the side in the fifth and seventh, to the delight of the 10,007 fans at Silver. The Wings won, 4–1, with Harrison contributing an RBI triple.

Harrison was hitting .342 after the eighteen-strikeout game, but the real hitters were Grich and Baylor. On June 11, they were named to the International League All-Star team along with Ferraro, who made the squad for a record fourth consecutive season. Grich was a unanimous choice at short and responded in true all-star fashion five days later, hitting three home runs in a seven-inning, 6–4 loss to Richmond. He homered in the first, fourth, and sixth to equal the three homers he had hit the year before in a 27–4 romp over Buffalo. He was in the on-deck circle when the Wings' rally against Richmond fell short in the seventh, leaving the crowd of 4,573 at Silver Stadium disappointed.

If fans felt they'd been left at the altar, the mood was appropriate. The next day Grich left for California to marry Martha Johnston, his high school sweetheart. Grich went from groom to best man when, eight days later, he slammed a towering home run off left-hander Mike Kekich and drove in another run as the International League All-Stars out-slugged the New York Yankees 15–13 before 11,001 fans at Silver.

The next day, June 25, Johnny Oates's wife, Gloria, gave birth to the couple's first child, Lauri Lane, at Rochester General Hospital. The Wings also found new life, splitting a doubleheader with Tidewater that night to go 33–33. It would be the last time they'd be stuck at .500.

Rochester won its next six games and strengthened its roster with the return of veterans Freddy Beene and Terry Crowley. "Everything started to jell around that time," Altobelli recalled. "We finally had our set lineup, and a solid pitching staff. We were a team." Beene had pitched with the Wings from 1966 to 1970 and had been the Wings' top pitcher in '69, going 15–7 with a 2.98 earned run average and a league-high four shutouts. The diminutive Beene—he stood five-foot-eight and weighed only 154 pounds—broke his leg in his first start in 1970, then posted a 9–3 record. Beene's arm troubles began in October 1970, when he was scheduled to pitch the season opener for Frank Robinson's San-turce club in the Puerto Rican Winter League. His arm had felt tight for three days, but he pitched anyway. In the fourth inning, he tried to throw a slider. "Everything broke loose," the Texas native said. He was diagnosed as having calcium deposits, and he was traded to the San Diego Padres two months later. The deal was made on condition that Beene recover fully.

He didn't. Beene never pitched with the Padres, complaining early in the season that "It hurts so much I could cry." San Diego sent him back to the Orioles, where he made three appearances for Dallas-Fort Worth before rejoining the Wings. "He pitched on pure guts," Altobelli said. "Every time he went out, we thought his arm might fall off."

Crowley was another key component in Rochester's turnaround. A Red Wing in 1968 and 1969, when he hit twenty-eight homers and led the International League with 246 total bases, he spent the 1970 season with the world champion Orioles and hit .257 in eighty-three games. Crowley thought he would stick with the O's in 1971 but pulled a ham-string in spring training and found himself headed to Rochester one week before the season opener. He hit .291 with five homers and 22 RBI in 26 games before being recalled on May 26 and was sent back in early July after outfielder Tommy Shopay came off the disabled list in Baltimore.

With the roster solidified by the addition of Crowley and Beene, the players began to draw closer. Hutto held regular Sunday parties at his house, inviting the entire team. Road trips also became something to look forward to. Like schoolchildren assigned seats by the teacher, the Wings would sit in the same place on planes and buses. "It was a very close team," Cullinane recalled. "They would stop at a restaurant on the way to another town, and the entire team would sit and eat together. You'd never see that today."

Altobelli added: "You could be the last guy on the bus and that seat you had was still open to you. And they carried on so much, kidded one another." Imitating animals was the club's favorite pastime. "Roric Harrison could imitate a mule," Altobelli said. "Then we had guys like Mickey Scott, who could imitate these birds from Africa, these big macaws. It got to be so funny I could hardly keep from laughing." Harrison also did an impersonation of John Wayne that was so dead-on that the pitcher earned the nicknamed "Duke."

Meanwhile, the Wings were doing their best impression of the '27 Yankees. On July 17, they crushed the Winnipeg Whips 17–4 at Silver Stadium in what could best be described as a profitable experience. Before the game, local businessman Morton Brodsky had offered $10 for every Red Wings hit and another $25 for each home run. Eight Red Wings made him pay; they pounded out sixteen hits—including three homers—for a $235 payday. The romp gave Rochester its fifteenth win at home in nineteen games since the all-star break.

That week, Bob Matthews, a rookie staff writer for the *Democrat and Chronicle,* proclaimed 1971 "the Year of the Rochester Red Wings." Matthews would go on to become a popular sports columnist and radio talk-show host. A lifelong Rochesterian, he always considered the '71 Wings the best minor-league team he had ever seen. "You had two-guys —Grich and Baylor—who probably could have started for any team but the Orioles," he said. "You had a manager who knew how to get the most from his club, and you had a team in which virtually every player had a career year. It was an unforgettable season."

On August 2, they took over the top spot by three percentage points over Tidewater, beating Syracuse 7–4. Harrison was the winning pitcher and, true to form, hit a three-run homer. But it was the smallest man on the field who got the Wings off and running as Richie Coggins hit his seventeenth home run. Only five-foot-eight, 170 pounds, the left-handed hitter had become what Altobelli called "day in and day out, our most unexpected surprise." Coggins was a Detroit All-City selection in football, basketball, and baseball. He went to UCLA on a football/baseball scholarship but a knee injury cut short his collegiate career.

Dynamic Duo

Right from the start, Bobby Grich and I were a little more than curious about each other. Being the Orioles' top two draft picks, I had heard about him and he had heard about me. I'd never met a surfer and beach bum from the Sunshine State. He'd never met a black cowboy from Texas.
We were a perfect match.
—Don Baylor *in his book* Don Baylor: It's Nothing But the Truth—A Baseball Life

They became teammates, roommates, and best friends, can't-miss prospects who forever will be linked together in Red Wings lore. "When I think of Don Baylor and Bobby Grich," Joe Altobelli said, "it's always in the same breath. They had to overcome some tough obstacles because there was just no room for them in Baltimore in 1971. But they didn't fall apart, they didn't cry in their beer, and they went on to have great careers.

"They were very close, very good friends. They were sent down on the same day in '71 and I know what Earl [Weaver] was thinking: 'Can I play Bobby Grich and Don Baylor four or five times a week up here?' The answer was no. He'd be wasting them."

Grich was the Orioles' number one pick in 1967, and Baylor was their second pick. For fourteen of their first fifteen professional seasons, they played together. From Bluefield to Stockton to Dallas to Rochester to Baltimore and finally to California. The only exception was in 1975, when Baylor was traded from Baltimore to Oakland in a spring-training deal involving Reggie Jackson. Baylor cried that night in the Orioles clubhouse at Miami Stadium. "How," he asked a friend, "am I going to tell Bobby?"

Both won Minor League Player of the Year honors with Rochester, Baylor in '70 and Grich in the magical '71 season. And both had been called up to the Orioles during their world championship season of 1970. In his 1989 book, Baylor recounted how a bases-loaded single in his first major-league at-bat at Washington's RFK Stadium was made possible in part by Grich:

> A lot of guys probably get that first hit and thank their high-school coach, their mother, their father or whatever. I thanked Grichie. Bobby had been called up about a month before me and had been playing off and on. A few days before he had also been faced with a bases-loaded situation. . . . Grichie was walking to the plate

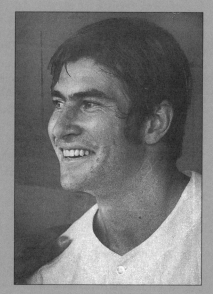

Don Baylor and Bobby Grich.
Courtesy of the *Democrat and Chronicle/Times-Union.*

when he heard a whistle. It was Weaver. Bobby looked back and saw
Brooks Robinson coming out of the dugout to pinch-hit.

Bobby was furious. He went back to the dugout and grabbed
Weaver by the throat, started strangling him and screaming, "How
do you expect me to hit in this league when you keep pinch-hitting
for me all the time?" I couldn't believe my eyes. There he was, a
rookie, trying to kill baseball's little genius. Elrod Hendricks had to
separate the two. After I got to hit with the bases loaded, I often
wondered if Earl thought I would try to kill him, too, if he had sent
up a pinch-hitter.

Grich played on six American League all-star teams during his
seventeen-year career with Baltimore and California. He finished with a
.266 lifetime average, 224 homers, and 864 RBI. Baylor, who seemed to
play in Grich's shadow in the minors, outdid him in The Show. In nineteen seasons, he batted .260, slammed 338 homers, and knocked in
1,276 runs, earning seven all-star selections and the 1979 American
League MVP award. On October 27, 1992, Baylor was named manager
of the National League expansion Colorado Rockies.

Coggins began his professional baseball career in 1968 and played in forty-three games with the 1970 Wings when he was only nineteen. He entered the '71 season with only fifteen homers in three seasons but wound up with twenty from the leadoff spot that summer. "A lot of managers didn't want Coggins," Altobelli said. "They thought he was too militant. I thought he was terrific. I don't know how he got that rap. He was wearing clothes that were different than the clothes being worn by the old people. I told the Orioles, 'How can you knock the clothes his mother made him?' His shoes were shined, his uniform was clean."

The Wings continued to sizzle throughout August, and no one grabbed more headlines than Harrison. He followed up a three-hit shutout in Louisville with a one-hitter in Syracuse on August 12, giving up a bloop single to Rusty Torres with two outs in the eighth. Three days later, Torres hit Harrison again, but this time the situation was far more serious. Harrison had just sat down next to Altobelli in the visitors dugout when Torres lined a foul ball that struck the star pitcher on the right side of the head. Harrison was rushed to St. Joseph's Hospital in Syracuse for X rays and was diagnosed as having a torn eardrum.

"Thank God he turned his head," Dr. Armand Cincotta said that night. "If he hadn't, the ball would have hit him flush in the face."

Shaken up but determined not to miss a start, Harrison was released from the hospital that night and made his scheduled start the next day. Incredibly, he tossed his second consecutive one-hitter against the Chiefs in a 1–0 Rochester win. The only Syracuse hit came from pitcher Dale Spier in the third. "It was a strange feeling, because I couldn't hear the ball hit the catcher's mitt," Harrison said afterward. "I've been having some trouble with my hearing and have a ringing sound in my ear." The win gave Harrison five shutouts and improved his record to 14–4. During his three-game hot spell, opponents had struck out thirty-three times and managed just five singles.

The Red Wings took a break from the pennant race to host the defending world champion Orioles in the annual exhibition on August 23. A crowd of 11,909 watched as backup catcher George Farson drilled a two-run single off Baltimore's Pete Richert in the eighth to lift the Wings to a 4–2 win. Grich provided the game's only homer, a solo shot in the first off Dave Leonhard.

After the game, Orioles right fielder Frank Robinson told reporters of his desire to be the first black manager in the majors. "If the right offer comes tomorrow, in Cleveland . . . in California . . . anywhere, I'll take it for next year," Robinson said. "I want the challenge. It can be a winner or a loser. I don't care." At the time, Robinson worried that superstars such as Maury Wills, Willie Mays, and Ernie Banks might have a better shot at landing a big-league job first, but it didn't work out that way. In 1975, Robinson made history when he took the field as player-manager for the Cleveland Indians. Three years later, he became the first black Red Wings manager.

Having knocked off the best team in the majors, the Wings set about securing their place atop the International League. The clincher came on August 28, when Grich hit three homers—numbers 29, 30, and 31—in a doubleheader sweep at Richmond to give Rochester its first pennant since Earl Weaver's 1966 club. When Dave Boswell forced Shaun Fitzmaurice to hit into a game-ending double play, the Wings rushed the mound and—long before it became fashionable in the National Football League—doused Boswell with a bucket of ice water. In the clubhouse, the exuberant Wings popped thirty quarts of champagne, courtesy of GM Carl Steinfeldt.

The alcohol did not go untouched. Later that night, several inebriated Wings snuck back on the field and turned on the fire hose, dousing home plate before the Parker Field grounds crew shooed them away. The players also hauled down the "Rochester" pennant that flew above the stadium.

The next day, Harrison won his fifteenth game in his final regular season start and Grich homered again in a 4–3 win. That gave Grich thirty-two homers, the most by a Red Wing since Boog Powell hit thirty-two in 1961. Eleven of Grich's homers came against Richmond.

That night, about five hundred fans welcomed the league champions to the Monroe County Airport when their chartered flight landed at 8:30. Many of the fans had waited for two hours to greet their heroes, and the Wings saved the best for last. After everyone else had entered the terminal, Grich and Baylor appeared from the plane. The fans reacted as if the Beatles had just landed in New York. They hugged, kissed, and grabbed the young heroes. It took fifteen minutes for Grich and Baylor to make it through. "I'd be lying if I said I've been happier than right now," Grich said, his new wife by his side. "This has to be the greatest feeling in the world."

The race was over, but there was one piece of history left to be written during this wild season. On August 31, Syracuse right-hander Mike Pazik no-hit the Wings 5–0 at MacArthur Stadium. The rookie from Holy Cross struck out nine and walked six against the regular Wings lineup. Rochester closed with a pair of home wins over Syracuse, drawing more than twenty thousand fans despite the irrelevance of the games to the standings. And so the season had finally ended. Rochester played .716 ball (53–21) after its shaky start, to finish 86–54 and outdistance Tidewater (79–61) by seven games.

The Tides met third-place Charleston (78–62) in the first round of the playoffs, while the Wings played fourth-place Syracuse (73–67). The best-of-five first-round series began on September 3 at MacArthur Stadium. The Wings rallied from an early 3–0 deficit to win 5–4 in ten innings, when Baylor singled home Fazio with the winning run. There was little celebrating after the game, however. In the sixth inning, Harrison pulled a hamstring muscle and suffered ligament damage in his left knee sliding into second base and had to be taken from the field on a stretcher. Later, he sat in the unusually quiet Red Wings clubhouse, his left leg propped up and an ice bag wrapped around his knee. "I don't know how long it will take to heal," the despondent right-hander said, "but it doesn't seem as bad as the last time." Harrison had missed most of the '69 season after tearing ligaments in his left knee. This injury was just below the knee, where the hamstring ties in. It would sideline him for the rest of the post season.

"Was I worried? Of course I was," Altobelli said. "You always worry when your ace goes down, but this was a funny pitching staff. It wasn't a great staff, but the guys knew that our offense was gonna get them runs. Subconsciously that helped. They didn't worry when the other team jumped on them for a couple of runs early."

Undaunted, the Wings took a 2–0 series lead, belting out thirteen hits in a 5–1 win before only 2,418 fans at MacArthur Stadium. Beene worked into the eighth, improving to 4–0 against the Chiefs, and Mickey Scott finished up. The steamy September afternoon took its toll on Beene, who vomited in the dugout in the third inning but stuck it out until the eighth. "I'm from Texas, but I guess you never get used to heat like that," Beene said.

The series switched to Rochester, with the Wings needing one win to advance to the Governors' Cup finals. It wouldn't come in game three. The Chiefs scored three unearned runs in the ninth—keyed by a Grich error—to win 8–5 before 9,339 fans. Rochester wrapped it up in game four as George Manz scattered six hits and Crowley homered in an 11–2 romp before 6,886 fans at Silver.

The Wings learned who their next opponents would be shortly after the game. Hank Bauer's Tidewater Tides had swept the Charleston Charlies three games to none to move into the best-of-five Governors' Cup final. The series would begin the next night at Silver. The Tides were led by outfielders Mike Jorgensen, who had hit .342 with 15 home runs in only 65 games (he'd spent part of the season with the New York Mets), Leroy Stanton (.324–23–101), and first baseman John Milner (.290–19–87), plus a deep pitching staff led by Jim Bibby (15–6, 4.04), league ERA champ Buzz Capra (13–3, 2.19), and Jon Matlack (11–7, 3.97).

With Harrison out and Dave Boswell summoned back to the Orioles, pitching depth became a problem for Altobelli. Because his pitchers were overworked, the Wings manager was forced to start veteran reliever Orlando Pena in game one. It was a disaster. Pena hit Lute Barnes in the face with a pitch to open the game and the Tides scored five first-inning runs in a 12–1 romp, winning their sixth consecutive game behind Matlack. Pena lasted just three innings, and Tidewater finished the job with a six-run seventh off Bill Burbach, handing Rochester its worst loss of the season. "I'll never forget this game," a dazed Altobelli said afterward.

There was good news for the Wings, however. Right-hander Wayne Garland joined the club from Double-A Dallas-Fort Worth, where he had gone 19–5 with a 1.70 ERA for Cal Ripken's Spurs. Altobelli set his rotation for the rest of the series: Beene would start in game two, followed by Garland, Bill Kirkpatrick, and George Manz. The blowout made game two crucial for the Wings because the final three games would be played in Virginia. The Tides appeared headed for another win when they took a 4–0 lead in the fourth, but the Wings fought back in the bottom half of the inning. Grich doubled, Baylor tripled, and Hutto hit a two-out single to cut the lead to 4–2. Sam Parrilla, hitting just .135 in the postseason, put the Wings ahead with a three-run single in the fifth, and Mickey Scott finished off the Tides to even the series.

It was on to Norfolk, where the Wings squeaked out a 2–1 win on Johnny Oates's sacrifice fly in the eleventh. Garland was sensational in his Triple-A debut, striking out seven and allowing only six hits in eight-plus innings, and for the second consecutive night, Scott put away the Tides by striking out former Red Wing Billy Scripture.

But the real hero was Parrilla, who made two sensational catches in extra innings. Parrilla, hardly known for his fielding, made a shoestring catch on Mike Jorgensen's liner in the tenth, then a backhanded diving grab of Jim Williams's drive to right. "Ron Swoboda catches," Tides second baseman Lute Barnes muttered. "I don't see how he caught either one of them."

Both teams were on the verge of losing key players. Jorgensen was recalled by the Mets after the game, and Oates was heading back to Fort Devens, Massachusetts, for two weeks of army duty. Facing elimination at home, the Tides rebounded to win game four 4–2 with a pair of runs off Ray Miller in the eighth. Grich homered, but the night belonged to Tides starter Don Rose, who fanned twelve.

Word reached both clubhouses that Denver had swept Indianapolis in a rare playoff doubleheader that night, winning the American Association series four games to three. The Bears would represent their league in the Junior World Series, but they had played their last home game. Because of a conflict with the National Football League's Denver Broncos, the Bears would be unable to use Mile High Stadium and would have to play all Junior World Series games in the International League champion's ballpark. That raised the stakes for the decisive game five, but the Wings and Tides first had to endure two days of rain. Frustrated, Wings GM Carl Steinfeldt tried to get the series switched back to Rochester, to no avail. Tides manager Hank Bauer had another suggestion. "Maybe we should toss a coin for it," he said.

The Wings tried to keep loose—most of them went to the local movie house to see *Billy Jack*—but at least one key player had had enough. "Sam Parrilla was getting itchy to go home," Altobelli recalled. "One of the players had told him 'There's no money in this,' and Sam wanted to leave. Hutto came to me and said, 'You'd better talk to Sam.' " Altobelli called the frustrated right fielder in and gave him his best sales pitch. "I said 'Sam, if we get in this Junior World Series, you are going to make some extra money,' " Altobelli recalled. "Well, he didn't believe me. He just stared at me and said 'Get out of here.' I said 'Sam, you are going to make some money.' "

It was like dangling a piece of cheese in front of a mouse. His spirits revived, Parrilla slammed a pair of homers in game five and Grich and Crowley each added one as the Wings rolled 8–5. Parrilla had hit just eleven homers during the regular season and was batting .194 in the playoffs. "This," the quiet Brooklynite said, "is the most important thing I have ever done in baseball."

Beene, who replaced scheduled starter George Manz because of the rainouts, picked up his third win of the playoffs, and Pena, who had been blasted by the Tides in game one, struck out Dave Schneck for the final out.

There was little time to celebrate the club's sixth Governors' Cup title. The team flew back to Rochester, ready to take on Denver in game one of the Junior World Series that night.

Del Wilber's Bears led the American Association with a .276 average, but they lacked a strong starting rotation. In fact, thirty-six-year-old sinker-ball specialist Garland Shifflett, a reliever, had been named league MVP after compiling a 12–7 record and eighteen saves. Denver had finished only 73–67 during the regular season and was led on offense by Richie Scheinblum, a switch-hitting outfielder who hit .388 and belted twenty-five homers. Wilber, called Scheinblum "the Bobby Grich of the American Association." The Bears' other powerhitter was Tom Grieve, a former number one draft pick who later became the general manager of the Texas Rangers. Grieve batted .272 with nineteen homers. The Bears grabbed an early 4–0 lead in game one but the Wings rallied to tie, then took the lead for good when Terry Crowley slammed a two-run homer off Cisco Carlos in the eighth. Scott, the fourth Wings pitcher, slammed the door on the Bears to pick up the 8–5 win, surrendering his first run in seven playoff appearances.

Oates had entered the game in the fifth, arriving from reserve duty in Fort Devens, Massachusetts. After the game, the catcher flew back to the Boston-area base, arriving at 5 A.M.—two hours before reveille. It was a practice he would continue throughout the series.

A crowd of 7,715 turned out the next night to watch the Wings again break from a 4–4 eighth-inning tie to win 6–4 and go up two games to none in the best-of-seven series. In keeping with their prior agreement to alternate the official home and road teams, the Wings batted first. Garland picked up the win, but the emotional story of the night centered on Orlando Pena, who pitched two perfect innings of relief. The veteran forkballer had learned earlier in the day that his father had died in Miami following a heart attack.

"I told Joe [Altobelli] I could pitch and I wanted to do my job if he needed me," Pena said that night. "When I came into the game, Bobby [Grich] said 'Win it for your father.' I think I wanted to do better than I ever had before." The next day, Pena flew to Miami for his father's funeral and returned before the series ended.

The Bears bounced back in game three, winning 3–2 as Jerry Janeski scattered ten hits in going the distance. Grich homered for the fifth time in five days but the Wings were done in by four errors.

Beene pitched the Wings to within a game of the Junior World Series title the next night, striking out twelve in an 11–3 win before 9,639 fans. Every Red Wings starter had a hit, and Baylor belted a two-run homer. Beene had endured the pain in his elbow all season and with Harrison out had become Rochester's most dependable starter. "It has been a nightmare," Beene said of his aching arm. "I feel it until I pitch again. It starts about an hour after I pitch. It hurts when I drive my car, when I comb my hair."

A crowd of 11,993 showed up the next night anticipating a series-clinching victory, but the Bears foiled those plans with a 9–5 win. Grieve and Scheinblum combined for seven runs batted in, but the real bad news for Rochester came after the game when Orioles personnel boss Harry Dalton phoned Altobelli in the quiet clubhouse. Shortstop Mark Belanger had gone down with a knee injury and the Orioles were calling up Grich. "We really can't argue," GM Carl Steinfeldt said after getting the news. "They have 11 games left and only a five-game lead. They need a shortstop."

Grich was in no hurry to leave, telling Altobelli he would stay until the Wings wrapped up the series the following night. "I told him, 'Bobby,

Dreamy numbers

1971 Final Statistics

Batting	G	AB	Runs	Hits	HR	RBI	Avg.
Don Baylor	136	492	104	154	20	95	.313
Rich Coggins	136	536	107	151	20	53	.282
Terry Crowley	78	259	56	73	19	63	.282
George Farson	36	60	4	13	1	3	.217
Don Fazio	95	294	40	80	4	37	.272
Mike Ferraro	120	408	59	111	7	65	.272
Bobby Grich	130	473	124	159	32	83	.336
Jim Hutto	128	432	58	123	15	73	.285
Larry Johnson	92	251	22	77	5	39	.307
Art Miranda	20	67	4	13	0	4	.194
Johnny Oates	114	346	49	96	7	44	.277
Sam Parrilla	111	375	54	125	11	70	.333
Ron Shelton	66	154	20	40	1	9	.260

Pitching	G	W	L	Saves	ERA
Mike Adamson	2	0	1	0	9.00
Greg Arnold	14	2	7	0	4.78
Dick Baney	9	1	0	0	5.79
Fred Beene	12	7	1	0	4.44
Dave Boswell	4	3	0	0	3.00
Bill Burbach	21	7	2	1	4.84
Ricardo Delgado	9	0	2	0	4.00
Roric Harrison	25	15	5	0	2.81
Steven Jones	2	0	0	0	18.00
Dave Leonhard	14	7	4	0	3.76
George Manz	27	8	5	1	5.10
Edwin Maras*	42	9	10	4	6.06
Ray Miller	44	3	2	11	3.16
John Montague	28	8	6	3	4.46
Orlando Pena	11	2	1	5	2.45
Mickey Scott	54	9	1	9	3.38
Richard Thoms	7	0	0	0	3.27
Mark Weems	11	0	1	0	6.88

* split with Winnipeg

they're not going to go for that,' " Altobelli recalled. "I said 'You've gotta go. Now go on and do something up there.' " Two nights later, Grich paced a five-run Orioles rally with a two-run single in the ninth as Baltimore beat the New York Yankees 8–4. He would never again play in the minors. Grich's final line with the '71 Wings was tremendous. He led the International League with a .336 average and 32 home runs, scored 124 runs, drove in 83, and had 26 doubles and 9 triples. He hit five homers in the postseason, one in the Orioles exhibition one in the All-Star game, and another for the Orioles in September, giving him an even forty. "I played out of my head that year," Grich said. "It was a storybook season. It couldn't have been any better." The star shortstop had missed ten games in 1971 because of military obligations, and the Wings had lost all ten. Still, Altobelli was undaunted. "We'll win it without him," the rookie manager said confidently.

Many Red Wings fans criticized the callup of Grich, who would not be eligible for postseason play in Baltimore, before the Denver series was over. The blow of losing the talented shortstop, who had gone 9-for-21 with 3 homers and 5 RBI in the series, was cushioned somewhat by two days of rain. But when the series resumed on September 21, the teams produced the wildest game of the season at Silver as Denver outlasted Rochester 12–11 to even the series at three. Ten pitchers surrendered thirty-three hits and both teams blew four-run leads. The Wings trailed 12–8 entering the ninth but fell short.

And so it all came down to Wednesday, September 22. Wilber sent out Janeski, who had stopped the Wings in game three. Altobelli countered with the little Texan, Beene, who had baffled the Bears in game four.

As they had throughout the series, the crowd of 9,043 gave the homeless Bears a huge welcome in pregame introductions. But they saved their biggest cheers for last. Richie Coggins had four hits and scored five runs, but the hero was Beene, who singled home the tying run in the sixth, allowed the go-ahead run to score by breaking up a double play and pitched into the eighth, leading the Wings to a 9–6 win. Pena ended a Denver threat in the eighth, then retired the first two hitters in the ninth on ground balls.

With the suspense building, one fan jumped onto the field and shook hands with Fazio, Ferraro, and Crowley. He then ran into left field and hugged Baylor, to the crowd's delight, before being taken off the field by police. Moments later, at 10:04 P.M., Pena struck out pinch-hitter Lou Klimchock to give Rochester its fourth minor-league championship and its first since Harry Walker's 1952 club.

This time, hundreds of fans jumped over the railings and swarmed

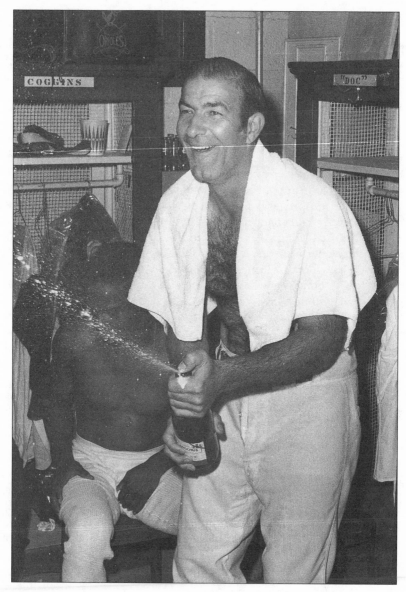

Joe Altobelli broke out the bubbly following the Wings'
Junior World Series clincher over Denver in 1971.
Courtesy of the *Democrat and Chronicle/Times-Union.*

the mound, where the exuberant Wings were celebrating. Some fans tried to pry home plate loose but were shooed away by ushers. Others were more successful, swiping the bases. Several fans tried to dig up the pitcher's mound, hoping to take away a souvenir, and others holed up in the Red Wings dugout, kept at bay by police. The Wings finally managed to slip into their clubhouse, but the loud chants of "We want Beene! We want Beene!" continued to bellow from the field.

The party continued into the night as hundreds of fans joined players at the Downtowner Motel. "It was quite a scene," Altobelli recalled. "It took me an hour to get to the bar to get champagne and another half-hour to get back to my table. It was really something, a feeling that was kind of mutual among everyone."

Oates, who had endured a rigorous schedule to keep his commitments to both the reserves and the Wings, led the Wings with a .529 average (9-for-17) in the series, with Parrilla and Baylor knotted at .481. Even coach Pete Ward, who had been activated for the series, finished 1-for-2.

Two days after game seven, a *Democrat and Chronicle* story on players' shares caught Joe Cullinane's eye. "Suddenly I see my own name," the broadcaster said. "They voted me a half-share. An announcer getting money? Insanity! I still remember the exact figure, too. It was $569.38."

Including the postseason, the Wings drew 436,947 in 1971, the top attendance figure in the minors. The seven-game Junior World Series drew 58,838 and the Wings made a net profit of $83,892 for the season.

"We made a lot of money," Steinfeldt said. "One of our best investments was the $106 it cost to fly Orlando Pena back up from Miami after his father's funeral." Pena threw the final pitch of the long and unforgettable season.

In 1993, *Baseball America* named the '71 Wings one of the top ten minor-league clubs of the past fifty years.

How good were the Wings? Richmond catcher Jim French, who played seven seasons with the Washington Senators, put it this way shortly after the '71 season: "Rochester's personnel is better than the Senators. Over a full season, Rochester would win. Take away Frank Howard and Dick Bosman from Washington and it wouldn't even be close."

11

A Successful Blend

*When I look back on my time managing the Red
Wings, I smile. I've been a lot of places in this game, but
those are some of the happiest moments of my life.*
                                    —*Joe Altobelli,* March 1995

A ltobelli would manage five more
seasons in Rochester, winning an-
other Governors' Cup title and twice finishing with better records than
his '71 club. But nothing could duplicate the feeling of that first championship season. "The other five years all blend together," he said. "I remember people, certain moments and incidents. But I remember
everything about 1971."

The key members of the Junior World Series champs—Grich, Baylor, Harrison, Crowley, Oates, Beene, and Scott—were gone in '72. Only
Richie Coggins and Sam Parrilla returned to the starting lineup, to be
joined by Don Fazio when school let out in mid-June. Pitchers Bill Kirkpatrick, George Manz, and Wayne Garland also were back. Replacing
Baylor in left field was Jim Fuller, a burly slugger from Bethesda, Maryland, who had slammed 33 homers and driven in 110 runs for Class A
Miami in 1971.

Six weeks into the season, Coggins was forced out of the lineup
when he was spiked in the hand during a play at second base. His
replacement was a speedy outfielder named Alonza Bumbry, who was
hitting .363 with twelve steals for Asheville of the Southern League. The
move was supposed to be just temporary, but Bumbry was hitting .333
when Coggins returned two weeks later, and the two formed a lightning-

quick tandem at the top of the Red Wings lineup. Bumbry was small (five-foot-eight) and old (twenty-five) for a rookie, but the left-handed hitter was one of the fastest men in baseball. "Of all the dudes I've seen," said his roommate, Enos Cabell, "he's the fastest dude."

Bumbry, one of ten children, grew up in Virginia and attended Virginia State on a basketball scholarship. Nicknamed "Bumblebee," he spent two years in the army as a first lieutenant in the reserves and blamed that experience for what scouts labeled a weak throwing arm. "I didn't throw for two years," he said. "We did have one glove and one ball, but being in the jungle [Vietnam] for 11 months, we had only 40 or 50 feet to play catch."

Bumbry did more than stay with the Red Wings in 1972. He won the International League batting title, finishing at .345 in 108 games. He also was named the league's Rookie of the Year and joined Wings third baseman Tom Matchick as a member of the postseason IL all-star team and Silver Glove recipient.

The Wings played slightly better than .500 ball and entered the final day of the season tied with Toledo for the last playoff spot. Kirkpatrick pitched a five-hitter as Rochester won 2–1 at Syracuse, finishing 76–68, while Louisville won the pennant and eliminated Toledo with a 1–0 win. The Wings had squeezed into the playoffs, but their hopes of repeating as Governors' Cup champions ended when they lost the finale of a three-game playoff series with Louisville in extra innings. The International League split into two four-team divisions in 1973, with Rochester joining Syracuse, Toledo, and the Pawtucket, Rhode Island, franchise (transplanted from Louisville) in the American League Division. Tidewater, Richmond, Peninsula, and Charleston formed the National League Division.

Kirkpatrick and Garland headed the starting staff, and outfielder Tommy Shopay returned after two seasons in Baltimore. Fuller also was back after hitting eleven homers in forty-nine games the season before, and third base was manned by a rookie named Doug DeCinces, who was being groomed to replace the legendary Brooks Robinson in Baltimore.

There were other changes at Silver Stadium in 1973: the bullpen behind the left-field fence, where fire barrels had kept idle pitchers warm on chilly nights, gave way to the simplicity of practice pitching mounds down both lines. And pitchers were no longer part of the regular lineup, having been replaced by the new designated hitter rule, which had been used only as an experiment in the 1969 International League.

One Red Wing dominated all season, for better or worse. At six-foot-three, 220 pounds, and with sideburns as wide as home plate, Jim Fuller was Paul Bunyan with a baseball bat. Only twenty-two, the first

Jim Fuller was strictly hit-or-miss in 1973,
slamming 39 homers and striking out 197 times to
earn league MVP honors. Courtesy of the
Democrat and Chronicle/Times-Union.

baseman/outfielder went to the plate with one purpose in mind: home runs. He hit thirty-three for Miami in 1971, capping a year in which he also batted .326 and drove in 110 runs to win MVP honors in the Florida State League. He split the next season between Double-A Asheville and Triple-A Rochester, slamming thirty-four homers. Fuller emerged as a Red Wings folk hero in 1973, when he hit thirty-nine homers, three short of Russ Derry's club record set in 1949. Fuller led the IL in homers and RBI (108), but he also struck out a whopping 197 times—including five in one game—to set a franchise record. Fuller became the third Red Wing to earn International League MVP honors in four seasons, joining Roger Freed (1970) and Bobby Grich (1971). "Fans would stick around late in a game just to see him bat one more time," longtime Wings official scorer Len Lustik said. "He's the only guy I remember them doing that for. You just never knew what he was going to do next." Fuller would entertain Rochester fans for three more seasons but never would recapture the home-run swing that made him one of the Wings' most memorable players in years.

Rochester moved into first place on May 1, 1973, and led its division throughout most of the summer, building a seven-game lead in mid-August. But six consecutive losses followed, and the lead over Pawtucket dipped to two when the Red Sox visited Silver for the final three games of the season. Pawtucket won the first two, locking both teams in a first-place tie at 78–67, but Rochester avoided a late-season collapse as Garland pitched a complete game for his tenth win in a 6–2 victory. That would prove to be the Wings' last win of the season. Hampered all season by so-so pitching and inconsistent hitting, they fell in three straight play-off games to the Charleston Charlies.

There was more bad news: Carl Steinfeldt announced he was leaving after two and one-half seasons as general manager to take over the same job with Charleston. Morrie Silver returned from Florida to help find a successor, but the Wings ultimately decided to operate without a GM. Instead, Sam Lippa, who had resigned as director of promotions one year before, was named business manager, and former Red Wing pitcher Ed Barnowski was promoted to director of sales and promotions. The Wings, who had turned a minor-league best profit of $71,382 in 1973, now had no front-office leader.

The 1974 season started off with a roller coaster of emotions. On April 20, Wayne Garland pitched the first opening day no-hitter in International League history, winning 5–0 before 2,188 fans at Watt Powell Park in Charleston, West Virginia. Four Charlies reached base against the right-hander, one on a walk and three on errors. It was the first nine-inning no-hitter by a Red Wing since Dave Vineyard in 1966, and Bill Lang, president of Rochester Community Baseball, Inc., promised to present Garland with a check for $100 when the Wings opened at home that Friday.

The Red Wings received more good news when they returned to Rochester. Outfielder Royle Stillman, who had been a holdout for three months, agreed to rejoin the club. But tragic news awaited them following their April 26 home opener, an 8–7 loss to Charleston before 6,256 fans: Morrie Silver, the man who had twice saved professional baseball

First base generally is regarded as the strongest position in Red Wings history.

But athletic trainer is not far behind.

Howie Haak, Danny Whelan, and Herm Schneider each got his start in the trainer's room at 500 Norton Street, taping ankles and massaging egos for the Rochester Red Wings. Each of them went on to enjoy major-league success.

Haak was such a good catcher at the University of Rochester that the Red Wings signed him to a contract in 1933. The premed major's official position was reserve catcher, but the Wings also were interested in Haak as an assistant trainer, a position he held until 1938 when he became the team's head trainer. Haak, though, would make his baseball mark in an entirely different role. Legend has it that everyone except him had left the clubhouse following a late-season game in 1941 when the phone rang. St. Louis Cardinals general manager Branch Rickey was on the phone. Haak recreated the conversation in a 1993 interview: " 'We need an outfielder up here right now,' he said. 'Is there anybody down there who you think can help me?' 'Sure, I said. We got this kid named Musial. You should call him up.' "

Stan Musial was indeed called up. A Hall of Fame player's career was launched. And a scout was born. When Rickey moved over to the Brooklyn Dodgers in the mid-1940s, he signed Haak to be one of his scouts. In 1950, Rickey moved to the Pittsburgh Pirates, and Haak followed. The Rochester native wound up becoming the first scout to successfully mine the rich ballplaying diamonds of Latin America. Haak signed scores of major-league players from there. His greatest find was Roberto Clemente.

Whelan succeeded Haak in the Red Wings trainer's room, and he, too, would go on to to bigger and better things. Whelan was the trainer on the Pittsburgh Pirates team that stunned the New York Yankees in the 1960 World Series on Bill Mazeroski's historic bottom-of-the-ninth-inning homer in game seven. Later, Whelan would switch sports, joining the National Basketball Association's New York Knicks as trainer. He picked up two more championship rings in Madison Square Garden as the Knicks won NBA titles in 1971 and 1973. Jack Buck, the nationally known sports announcer, remembers Whelan for more important reasons than being involved with championship teams. During the summer of 1953 when Buck was announcing Red Wings games, Buck and his family joined Whelan for a picnic on a Lake Ontario beach. Whelan wound up saving Buck's daughter from drowning.

Schneider was a trainer with the Wings in the early '70s. He grew up a block from Silver Stadium, and often would play hooky from school and attempt to sneak into games. "I was what the cops called a nuisance kid," he recalled. "The Red Wings finally got so sick of me trying to sneak in that they offered me a job." Schneider swept clubhouse floors, polished spikes, picked up dirty towels, washed uniforms, and taped ankles. After graduating from high school in 1970, he became the Wings assistant trainer and climbed to the head position after earning a sports medicine degree in college.

He later became an assistant trainer with the New York Yankees before becoming the White Sox head man. Schneider gained the respect of the athletic training community for the rehabilitation work he did helping Bo Jackson make his unprecedented comeback to baseball following hip replacement surgery. Schneider also coaxed White Sox short-stop Ozzie Guillen back from a career-threatening knee injury and was credited with devising a preseason training program for Michael Jordan's brief conversion from basketball to baseball.

in Rochester from extinction, was dead. Silver had passed away at 7:15 that night in Miami Beach, Florida, hours after the home opener at the ballpark bearing his name. He had been hospitalized for five days following his third heart attack in a decade.

Silver had moved to Miami Beach in 1968 with his wife, Anna, and daughter, Naomi, following his second heart attack, but he had continued to play a significant role in the club's operations. General managers Bob Turner and Carl Steinfeldt would faithfully phone Silver to report on each game, and Silver routinely flew into Rochester for important business matters. Just two months before, he had returned to negotiate a radio deal and a better concessions contract.

News of his death stunned the community. "I've always thought no one is irreplaceable in this world," Turner said, "but Morrie Silver is the exception. There can be no one of his combination of dedication and talent. I fear for Rochester baseball now that he's gone."

Hundreds turned out for Silver's funeral services in Rochester at Temple B'rith Kodesh and Mount Hope Cemetery. Earl Weaver, then managing the Baltimore Orioles, returned with his wife, Marianna. Orioles GM Frank Cashen and California Angels GM Harry Dalton also paid their respects, along with Altobelli and his team. The Red Wings had postponed their game with Richmond the night before and decided to wear black armbands the rest of the season in tribute to Silver.

It would turn out to be a season to remember. The Wings stumbled early, hampered by injuries and the late May callup of Garland. But a 13–3 June spurt pushed Rochester into first place. The Wings were 42–26 at the all-star break, just .004 points ahead of Syracuse, but seven consecutive wins over the Chiefs the next two weeks pushed the lead to seven and one-half games and eventually to twelve. On their way to the pennant, the Wings were making history. Tidewater's Hank Webb tossed a seven-inning no-hitter against them on June 7. Pawtucket's Charles Ross turned the trick six weeks later.

The season's masterpiece was turned in on August 16 during the second game of a doubleheader at Silver. Rochester's Gary Robson, a twenty-three-year-old right-hander from UCLA, entered the game with a 4.62 ERA and 51 walks in $50^{2}/_{3}$ innings, but on this night he was flawless. Robson struck out eleven and threw a seven-inning perfect game as the Wings beat Charleston 2–0 before 10,272 fans on Gannett Carrier Night. Bobby Bailor had started in center during the first game of the doubleheader and sat out the nightcap. His replacement, Tommy Shopay, cracked a two-run homer off Charleston starter Kent Tekulve for the only runs Robson would need. Robson's gem was the fourth no-hitter in the International League in 1974, and all four involved the Wings.

Rochester clinched the title with two weeks left in the season and finished 88–56, the most wins by the franchise since Harry Walker's 1953 club went 97–57. Rochester split the first two games of its best-of-seven playoff series with Memphis, and Blues catcher Gary Carter stole the show in game three. The future major-league star drove in six runs with a single, triple, and home run as Memphis rolled 6–4. It would be the Blues' last win. Strong pitching performances from starters Bill Kirkpatrick, Dyar Miller, and Paul Mitchell gave the Wings three straight wins and pushed them into the Governors' Cup finals against Syracuse.

The Wings had taken the regular season series 17–7, but the Chiefs won game one 11–5 in thirteen innings at Silver Stadium, then rallied from a 6–1 deficit to win game two 10–6. Miller and Mitchell pitched complete-game victories in Syracuse to tie the series at two, but the Chiefs romped 8–1 back at Silver to move one win from the championship. Back in Syracuse, Altobelli called on Kirkpatrick and his ace responded with a complete-game 6–2 win to even the series. It was the tenth consecutive win for the right-hander, who had finished the season 15–7. The visiting team had won each of the first six games, but the tide turned in game seven. With the red-hot Miller pitching, the Wings rolled

5–1 and won their second Governors' Cup title under Altobelli, who was named Minor League Manager of the Year by *The Sporting News*.

There was more news in the off-season. In October, Ed Barnowski finally filled the general manager's position left vacant by Steinfeldt's resignation. Three months later, Bill Lang retired as club president after seven years. Vice president Vincent Stanley was named as his successor, and Anna "Bert" Silver, the widow of Morrie Silver, became the first woman named to the RCB executive board.

The 1975 team was a mixture of veterans and newcomers. Fuller was back, Royle Stillman returned and was shifted to first base, and Dyar Miller and Paul Mitchell anchored a pitching staff weakened by the off-season trade of the dependable Kirkpatrick. Rich Dauer, the Orioles' number one draft pick in 1974, began the season at third base but was demoted to Asheville in May after hitting just .191. Stillman led the club in batting (.313) and RBI (75), and Fuller's seventeen homers—twenty-two fewer than in 1973—were good enough to pace the club again.

The recalls of Miller and Mitchell were compensated by the emergence of rookies Mike Willis and Mike Flanagan. Willis would finish 14–8 with a 2.58 ERA, tying for the league lead in wins. Flanagan, a twenty-three-year-old left-hander from Manchester, New Hampshire, would go 13–4, 2.50. The Wings finished tied for first with Tidewater at 85–55, then lost a one-game playoff in Norfolk 8–0. Rochester opened its best-of-five playoff series against Syracuse with a 5–0 win behind Willis, but the Chiefs outscored the Wings 23–4 in the next three games to win the series.

Altobelli continued to hope for a major-league job offer, but with none forthcoming he reluctantly agreed to return to Rochester for a sixth season in 1976. Still, he made it clear to the Orioles that this would be his final season in Rochester. "I just felt six years was enough," he said. "I told them I would stay in the organization—I'd even be a roving instructor if they wanted me to—but I just felt it was time to give someone else a chance to manage here."

The '76 season would be filled with cheers, farewells—and controversy. The Red Wings were loaded, with seventeen players returning. First baseman/outfielder Tom Kelly, who would lead the Minnesota Twins to World Series titles in 1987 and 1991, joined the club on loan from the Twins. Snow and rain forced cancellation of the Wings' first home series, and they were rained out in Norfolk, Virginia, as well. After eleven days, they finally returned to action with a doubleheader sweep at Richmond. The home opener finally was played on May 8, with Memphis beating the Wings 10–7 before 6,949 fans. The club struggled

Take Me Out to the Cow-Milking Contest?

They never suited up a midget to pinch-hit for them. Nor did they hold a "Disco Demolition Night" in which a truckload of records was blown up on the field. But the Red Wings have staged a number of promotions through the years that surely would have brought a smile to the face of baseball's late P. T. Barnum—Bill Veeck.

There have been beer nights and cow-milking contests and egg races and parachutists and Italian nights and free tickets for young fans who bring home good report cards. Home run derbies have always been a big draw at Silver Stadium. Babe Ruth, Willie Mays, Mickey Mantle, and Frank Robinson are among the heavy hitters who have taken swings there.

Jesse Owens, the Olympic gold medal sprinter, competed in several races at 500 Norton Street, easily outdistancing speedy Red Wings foolish enough to think they could beat the world's fastest human. Owens never raced a horse but Red Wing Ken Smith did—and won. On June 17, 1986, he beat thoroughbred Eighty-Proof, ridden by jockey Rod Markbraf, in a thirty-yard sprint from first to second.

The Grateful Dead and the Beach Boys are among the numerous musical groups to harmonize at the ballpark. Evangelist Billy Graham has crusaded there. He was looking to save something that can't be found in a box score.

Long before they became world boxing champions, Sugar Ray Robinson and Carmen Basilio fought outdoor bouts at the Rochester ballpark. Wiley Post, one of America's most famous aviators, stopped by for a visit in the 1930s.

Of all the great performances, it would be tough to top—literally —the show Karl Wallenda put on the evening of May 12, 1976. A crowd of 2,736 watched seventy-one-year-old Wallenda successfully walk a tightrope five hundred feet from the center-field fence to the grandstand roof—sixty feet above ground. The performance must have inspired the Wings; they swept a doubleheader from the Rhode Island Red Sox.

Silver Stadium also has played host to several home-plate weddings, the most recent coming during the 1982 season when Wings catcher Tim Derryberry married Cheryl Toxey.

Karl Wallenda. Courtesy of the *Democrat and Chronicle/Times-Union*.

Derryberry wedding. Courtesy of the
Democrat and Chronicle/Times-Union.

through May, falling to seventh place at 12–18. But old faces were returning to the Wings, and so were victories.

Tommy Shopay was sent down when Reggie Jackson, traded by Oakland to Baltimore, finally joined the Orioles. Terry Crowley, who had last played for Rochester in 1971, was released by the Atlanta Braves in spring training, picked up by Baltimore, and reassigned to Rochester. And Bill Kirkpatrick, who was 41–36 for the Wings from 1970 to 1974, was picked up after being released from the Montreal Expos' Triple-A team in Denver. On June 20, the Red Wings were in fourth place, four and one-half games behind Syracuse. By July 6, Rochester was in first, five and one-half games ahead of the Chiefs. In between, they won sixteen consecutive games, just three shy of the club record set by Harry Walker's 1953 squad. "It's like parting with a good friend," Altobelli said after the streak ended with an 8–4 loss in Pawtucket. "We sure got a lot of mileage out of it, though." Streaking would become a fad in Rochester in 1976. Besides the sixteen-game run and two seven-game streaks, the Wings reeled off fourteen straight from late July through August 3. By that time, they had won 37 of their last 43 to post a remarkable 70–36 mark and a twelve-and-one-half-game lead.

Altobelli was blessed with the best pitching staff of his six-year stint in Rochester. Wings hurlers posted a league-best 3.51 ERA and threw a gaudy fifty-seven complete games. The ace was Dennis Martinez, a right-hander from Granada, Nicaragua. Martinez had pitched only five innings for the Wings in 1975 but dominated the league in 1976, winning the International League pitching Triple Crown by leading in victories (14), ERA (2.50), and strikeouts (140). The lefty ace was Scott McGregor, a Californian who had joined the Red Wings from Syracuse on June 15 in a ten-player deal between the Orioles and New York Yankees. McGregor had pinpoint control and used it to forge a 12–6 record (8–1 with the Wings) and 3.06 ERA, walking only forty batters in 162 innings and leading the league with six shutouts. The rest of the potent staff included Bob Galasso (13–5), Mike Willis (12–6), and Mike Flanagan, who went 6–1 with a 2.12 ERA but spent most of the season with the Orioles. The bullpen was led by Dave Johnson (11–5 with seven saves) and Earl Stephenson, who recorded a 1.17 ERA in forty-six innings.

Four days after their sixteen-game streak was snapped, the Wings lost Fuller to a broken right thumb. Despite his .235 average, the slugger was leading the team with 18 homers and 53 RBI. With Fuller expected to miss more than a month, the Orioles promoted twenty-year-old Eddie Murray from Double-A Charlotte to the Wings. A Los Angeles native, Murray came from a family rich in baseball talent. Three older brothers had played professional baseball, and another, Rich, would make it to the majors in 1980 and 1983 with the San Francisco Giants, but none could match Eddie's skill and determination. The Orioles' third-round pick in 1973, he had played mostly first base before giving third a shot at Asheville in 1975. Recently he had been seeing time in the outfield.

Murray had worked his way steadily through the system since being drafted, but his numbers were unspectacular. He had never hit .300, never driven in more than sixty-eight runs, and never slammed more than seventeen homers. He did everything well, nothing great. In 1976, Murray blossomed. At Charlotte, he was hitting .294 with 12 homers and 44 RBI when he got the call. The Wings were 49–32 when Murray joined the club on July 15. He played first base and batted sixth in his Red Wing debut, going 0-for-2 in a 4–3 loss to the Charleston Charlies in game one of a doubleheader at Silver. He was a late-inning replacement for left fielder Royle Stillman in the nightcap and scored a run in Rochester's 7–6 win.

A quiet man with unlimited power and a workmanlike attitude, Murray's stay in Rochester would be brief. He hit .274 in 54 games, with 11 homers and 40 RBI in his final minor-league stint. The next year, he earned American League Rookie of the Year honors with Baltimore, the start of a tremendous career that would peak on June 30, 1995, when he became the twentieth player in major-league history—and the second former Red Wing, joining Stan Musial—to join the 3,000-hit club.

The Red Wings continued to win, and Rich Dauer continued to hit. The second baseman found himself locked in a battle with Charleston's Miguel Dilone for the batting title as the season wore down. Every at-bat became important, and the stress began building in the competitive Dauer. Late in the season, he reached first on a sharp grounder at Silver Stadium, then became livid when he saw the scoreboard flash "E" for error. When he scored minutes later, Dauer pointed up to the press box behind home plate and began screaming at official scorer Len Lustik. "He got me so angry," Lustik recalled, "that when he was in the on-deck circle his next time up, I went down to the box seats and started yelling back at him. I told him, 'If you're gonna win the damn thing, win it the right way.' "

The controversy began on September 1, when the Pittsburgh Pirates called up Dilone. With the Charleston outfielder's average frozen at .33498, Dauer needed two hits in less than four at-bats to win the International League title. The next day at Silver, he singled and doubled in his first two at-bats against Syracuse and was pulled from the game by Altobelli to a standing ovation. His average stood at .33526. One game remained, but the batting race appeared over. Dauer had the lead, and Dilone was in Pittsburgh.

Or was he? The next morning, Wings broadcaster Pete Brown placed a call to Memphis to check on some other players' averages. To the surprise of everyone—the Wings, the media, IL president George Sisler, and especially Dauer—Brown learned that Dilone was still with the Charlies. His recall would not take place until the season ended. The speedy Dilone had played in a doubleheader the night before, going 1-for-6. That was the good news for Dauer. The bad news was that league statistician Ed Williams reported that a mistake had been made in calculating Dilone's average. With one game remaining, it now stood at .33578—barely ahead of Dauer.

Dauer had planned to sit out the finale in Syracuse that night. Now he was so distraught at the change of events that he told Altobelli he would not play, even though he trailed Dilone. When Dilone reported from Memphis that he would play, Dauer changed his mind, ten minutes before the start of the Wings' game.

"If I was going to lose the title, I wanted to lose swinging," Dauer said.

Dauer fell further behind when he went hitless in his first three at-bats, then learned that the Charleston-Memphis game had been rained out. Dilone's season was over. Dauer needed to go 2-for-2 over the final four innings to win the crown. "I thought it was a lost cause," he admitted afterward. "I was very depressed."

Dauer stayed alive with a single in the seventh, then stepped into the on-deck circle with two outs in the ninth, with the Chiefs leading 6–5. On the mound was rookie right-hander Scott Delgatti, a Rochester native who had just been called up to Syracuse. Delgatti didn't know about Dauer's situation—at least until Chiefs third baseman Tom Matchick told him.

Matchick, who had played for the Wings before being traded that summer, gave Delgatti some special instructions. "He told me, 'Look, we want Dauer to win this thing,' " Delgatti recalled. "He said, 'Walk this next guy and give Dauer something to hit.' The whole team wanted Dauer to win. They saw him as a pure hitter, a guy who got line drives. Dilone got half his hits on bunts. The guys didn't respect that."

Reluctantly, Delgatti walked Larry Harlow.

"Then I looked at [Chiefs manager] Bobby Cox in the dugout and he just nodded," Delgatti said. "I looked to my right. . . . My shortstop was playing behind second base. Matchick was [practically] in left field."

The Chiefs were giving Dauer an open invitation to bunt. Dauer was too proud to accept, but catcher Rick Stelmaszek mentioned to him that the next pitch might be worth swinging at. Delgatti's first pitch was a fastball down the middle of the plate. Dauer drilled it to left and outfielder Rick Bladt never moved as the ball bounced off the wall for a double. The batting title belonged to Dauer by the slimmest of margins:

Dauer: .33587

Dilone: .33578

"I didn't throw it at batting practice speed or anything," Delgatti said. "But if you throw that kind of pitch at Triple-A—and the hitter knows it's coming—he's going to hit it."

The Syracuse crowd gave Dauer a standing ovation, aware of his feat but not the circumstances surrounding it. Delgatti was so upset at being the "hitman" in the incident that his first pitch to the next batter landed about ten feet in front of home plate. After the game, the jubilant Wings invited Delgatti into their clubhouse to thank him. The twenty-eight-year-old pitcher didn't cross paths with Dauer, but the two did meet up three years later in Miami, when Delgatti was trying out for the Orioles and Dauer was their starting second baseman. "He didn't say much," Delgatti recalled. "Just something like 'I appreciate you trying to help me out.' "

Delgatti's youthfulness was apparent the morning following the Dauer incident, when he was quoted in the papers admitting his role. "We wanted to give it to Dauer," he said, "so I sort of threw it down the middle."

International League president George Sisler, Jr., was furious and vowed to investigate the matter, though he said Dauer's title would stand. "Some guys can't hit a fat pitch in batting practice," Sisler said. "Dauer did what he had to do. He didn't bunt. He hit the ball off the fence."

In the end, no penalties were handed out and the matter was dropped. Dauer wound up the league MVP and went on to play ten seasons with the Baltimore Orioles. The 1976 Red Wings finished 88–50, Altobelli's best record in his six seasons and the franchise's best since Harry Walker's 1953 club finished 97–57.

The '76 team might have been considered the best in Red Wings history if the games had stopped after the regular season. But the playoffs proved to be the undoing of the club—and the end of one of the Wings' most glorious eras.

Rochester's opponent in the best-of-five playoffs was Richmond. The Braves had needed a late-season run just to make the postseason, but they stunned the Wings 7–3 in game one at Silver, with Martinez lasting just one and one-third innings. Martinez had not won since August 6, and when he showed up for the 2:00 P.M. playoff opener at 1:20, teammates began to whisper about his late-night habits. In fact, Martinez was battling an alcohol problem, one that would become public after he was traded from Baltimore to the Montreal Expos in 1986 for infielder Rene Gonzalez.

The Wings' hopes of a third Governors' Cup title in six seasons continued to unravel with a bitter 5–4 loss in game two, when Richmond scored two runs in the ninth. Martinez missed the team flight to Richmond, and a furious Altobelli threatened to keep him out of the rotation. The situation never came to a head, as Richmond completed its stunning sweep with a 6–0 home win to eliminate the Wings.

It would be Altobelli's final game as manager of the Red Wings. Two weeks after the playoffs, he was in St. Louis interviewing for the Cardinals job as manager. "Bing Devine was the general manager at the time and he asked me to fly in to talk," Altobelli recalled. "I only brought one suit, because I was only going to be there a day."

While in St. Louis, Altobelli received a call from San Francisco Giants owner Bob Lurie. The Giants were also looking for a manager, and Lurie liked what Altobelli had done with the Red Wings. "The Cardinals really wanted me to join their organization," Altobelli said. "They told me, even if we don't hire you as manager we'll pay you $50,000 a year to be an instructor. But when I went out to San Francisco and they made me an offer, I just couldn't turn it down. It was a better opportunity, and a club with better talent."

And so one of the Red Wings' golden eras had ended. In six seasons as manager, Altobelli had won 502 games and lost 350. His teams had never produced a losing season and had won two pennants, two Governors' Cups, and one Junior World Series. Shortly after Altobelli left the Red Wings, the club announced it was retiring his number 26. It is the only number retired in Red Wings history.

12

Life after Alto

No matter what happens, there's no way I'd come
back to Rochester now.
—Frank Robinson, 1978

Altobelli's departure left a void in
the Orioles minor-league system.
Other organization men such as Jim Schaffer, Billy Hunter and George
Bamberger had been plucked away by other teams, leaving the managerial cupboard bare. The Orioles went outside the organization, hiring
longtime St. Louis Cardinals star Ken Boyer to lead the Wings. The
Missouri-born third baseman was a model of consistency with the
Cardinals. After hitting a career-high 32 home runs in 1960, he hit 24 in
each of the next four seasons. He also drove in 90 or more runs from
1958 to 1964, leading the National League in 1964 with 119 to power
the Cardinals to a seven-game World Series victory over the New York
Yankees.

With the heart of Altobelli's pitching staff—Flanagan, McGregor,
and Martinez—now in Baltimore, Boyer's 1977 club struggled to a sixth-
place finish. At 67–73, the Wings finished below .500 for the first time
in twelve seasons. Boyer was optimistic about turning things around in
1978, but he never got the chance. On April 28, the St. Louis Cardinals
fired manager Vern Rapp with the club off to a 5–10 start. They chose
the popular Boyer as Rapp's successor.

Boyer became the first Red Wings manager to leave the team during
the season since Harry "The Hat" Walker was promoted—also by the
Cardinals—in 1955. While Orioles minor-league pitching coach Al

171

Widmar took over as interim manager, the search for Boyer's replacement intensified. The short list included former New York Mets manager Joe Frazier and former Texas Rangers manager Frank Lucchesi, but speculation centered on Orioles coach Frank Robinson. Orioles general manager Hank Peters met with Robinson in Boston and admitted, "If he wants the job, we'd like to offer it to him."

"It's up to me whether to say yes or no, and I'm still not sure," Robinson said three days after Boyer's departure. "It's still in a holding pattern. Usually, I have a feeling for something, but this just seems to kind of hang. I don't have a bad feeling about it, and I don't have a good feeling." Robinson had been one of the finest players in baseball history. His 586 home runs were fourth on the all-time list, and he was the only player to win MVP awards in both leagues. He was the National League Rookie of the Year in 1956, won the Triple Crown in 1966 with Baltimore, and played in five World Series and eleven All-Star games. In 1975, Robinson became the major leagues' first black manager when he took over the Cleveland Indians, a job that lasted two and a half seasons.

After a brief coaching stint with the California Angels, Robinson returned to Baltimore as a coach in 1978. Still, he wanted another shot managing in the big leagues and finally decided that guiding a Triple-A club would be the faster way to achieve his goal. After all, it had worked for Boyer. On May 3, 1978, he accepted the job in Rochester and thus made history again, becoming the first black manager in Red Wings history. Calling it "the toughest decision I ever had to make," Robinson phoned Peters and took the job after receiving assurances that he could rejoin the Orioles coaching staff in 1979 if he did not return to Rochester or land a major-league job. His salary with the Wings would remain the same as with Baltimore—$30,000. "Robinson's hiring is not great," Wings general manager Don Labbruzzo said, "it's fantastic. This is one of the greatest things ever to happen to Rochester baseball. I guarantee you no minor-league team ever had two players as great as Ken Boyer and Frank Robinson as managers in the same season."

Robinson admitted he would not have accepted a job with just any minor-league team, saying he was "impressed with the fans and the baseball atmosphere" during his visits to Silver Stadium for Orioles exhibitions. The Red Wings were in Toledo when Robinson's hiring was announced. He didn't take over until they returned home four days later. Red Wings center fielder Mike Dimmel felt it was the right move for Robinson, saying "He's coming to a town where managers flock to the big leagues." Pitcher John Flinn called the appointment "super." "It's neat when you can call home and tell people you're playing for Ken Boyer, and now Frank Robinson," Flinn said. "That's a thrill in itself."

Hall of Famer Frank Robinson's stint as Red
Wings manager was short, and not always sweet.
Courtesy of the *Democrat and Chronicle/Times-Union.*

Robinson had not worn a minor-league uniform in twenty-three years, and many wondered how such a tremendous talent would adjust to life in the bushes. He did have minor-league experience, however dubious: two years before, when he was still Cleveland's manager, Robinson had created a stir in Toledo by decking Mud Hens pitcher Bob Reynolds during an exhibition game. Robinson pulled no punches when he met with his new club in Rochester. He promised no wholesale changes and said he would evaluate each player individually. "I will adjust to the players," he said at a standing-room-only press conference. "They won't have to adjust to me. I manage what I have." He did promise to bring "a wide-open, aggressive game" to the Wings. "I don't like to go by the book," he said. "I'm not a book manager. I like to take chances."

Robinson took over a 10–8 club. His first game was rained out, but the wait proved worth it. On May 9, the Columbus Clippers took a 9–4 lead into the bottom of the ninth but the Wings rallied for six runs to hand their new boss one of the most dramatic comebacks in Silver Stadium history. Robinson wore number twenty, the number he had worn every season in pro ball except for 1972, when Los Angeles Dodgers teammate Don Sutton wore it. Through his first month on the job, Robby's Red Wings were 12–16 under his leadership. He admitted to spending more than one sleepless night recounting a tough loss, but he was thrilled to be in Rochester. "I'm certain I made the right move," he said. "I'm enjoying it. The team has a super overall attitude and we're going to win. My only regret is that I wasn't here when the season started."

The Wings showed little power all season—outfielder Gary Roenicke led the club with thirteen home runs—but Robinson and an old friend provided the hometown fans with a night to remember on August 24. Willie Mays, whose 660 homers trailed only Hank Aaron (755) and Babe Ruth (714) on the all-time list, engaged in a pregame home-run contest with Robinson before a game at Silver Stadium. Mays, who received $2,000 for his appearance, failed to clear the fences in ten swings against Wings catcher Dave Criscione but drew wild cheers with his routine fly balls. Robinson smashed two homers to left to win the contest. "My arms were so tired I couldn't even raise them over my head," said Mays, who was then forty-seven. "But the fans appreciate it. They know I'm too old to come here and hit home runs. They like to see me for what I was before."

The Wings stayed in the playoff hunt until the final week, finally settling in sixth place at 68–72, 58–64 under Robinson. The first-year manager had expressed an interest in returning for 1979 as early as August, and he officially told the Orioles of his desire on October 27.

Robinson made the call from Puerto Rico, where he was managing, and farm director Clyde Kluttz told him he would make a decision within the week. Kluttz indicated money would not be an issue. "If it is," he said, "Robinson will not get the job. Last year we paid him a lot more than the going rate for a Triple-A manager and I'm prepared to offer the same."

The offer never came. One week after Robinson made his request, former Detroit Tigers coach Fred Hatfield rejected an offer to manage the Wings, taking a job with the Tigers' Class A team in Lakeland, Florida, instead. Robinson was furious that someone else had been offered his job.

> No matter what happens, there's no way I'd come back to Rochester now. The day before the season was over [Wings general manager] Don Labbruzzo rambled on and on about how he understood the injuries we had and said under the circumstances that he thought I did a good job and he'd be happy to have me back. Now I'm told that Labbruzzo and [Wings president] Bill Blackmon told the Orioles at the end of September that they wanted a change. . . . I want the fans and everyone to know that I would have loved to come back. But there's no way now, under any circumstances.

Robinson quickly landed a coaching job with the Orioles, and in 1981 he got his second chance when he was named manager of the San Francisco Giants. One year later, he was inducted into the Baseball Hall of Fame. Robinson later managed the Orioles before moving up to the front office.

With Robinson rejected and Fred Hatfield out of the picture, the search for a new Red Wings manager continued. Finally, in late November 1978, the Orioles and Wings agreed on a choice. The new man was Howard Edwards, nicknamed "Doc" for his service in the U.S. Navy medical corps. The son of a West Virginia coal miner, Edwards had spent parts of five seasons in the majors, hitting .238 as a backup catcher with the Cleveland Indians, Kansas City Athletics, and Philadelphia Phillies. Kluttz had hired Edwards five years earlier to manage Double-A West Haven in the Eastern League. He led West Haven to a second-place finish and then a fourth, before moving on to manage in the Chicago Cubs and Montreal Expos organizations. Edwards led Denver to a second-place finish (64–71) in 1977.

Labbruzzo lauded the move, saying "We now have the kind of manager who follows in the Joe Altobelli mold." But Edwards would not enjoy Altobelli's success in Rochester. This "Doc" could not cure what

Lustik's Law

Len Lustik was so thrilled at becoming the Red Wings' official scorer in 1973 that he gladly would have done the job for free. In fact, he thought he was doing it for free.

"I had no idea I got paid for it," he said. "When the season was over, I received a check from the International League for $600. It turned out I had scored 40 games at $15 per game. I thought they'd made a mistake."

Lustik had no previous experience as a scorer, but when veteran sportswriter George Beahon asked him to fill in throughout the year, the tax accountant agreed. More than twenty years later, Lustik is still on the job as full-time scorer. He has watched close to two thousand games from his front-row seat in the press box and has had more run-ins with players than he'd care to remember. Lustik has sent notes down to only two players: Iowa Cubs infielder Gary Varsho and Red Wings shortstop Kelly Paris. "In two preceding nights, there were errors called on balls that Varsho had hit," Lustik said. "The one night I wasn't here, he came up to the press box. When the attendant asked, 'Who are you?' he sarcastically said, 'I'm Gary Varsho. I just came to see what the view looked like from up here.' "

That night, Varsho struck out five times, and Lustik was quick to react. "I sent a note down with the press box attendant saying 'Dear Gary, How's the view from down there? Signed, the official scorer.' Two weeks later, he was called up to the majors, and he's never been back." Paris was one of Lustik's least favorite Red Wings. "He bitched and moaned all the time," Lustik said. "One time I really got tired of it, so I took a bottle of wine and covered the label with a note saying 'This should appeal to you, 'cause it's made from sour grapes.' He sent it back up with a note telling me where I could put it."

Once, Paris was in a foul mood because his batting average had fallen below .200 and he blamed much of his trouble on Lustik's rulings. The shortstop spotted the official scorer on the dugout steps before a game and approached him with a bat in his hand. "I wish I could take a swing at your head," Paris said angrily. "Go ahead," Lustik countered. "The way you've been hitting, you'll probably miss."

The worst player Lustik ever dealt with was Red Wings third baseman Doug DeCinces. "Doug had an excuse for everything," he said. "The ball hit him in the cup, he lost a grounder in the sun, the temperature was too warm. . . . We would argue and argue and I'd always go down into the dressing room afterwards to try and be a nice guy.

My happiest moment came when he finally got called up to the Orioles, and he came back his first year for the exhibition. He made three errors. The first two were on ground balls that he fumbled, and the third was a popup to the catcher. The catcher calls for it and he's under it, and Doug comes barreling in from third yelling "I've got it! I've got it!" And the ball pops out of his glove for the error. Three fielding chances, three errors. I was smiling from one end of the press box to the other.

After DeCinces retired, Lustik went to a baseball card convention in Anaheim, California, and discovered DeCinces was the keynote speaker. "Afterwards, I went over to say hello and he said 'Oh my God, what are you doing here?' and I said 'I wanted to see if you were going to drop your speech.' "

Lustik has never been physically confronted by a player, but he thought he was a goner after a game back in 1974. Red Wings slugger Jim Fuller lined a ball so hard that it went through the legs of Tidewater shortstop Leo Foster and rolled all the way to the wall. "I called it an error and I had all the Red Wings looking up. Everyone felt it was a hit," Lustik said. "I thought he should have made the play.

Lustik was walking alone to his car in the deserted media lot at around eleven o'clock that night when a figure suddenly emerged from the phone booth near the exit and approached Lustik. "I'm scared out of my wits. I figure, 'This is it. I'm going to get mugged. I'm history.' The guy asks if I'm the official scorer, and like a fool I say yes. He says 'I'm Leo Foster, and I just want you to know that was one hell of a call. I know you took some heat for it, but if I want to play in the major leagues I've got to make that play.'

"Needless to say, I followed Leo Foster's career for as long as he played. He finally got up to the Mets."

When catcher Harry Saferight played for Richmond, he was put into right field in the ninth inning as a defensive replacement and dropped a ball. After the game, Saferight showed up in the press box in full uniform to complain about the error. "He insisted that he shouldn't have gotten an error because he was in right field and he's normally a catcher," Lustik said. "He felt that because he was a catcher and they had asked him to play in the outfield that he was immune from errors. Years later, we got him here in Rochester."

Most of the games Lustik has scored have been uneventful. One exception was August 16, 1974, when Gary Robson threw a seven-inning perfect game for Rochester. So thrilled was Lustik that he gave

Robson a $100 bonus out of his own pocket immediately following the game. He also gave catcher Jim Hutto and outfielder Tommy Shopay—who had homered in the game—$25 each. "It was a $150 night," Lustik said. "But it was worth it."

ailed the '79 Wings. After opening the season with a 13–1 romp, Rochester limped to its first eighth-place finish since Burleigh Grimes's 1945 squad, finishing at 53–86. The Wings offensive "leaders" were modest—13 homers by Ron Diggle, 60 RBI by Tom Chism—although the club finished second in team batting. But shoddy pitching, virtually no speed or clutch hitting—they hit into 125 double plays—doomed the Wings. Only 200,013 fans bothered to show up, the lowest figure at Silver Stadium since community ownership began in 1957.

Edwards's clubhouse support was shaky, with many players charging favoritism. After seeing a *Times-Union* headline in late August that predicted a poor 1979 finish as well, Diggle commented, "He [the writer] knew Doc would be back." Another player complained that "Players didn't know what to expect. Nobody knew who had a job or who didn't." Edwards took issue with the comments in a guest column he wrote for the *Democrat and Chronicle.* "I'm embarrassed by what happened at Silver Stadium this year," Edwards wrote. "We had a lot of injuries and lost the heart of our club in the first month, but I couldn't call off the games. It was disappointing reading [the players' comments]. That kind of stuff should never leave the clubhouse. I was very mad, but I had a talk with Ron and it's all over. The case is closed."

Edwards couldn't turn the club around despite acquiring four veteran players from the defunct Inter-American League: pitcher Mike Wallace, infielder Wayne Tyrone, catcher-outfielder Larry Doby Johnson, and outfielder Tommy Smith. "I did try to bring in some help from the Inter-American League," Edwards wrote. "There was still time to turn it around then. But we lost three weeks and played about 25 games before they arrived. Then it took them about two weeks to get back in shape, and by then it was too late for them to really help us."

Edwards promised a winning team in 1980 and he delivered, leading the Wings to a 74–65 third-place finish—their best record since Altobelli left in 1976. The Wings slipped to 69–70 in 1981, finishing fourth but making a quick playoff exit for the second consecutive year. Speculation had begun as early as August 1981 that Edwards would not be asked to return—new Orioles farm director Tom Giordano had publicly criticized Edwards's handling of the pitching staff—but his status remained in limbo for weeks following the season finale. Finally, on September 29, Edwards announced he was leaving the organization to become manager of the Cleveland Indians' top affiliate in Charleston, West Virginia. "I felt Tom probably wanted to do some things differently, and he has that right," Edwards said. "I felt it was best for everyone concerned that I make this move."

Even though he was leaving the Wings, Edwards promised to return one day. "I enjoyed three super years in Rochester," he said. "I loved the people there. I'm going to make Rochester my home when I get out of this game." Edwards would eventually land a job as the Indians' bullpen coach in 1985, then take over as manager when Pat Corrales was fired midway through the 1987 season. Edwards himself would be dismissed on September 12, 1989, when his once-contending club fell into an 11–24 slump. He left the Indians with a 173–207 record, replaced by John Hart. Edwards later managed the Buffalo Bisons, top farm club of the Pittsburgh Pirates.

His final season in Rochester would be highlighted by one player —and one game.

13

The Game That Wouldn't End

| Rochester | 000 000 100 000 000 000 001 000 000 000 000—2 18 3 |
| Pawtucket | 000 000 001 000 000 000 001 000 000 000 001—3 21 1 |

—Linescore from the longest game
in professional baseball history

Dave Huppert lost track of how many times he got in and out of his catcher's crouch that raw New England night in the spring of 1981. All he knows is that when Rochester Red Wings manager Doc Edwards mercifully pinch-hit for him in the top of the thirty-second inning, his knees were as stiff and creaky as the Tin Man's rusty joints in The Wizard of Oz. "The game was dragging so bad that at one point I looked back at the home plate umpire and said, 'Would you please call 16 straight balls so we can end this thing and get some sleep?' " Huppert recalled in an interview ten years later. Umpire Jack Lietz refused to grant the catcher's request, and the game between the Red Wings and the Pawtucket Red Sox staggered on.

And on.

And on.

And on.

Finally, at 4:07 Easter morning, April 19, 1981, Lietz, under orders from International League president Harold Cooper, suspended the game before the start of the thirty-third inning with the score tied at two. The players, coaches, and two dozen fans who persevered for eight frigid hours at Pawtucket's McCoy Stadium drove off into the sunrise.

Sixty-five days later, on June 23, the teams resumed play before

180

5,756 spectators at the tiny Rhode Island ballpark, and millions more listening worldwide on the Armed Forces Radio Network. The final chapter of one of the most bizarre baseball sagas took all of eighteen minutes to write. Dave Koza stroked a bases-loaded single off Cliff Speck and Pawtucket won the longest game in professional baseball history, 3–2. "It was kind of disappointing when it ended that quickly," said Bob Drew, the Red Wings general manager and backup broadcaster. "We knew we were part of history and we all wanted to keep the thing going." Some, though, were happy to see it end. Red Wings center fielder Dallas Williams, for example, went hitless in thirteen at-bats. Pawtucket designated hitter Russ Laribee didn't fare much better. He struck out seven times and finished 0-for-11.

Nobody, though, felt worse than losing pitcher Steve Grilli. He had been with the Toronto Blue Jays when the first thirty-two innings were played, but the Jays released him and he signed a free agent contract with the Wings before the longest game resumed. Grilli started the thirty-third inning and promptly loaded the bases. Edwards brought in Speck, who gave up the decisive hit, and Grilli became the answer to a trivia question: Who was the losing pitcher in the longest professional baseball game? "I was in the right place at the right time doing the wrong thing," he lamented. The game, though, helped immortalize Grilli and all its participants. The losing pitcher's Red Wings cap is on display at the Baseball Hall of Fame in Cooperstown, as is a tape of Drew's broadcast and the strangest-looking boxscore ever. "Steve was much too hard on himself," Huppert said. "Nobody blamed him for the loss. It was a real downer when it ended that way, but that game made us a part of baseball history and no one can take that away from us, unless they play a longer game, which I don't see happening."

No one who showed up at antiquated McCoy Stadium that windy April night had an inkling one of the more bizarre games in the long history of professional baseball would be played. However, there were indications even before the first pitch that this was going to be a long night. The start of the game was delayed a half hour while maintenance men worked to fix a bank of lights. "It was an omen," Huppert would later joke, "but we didn't pick up on it." Although McCoy had a reputation as a hitter-friendly park, pitching ruled on that historic night as starters Larry Jones of Rochester and Danny Parks of Pawtucket made zero the most popular number on the scoreboard. The Wings broke the scoreless tie in the seventh when Chris Bourjos singled home Mark Corey. Pawtucket tied the game in the bottom of the ninth. Chico Walker

A Final Tune-up for Junior

It didn't take long for anyone in Rochester to realize what lay ahead. One look was all you needed to realize that Cal Ripken, Jr., was destined for greatness. The player who broke Lou Gehrig's consecutive games played record of 2,130 on September 6, 1995, was the real deal the minute he trotted onto the diamond at Silver Stadium. "I'm no baseball GM, but you can tell when an athlete has that look about him, and Cal had that look," said former *Democrat and Chronicle* baseball writer John Kolomic. "His movements were so natural, so smooth, and he had that uncanny knack of anticipating things before they happened."

Heading into the 1981 season, *Sport* magazine predicted that Ripken would be the American League rookie of the year. Its editors were one year premature. He won it the following season. But he might have captured those honors in '81 had major-league baseball not gone on strike because he probably would have been called up by the Baltimore Orioles early in the season. As it was, Ripken spent 114 games with the Wings, and—surprise, surprise—did not miss a single game, despite a severely sprained ankle and a sore throwing shoulder that sidelined him briefly in spring training. Interestingly, the shoulder injury prompted some to forecast a slow start for the twenty-year-old third baseman-shortstop.

The predictions couldn't have been more off-base. Ripken homered in his first Triple-A game, a 6–5 victory against Pawtucket before more than nine thousand fans in the '81 season opener at Silver. He wound up hitting safely in eleven of his first twelve games and had seven home runs in his initial nineteen games. The player they called "Junior" wound up batting .288 with 23 home runs, 31 doubles, and 75 RBI to earn International League rookie of the year honors. The minute the strike ended on August 8 that summer, the Orioles promoted him.

Ripken's dedication to the game was obvious even back then. He was always taking extra grounders and batting practice. "He was the first one at the park and the last one to leave," Kolomic recalled. "He was your classic gym-rat, only his gym was a ballpark."

Former *Times-Union* baseball reporter Bill Koenig recalled the time when Ripken was coming off a mediocre road trip and headed to Silver for some additional work in the batting cage. When he showed up at the park, there were several other Wings hoping to do the same thing. Ripken volunteered to pitch, and by the time his teammates had completed their swings it was time for regular BP to begin. Ripken never did get to take his extra cuts. As Koenig noted, it didn't matter.

"Ripken needed the extra BP as much as Hannibal needed another elephant," he wrote in the next day's *Times-Union*. "Several hours later, he ripped three gigantic home runs and drove in four runs as the Red Wings beat Charleston 6–3 before 2,353 fans."

Floyd Rayford, the man who Ripken replaced in the Orioles lineup on May 30, 1982, to start the most famous streak in sports, chuckled when reminded of that session that preceded the three-homer performance. "It showed how unselfish Cal was," said Rayford, who later became a hitting instructor with the Batavia Clippers of the New York-Penn League. "He was the super prospect. He could have big-leagued people that day, and made sure he got his extra swings. But that's not Rip. He is a superstar, but he also is the ultimate team player."

Even at the age of twenty, Ripken was keenly aware of his image. John Valle, a former teammate of Ripken's, can't recall any stories of his teammate raising hell. "He wasn't one to go out and carouse," Valle said. "I think he was mature enough to realize all the things that awaited him if he kept his nose clean and to the grindstone. It's amazing, but I've never seen or heard of any incidents involving Cal, and that's pretty remarkable, considering the microscope he's been under, especially in recent years. I think it says a lot about his character."

That's not to say Ripken was an angel. There was a devilish side to him, especially when it came to practical jokes. "He and [John] Shelby were always pulling pranks on each other," Valle said. "He would put shaving cream in Shelby's jockstrap and street clothes, and there was one time when he nailed his spikes to the clubhouse ceiling. Shelby would return the favor, and Cal would take it in stride."

Both Kolomic and Koenig remember him as a delight to deal with from the media's perspective. "He was a standup guy," Koenig said. "Win or lose, he would talk. The only anger I ever saw was anger he directed at himself. He was a perfectionist, and he would get mad at himself when he did something that wasn't fundamentally correct. As a ballplayer and a person, Cal was the same. He was someone you could expect consistency from."

smashed a double off the center-field wall, moved to third on a wild pitch by Jones, and scored on Russ Laribee's sacrifice fly. The stage was set for extra innings—twenty-four of them, to be exact.

A crowd of 1,740 fans was on hand for the first pitch, but fewer than 100 remained by the time the game crawled into its twentieth in-

Cal Ripken, Jr. Courtesy of the *Democrat and Chronicle/Times-Union*.

ning. In the top of the twenty-first, Huppert doubled home a run (it was his first Triple-A hit) to put the Wings up, 2–1, and players from both teams seemed pleased. Maybe this thing was going to end after all. But in the bottom of the inning, Wade Boggs doubled in Koza to even the score. "After 15 innings it was kind of comical, but then they tied it, and everybody thought, 'God, will it ever end,' " recalled Cal Ripken, Jr., the Orioles iron-man shortstop who played third base that night for the Wings. Huppert called Boggs's hit "demoralizing. We weren't thinking history at the time. We were thinking abut getting some food and some sleep. I was starving, freezing and dog-tired." In the broadcast booth, Bob Drew had other concerns. "My voice was starting to give out when we hit the 20s," he said, referring to the inning count, not the temperature. "I just kept pouring coffee down me, and I got my second wind." He had another concern—Pawtucket had the only press box in the International League without a bathroom. "Needless to say," recalled Drew, "I was in plenty of pain."

PawSox reliever Luis Aponte pitched the seventh through tenth innings, striking out nine of the fourteen batters he faced. At 2 A.M., he was given permission to go home.

"Where have you been?" his wife, Xiomara, asked angrily upon his arrival.

"At the ballpark," he said.

"Like hell you have," she snapped. "You're lying."

Aponte reportedly spent what was left of the night on the couch.

If it hadn't been for an umpire's refusal to enforce the league curfew rule, the game never would have lasted into the wee hours, and Aponte might have gotten home at a reasonable hour. The rule said no inning should start after 12:50 A.M., except in the final series between two clubs. When the action went beyond the deadline, Pawtucket general manager Mike Tamburro reminded Lietz of the rule. The umpire produced his preseason manual, which did not contain the curfew notice. Tamburro then showed Lietz the league constitution, but the nine-year veteran umpire decided it wasn't applicable. "Play ball," he shouted. Boggs, who was lying on the field using third base as a pillow, dragged himself to his feet, and the game resumed. A furious Tamburro headed for a press box phone and called IL President Harold Cooper at his home in Columbus, Ohio. The phone rang and rang, but no one answered. Tamburro kept trying every five minutes or so, to no avail.

Meanwhile, down on the field, pitchers continued to dominate against groggy hitters who felt as if they were swinging telephone poles rather than Louisville Sluggers. "It seemed like every pitcher was better than the last one," said Floyd Rayford, who pinch-ran for Red Wings outfielder Tom Chism in the eighteenth inning and wound up staying in the game and going 0-for-5. "Bruce Hurst is out there throwing 95 mph fastballs at four in the morning, and his curveball is dropping off the table. Man, at four in the morning, I don't want to see any curveball breaking six feet." Added Red Wings second baseman Tom Eaton: "I don't know if the pitchers were really that good or if it was because we were so tired, but everyone out there began looking like Nolan Ryan." Among the Ryan impersonators was Jim Umbarger. The Red Wings reliever entered the game in the twenty-second inning to relieve Steve Luebber, who had completed an eight-inning shift. Umbarger wound up pitching the final ten innings that night, yielding no runs on four hits and striking out nine. "Now, I know," he joked afterward, "what they mean by long reliever." Umbarger remembered sitting in the bullpen when, at about the sixteenth inning, fellow reliever Don Welchel told him in jest: "Jim, you've got the 25th and 26th innings. I've got the 27th and 28th." Little did they know.

Umbarger was indeed pitching in the twenty-sixth inning when Pawtucket's Sam Bowen smashed a two-out fastball that appeared headed over the right-field fence. But the strong winds blew what every-

one hoped would be the game-ending home run back onto the field and
into the glove of right fielder John Hale. "The umpires and everybody
were trying to blow that one out of the park," Rayford said.

At about 2:30 in the morning, a doctor who just an hour earlier
had delivered a baby at the hospital across the street spotted the lights
still on and sauntered into the nearly empty ballpark.

"What's going on here?" the stunned physician said to no one in
particular.

"We're playing a ball game," replied Pawtucket manager Joe Morgan. "Have a seat. There's plenty of good ones left."

The game dragged on so long that one Rochester player, who was
pinch-hit for in the ninth inning, showered, got drunk, fell asleep in the
clubhouse, and woke up astonished to discover that the game was still
plugging along. At one point, Larry Jones, Rochester's starting pitcher,
joked to a teammate: "It's been a couple of days since I pitched. I'm
ready to go back in." As the innings and zeroes mounted, Tamburro
continued his attempts to reach the league president. At 3:45 A.M., Harold Cooper finally answered. "Some guy's telling me that the game in
Pawtucket is still going on, and I'm thinking, what is this, some kind of
crank call?" Cooper recalled in a 1991 interview. When Cooper realized
it was legitimate, he told Tamburro to put Lietz on the line. "After this
inning," the president instructed the umpire, "call the damn thing." The
Red Wings almost won the game in the thirty-second, but the rally died
when center fielder Bowen's throw to the plate nabbed Hale by a good
ten feet. Pawtucket failed to score in its half of the inning, and the game
was suspended. There had been talk about resuming it that afternoon
before the regularly scheduled game, but Cooper thought that wouldn't
be fair. He said the game would be completed during the Red Wings next
visit in late June.

About two dozen fans were still in the park when Lietz blurted that
the marathon had been suspended. The hardy souls were rewarded with
season passes, although a couple said they had had their fill of baseball
—for a lifetime. Announcer Drew and pitcher Umbarger hopped a cab
back to the Howard Johnson's where the club was staying and ordered
breakfast. Umbarger apparently had worked up quite an appetite while
working his ten-inning shift. As Drew looked on in disbelief, Big Jim
ordered oatmeal cereal with bananas, a ham-and-cheese omlette, home
fries, toast, pancakes, sausage and eggs, and a pot of coffee to wash it all
down.

There wasn't much time for sleep—the teams had a two o'clock game that afternoon. Huppert showed up at the ballpark fully expecting to take the day off, but his backup had pulled a groin muscle, so Hup was forced to catch again. That day's game was tied going into the bottom of the ninth. Recalled Huppert: "We're thinking, 'Oh, no. Please, Lord. Not again.' " They breathed a collective sigh when Bowen's game-winning homer mercifully prevented extra innings.

Drew was fired by the ball club when he returned from the historic road trip, but he still was able to broadcast the thirty-third and final inning on the Orioles network, because the major leagues were on strike. "I guess you could say I'm the only broadcaster to be fired between innings," he would joke years later.

A carnival atmosphere prevailed when the game resumed on June 23. In a story in that morning's *Democrat and Chronicle* reporter Bob Minzesheimer wrote: "Not since the time they had to shoot the drunken camel at the city zoo has there been this much excitement in Pawtucket, where tonight the Rochester Red Wings and Pawtucket Red Sox are to resume a baseball game in the top of the 33rd inning." Interest in the game was heightened by the void caused by the major league strike. Nearly 140 press credentials were issued. Many national sports columnists and baseball writers who normally would be at big league parks descended upon the tiny Rhode Island town. Four networks, including the British Broadcasting Company, were on hand, as was a photographer from a Japanese magazine. The game was broadcast worldwide over the Armed Forces Radio Network. Even novelist Philip Roth requested a press pass. The author of *Portnoy's Complaint* was said to be interested in scripting a play about the game, but it was never proven that Roth ever showed. PawSox manager Joe Morgan summed up the magnitude of the event when he said: "The World Series comes to Pawtucket for a day."

A crowd of 5,756—4,000 more than were on hand for the first inning back in April—stuffed McCoy Stadium that day. "There was a buzz of excitement in the air," Huppert recalled. "I was thankful [Wings manager] Doc [Edwards] had pinch-hit for me back in April, but when the game resumed in June, I was disappointed that he had because I wanted to still be a part of it."

It didn't take long for the Wings and PawSox to finish what they had started. Cal Ripken singled in the top of the thirty-third, but his Rochester teammates left him stranded. Edwards decided to pitch Grilli,

Red Sox 3, Red Wings 2

Rochester	ab	r	h	bi	Pawtucket	ab	r	h	bi
Eaton 2b	10	0	3	0	Graham cf	14	0	1	0
Williams cf	13	0	0	0	Barrett 2b	12	1	2	0
Ripken 3b	13	0	2	0	Walker lf	14	1	2	0
Corey dh	5	1	1	0	Laribee dh	11	0	0	1
Chism ph	1	0	0	0	Koza 1b	14	1	5	1
Rayford c	5	0	0	0	Boggs 3b	12	0	4	1
Logan 1b	12	0	4	0	Bowen rf	12	0	2	0
Valle 1b	1	0	0	0	Gedman c	3	0	1	0
Bourjos lf	4	0	2	1	Ongarafo	1	0	0	0
Hale ph	7	0	1	0	LaFrancois	8	0	2	0
Smith lf	0	0	0	0	Valdez ss	13	0	2	0
Hazewood rf	4	0	0	0					
Hart ph	6	0	1	0					
Bonner ss	12	1	3	0					
Huppert c	11	0	1	1					
Putman ph	1	0	0	0					
Grilli p	0	0	0	0					
Speck p	0	0	0	0					
Total	105	2	18	2	Total	114	3	21	3

Rochester   000 000 100 000 000 000 001 000 000 000 000—2
Pawtucket 000 000 001 000 000 000 001 000 000 000 001—3

No outs when winning run scored.

E—Eaton, Logan, Bonner, Valdez. DP—Rochester 4, Pawtucket 3. LOB—Rochester 30, Pawtucket 23. 2B—Koza 2, Walker, Boggs, Huppert. SB—Eaton. S—Williams 2, Logan, Hart, Huppert 2. SF—Laribee.

	IP	H	R	ER	BB	SO
Rochester						
Jones	8 2-3	7	1	1	2	5
Schneider	5 1-3	2	0	0	0	8
Luebber	8	6	1	1	2	4
Umbarger	10	4	0	0	0	9
Grilli L, 0-3	0	1	1	1	1	0
Speck	0	1	0	0	0	0
Pawtucket						
Parks	6	3	1	1	4	3
Aponte	4	0	0	0	2	9
Sarmiento	4	3	0	0	2	3

Smithson	3 2-3	2	0	0	3	5
Remmerswaal	4 1-3	4	1	1	3	3
Finch	5	3	0	0	1	3
Hurst	5	2	0	0	3	7
Ojeda W, 9-5	1	1	0	0	0	1

Parks pitched to 3 batters in the 7th.
Grilli pitched to 3 batters in the 33rd.
Speck pitched to 1 batter in the 33rd.
HBP—By Schneider (Laribee). By Parks (Eaton). By Aponte (Bonner), by Grilli (Barrett).
WP—Jones, Hurst, Smithson. T—8:25. A—1,740

who had opened the season in the big leagues with the Blue Jays. The veteran hurler was nervous from the start. He hit Marty Barrett with his first pitch, then surrendered a three-ball, two-strike single to Chico Walker that sent Barrett to third. Edwards instructed Grilli to walk Russ Laribee intentionally to load the bases. Cliff Speck was brought in to snuff out the rally, but he failed. Pawtucket's Dave Koza slapped a Speck curveball into short left field, scoring Barrett with the decisive run. As winning pitcher Bobby Ojeda hugged Barrett at home plate, the strains of Peggy Lee singing "*Is That All There Is?*" could barely be heard above the cheering crowd. While the celebration continued on the field and in the stands, Grilli sat alone in the visitor's dugout and cried. "I just feel like I've let these guys down," Grilli told John Kolomic of the *Democrat and Chronicle*. "They were here for the whole 30-something innings, then I come in and in one inning I blow it all down the drain. I just wanted to make do for the efforts they put in for 32 innings and I blew it." Speck, who threw the ill-fated curveball, was equally despondent while answering reporters' questions in the clubhouse. "I guess I'll be like the fellow who gave up that homer to Bobby Thomson," he said. "What's his name?" "Ralph Branca," someone answered, referring to the old Brooklyn Dodgers pitcher whose gopher ball in a 1951 playoff game enabled the New York Giants to win the pennant.

Huppert was disappointed, too. So much work, and nothing to show for it, except a loss and a pair of sore knees. But with the passage of time, Huppert came to appreciate that historic game. In his mind, no one was a loser in baseball's greatest endurance test. "Hey," he said. "Everyone associated with that game is in Cooperstown. That's the desired destination of everyone who ever plays this game."

The Long and the Short of It

The Rochester Red Wings–Pawtucket Red Sox thirty-three-inning baseball marathon during the 1981 season exceeded by four innings the previous record established fifteen summers earlier by Miami and St. Petersburg of the Florida State League.

The time of the Wings-PawSox game was officially listed at 8 hours, 25 minutes, though, in reality, it took 65 days to complete the contest.

The game was the equivalent of a basketball or football game that went ten overtimes.

The teams went through roughly 160 baseballs, costing the host PawSox nearly $600.

The fourteen pitchers combined to throw more than a thousand pitches. They struck out sixty batters and teamed up for twenty-nine scoreless innings.

The batters combined for just 39 hits in 219 at-bats, a .178 average.

Pawtucket's Bobby Ojeda was credited with the win, and Steve Grilli was saddled with the loss. The best pitching performance, though, was turned in by Red Wings long reliever Jim Umbarger, who struck out nine and yielded just four hits and two walks in ten scoreless innings.

Wings center fielder Dallas Williams had a looooong game, going hitless in thirteen at-bats.

In all, forty-one players participated, including Baseball Hall of Fame hopefuls Cal Ripken, Jr., and Wade Boggs. Ripken, who would go on to win two MVP awards and set baseball endurance records as the Baltimore Orioles shortstop, played third base for the Wings, and had two hits in thirteen at-bats. Boggs, who would win five American League batting titles with the Boston Red Sox, played third for Pawtucket, and went 4-for-12 with a run batted in.

14

The Good, the Bad, and the Ugly

*Because it's Morrie Silver Stadium, I can't say that
doesn't make me feel good. My husband worked so hard
for it. But I still say the main thing was, I felt the stadium should be there for the people. Some day they're
going to change it. Life goes on. But they're not going
to build [a new stadium] as long as I'm alive.*
                                        —*Anna Silver,* 1982

For twenty-five years, many of the
stock certificates that had been
purchased to save the Red Wings in 1956 languished in sock drawers,
file cabinets, and attics. Shareholders passed away, or passed on their
stock, and keeping track of the many stockholders became increasingly
difficult. In 1977, a Syracuse consulting firm determined that Silver Stadium, then forty-eight years old, needed structural work. Some politicians wanted to spend the minimal $2.5 million for the safety repairs.
Others wanted to completely renovate the ballpark with new lighting,
seats, roof, scoreboard, and parking facilities for $8 million and turn
Silver into a multipurpose facility.

The aging stadium would become the catalyst for a bitter proxy
fight. "We took a survey of shareholders last May," Rochester Community Baseball treasurer Larry Edwards said in January 1982. "We had
534 people respond and 92 percent wanted to renovate Silver Stadium.
And 68 percent said they wanted to go beyond the minimum safety
requirements and make the stadium attractive and available for other
events."

191

Anna "Bert" Silver was not among them. The wife of Morrie Silver had joined the board of directors following her husband's death in 1974 but soon found herself at odds with her colleagues on several issues. Foremost among them was the future of Silver Stadium.

"We'll keep our options open," she said in response to Edwards's comments, "but right now we see no need for anything but baseball [at Silver]."

During an RCB board meeting one night in 1981, president Bill Farrell brought up the possibility of building a new stadium in the Rochester suburb of Henrietta. The suggestion did not sit well with Mrs. Silver, who saw no need to leave the facility on Norton Street. A divisiveness began within the club's leaders, one that would grow deeper.

Longtime Wings radio broadcaster Pete Brown had undergone bypass surgery during the winter of 1979–80, then returned for the 1980 season. His duties were curtailed, yet he continued to be paid in full, a situation that concerned the board. At Farrell's command, Drew gave Brown three options: resume his previous duties, take a cut in pay, or expand his duties to assistant GM. Instead, he resigned under pressure in February 1981.

"What more could they want from him?" Anna Silver asked at the time. "He had sold all the ads [actually 80 percent] for the upcoming season. They offered him a choice as assistant GM? They didn't need an assistant GM; they had a good GM already. Pete wasn't qualified to be GM, anyway. Then they suggested a cut in pay for radio work only? He was only making $13,000 to begin with. How much of a cut can you take?"

Larry Edwards said Drew's problems with Farrell intensified after Brown left. "Bob suddenly began not communicating with Bill," Edwards said at the time. "One day Farrell came to me and said, 'I can't handle this guy anymore.' Then before we could even straighten it out, Drew announced he was resigning. He cited personal reasons. He told us of his problems and, believe me, they were real."

Bob Drew had been the Red Wings' general manager since the spring of 1979. Drew was a popular and hard-working GM who resented Farrell's increasingly active role in the day-to-day operation of the club. Frustrated, Drew resigned "for personal reasons" on March 4, 1981, effective October 31. The board accepted his resignation by a twenty-five-to-one vote. When Drew had a change of heart and wanted to rescind his resignation—on condition that he wouldn't have to report to Farrell—the board fired him. Many loyal fans threatened to boycott the

Overflow crowds like this one in late August 1980 would be few and far between at Silver Stadium in the tumultuous '80s. Courtesy of the *Democrat and Chronicle/Times-Union*.

1981 season and several sponsors threatened to withdraw, but the Wings continued on, with Bill Terlecky and Bob Goughan taking over as co–general managers.

Frustrated by Mrs. Silver's resistance to renovating the aging ballpark, the board of directors offered to buy her shares, but she refused to sell. On October 14, 1981, the executive committee of Rochester Community Baseball recommended to its board that Silver Stadium be renovated for "multi-purpose as well as other public events." Conspicuously missing from the meeting was Anna Silver, and committee members soon learned why. Midway through the meeting at Locust Hill Country Club, her resignation was delivered by courier. In the letter, she wrote, "Mr. Farrell can save his time and energy. Neither my shares nor Naomi's [her daughter] are for sale."

The next day, Silver threw her 6,220 shares of stock—17 percent of the total—behind a group of thirty-five dissident shareholders whose goal was to keep Silver Stadium a baseball-only facility. The group, which called itself the Shareholders Committee, declared a proxy battle seeking control of the club from the existing board.

The growing feud did not sit well with New York State senator Fred Eckert, who had sponsored a bill in July appropriating $150,000 in state aid toward a feasibility study for renovating Silver Stadium. The study might result in $2 million in state aid toward the fifty-two-year-old ballpark—money the Shareholders Committee said it would not accept —and Eckert warned that the proxy battle might jeopardize such aid. "I, along with thousands of other baseball fans, am growing more than a bit tired of this hassle," Eckert said. "This fan is telling the Red Wings they better get their house in order. If aiding the Red Wings means aiding baseball, we [the state legislature] will proceed with an appropriations bill for renovation of the ballpark. But if aid means aiding silly games, and not baseball games, there may be no bill."

Farrell was at the center of the storm. His impressive résumé included organizing the highly successful regional high school boys basketball tournament and bringing the Ladies Professional Golf Association to Rochester for an annual tour stop. Farrell had taken over as president of Rochester Community Baseball in 1978.

The Shareholders Committee had a three-man executive committee that included Raymond Sorg, a delicatessen owner and president of the Monroe County Food Merchants Association; Charles Stauber, former mayor of Fairport and owner of an advertising and public relations agency; and Richard Huggler, a science teacher in Spencerport for thirty-two years. The Shareholders Committee wanted Farrell out as president, feeling that Drew's firing had been calculated.

"The timing of that was terrible," Mrs. Silver said. "He had retired, the board had accepted his resignation as of October 31. They should have let it stay that way. Instead they felt they had to get rid of him now. I felt it was done so nobody would be general manager and Farrell could step into the job.

"He doesn't have time to devote to the Red Wings if he stays with Locust Hill on the LPGA. In minor-league baseball, we should have younger people who can work from 9 in the morning until late at night. He can't do this."

Farrell dug in for a long fight. "They're not going to win this proxy fight, no way," he said. "The shareholders and the entire community will wake up to this thing. We'll produce evidence showing our board acted in nothing but the best interests of baseball and this community. We're fighting for a principle."

> Considering his track record—including the financial success of Rochester Community Baseball, Inc., during his three years in control—there is no reason for

anyone to expect Red Wings president Bill Farrell to retreat with his tail tucked between his legs. The members of the newly formed dissident Shareholders Committee, all devoted Red Wings fans eager to see baseball thrive in our community, are completely within their rights to attempt to overthrow Farrell and the current board of directors via a proxy fight.

Unfortunately, the war is going to have some casualties.

—Bob Matthews, *Times-Union,* Oct. 16, 1981

Two weeks after vowing to fight the Shareholders Committee to the bitter end, Farrell offered to resign if Silver would sell her 6,220 shares. "As things stand now, she has total control," he explained. "It's no longer community baseball. If it would help restore baseball to the community, I think the entire board might resign to resolve this proxy fight." Farrell said the board would pay Silver the original fee, $10 per share, for a total of $62,200. Silver ignored the offer, saying "My stock is not for sale. I love this ball club."

Meanwhile, the Shareholders Committee continued to work the phones trying to drum up support. "They phone the stockholders and ask, 'Will you support Mrs. Silver?' " Farrell said angrily. "They don't even explain the issues and what is at stake."

Farrell denied ever throwing his support behind building a new stadium in Henrietta. "In fact, I've personally felt all along that renovation of Silver is the only reasonable solution to our stadium crisis," he said. "Sorg and his people know this, but they don't care. They just want to take over."

By the end of October, the Shareholders Committee claimed to have obtained more than 15,000 proxy votes from the 21,076 shares accounted for. The other 21,000 shares were considered untraceable.

"All they need is a simple majority to win," said Don Adair, executive director of the incumbent board of directors. "So if they have as many as they claim then we're in trouble."

The existing board believed that stockholders who had signed proxies supporting the Shareholders Committee would be able to change their vote at the annual stockholders meeting. Seeking to buy time to send out their own proxies, they succeeded through a court order in getting the meeting pushed back to February 27.

"We need time to get our message out," treasurer Edwards said. "Our purpose is to fully inform the shareholders so they can make an intelligent decision."

There would be one bombshell dropped before that meeting, and it occurred on January 7, 1982. At a festive news conference at the down-town Genesee Plaza Holiday Inn, at which the Farrell-friendly board announced record profits of $117,836, Farrell stunned everyone by re-signing as RCB president. He had greeted reporters at the news confer-ence, then departed for a friend's house. Moments later, a four-page prepared statement was distributed to reporters announcing Farrell's res-ignation after nearly three years as president.

"We had a shot at success," the statement said. "Things were look-ing good and I thought I could help. Unfortunately, that success has been clouded by events which began last February—the whole proxy fight started by the so-called Shareholders Committee. I'm afraid it just hasn't been any fun since then."

Suddenly, the Red Wings had no field manager, no general manager, no radio contract, and no president. "After a while," Bob Goughan said sadly, "it becomes just another day in the life of Rochester Community Baseball."

There was speculation that the timing of the resignation might have been a calculated effort to persuade shareholders to side with the current board. At the same time that the controversial Farrell had been removed, record profits had also been announced. Why change boards now?

Ray Sorg of the Shareholders Committee would have none of it. "This was a last-ditch effort on their part to get sympathy on their side," Sorg said. "But we have the votes, and it won't make any difference. Bill Farrell's resignation means nothing to us."

One week later, the incumbent board named V. M. "Wallie" Lord to replace Farrell as president. Lord, a board member since 1979, hoped to reach a compromise with the Shareholders Committee, but nothing had been accomplished by the time stockholders convened on February 27. The meeting lasted three hours and was attended by three hundred people at the Downtown Chamber of Commerce. The tone was calm, and Arthur Andersen and Co., a certified public accounting firm that had been appointed as election inspectors by the current board, promised to provide final results within the week.

The Shareholders Committee placed its strength at about 22,000 votes, with current management estimating about 16,000 in support. But several thousand stockholders had returned proxies to both sides, and it remained unclear which side would be awarded the votes. The tallies were announced five days after the vote: The incumbents had won by 194 votes—16,604 to 16,410—a margin so close that both sides admitted the results could change. Eastman Kodak cast its 1,500 votes in favor of the incumbents, but the linchpin to success was 3,337 votes that originally had been cast in favor of Silver's group. These shareholders had initially decided to give the current board the boot, signing proxies supporting the Shareholders Committee. But when the incumbents sent out their own proxies, the same stockholders gave them votes of confidence—a 6,674-vote swing.

Arthur Andersen and Co. chose to put the 3,337 crossover votes on the side of current management, but Shareholders lawyer Adam Bernstein vowed to fight the decision in court, saying "No one should celebrate yet."

On June 2, 1982, State Supreme Court Justice Richard Rosenbloom ruled that the controversial "irrevocable proxies" belonged to the Shareholders Committee, not current management. The decision shifted the vote tally to 19,747 for the challengers and 13,267 for the incumbents. "At this point you want to say you're going to fight on," Wallie Lord said, "but I don't know if there is a way to do it."

In the end, the incumbent board decided there wasn't. One month after Rosenbloom's ruling, the board announced it was dropping its appeal. The Shareholders Committee took control immediately, with Silver becoming the board's chairwoman and Charles Stauber its new president. At this point, the Bob Drew saga had become a moot point—"he's not available now," Silver said—and the issues dividing the two groups focused on renovation of the stadium and the not-for-profit status of the corporation. The Shareholders Committee opposed not-for-profit status and wanted limited renovations to the ballpark.

In the end, the proxy fight lasted nine months, cost $300,000 in legal fees and shattered friendships forever. On December 18, 1982, the thirty-four members of the new board were overwhelmingly re-elected at the annual shareholders meeting.

The war was over, but for many the wounds would never heal.

The operative word surrounding the 1982 Red Wings was "new." They had new uniforms (pinstripes for the first time), a new manager (Lance Nichols), and a new radio announcer (Jay Colley). By midsummer, they would have a new board of directors.

Nichols was a manager by necessity, not choice. A resident of Dodge City, Kansas, he had come to the Orioles organization in 1978 to manage Double-A Charlotte. He then spent two seasons at Miami and one at Bluefield before landing in Rochester. In 1979, Nichols had spent considerable time working with an eighteen-year-old rookie on his batting stroke. The rookie was Cal Ripken, Jr., and he credited Nichols as a major influence long after becoming a star with the Baltimore Orioles. Nichols considered himself an organization man who hoped to move into an administrative position. Orioles farm director Tom Giordano had penciled Nichols in as the club's scouting head the previous two seasons but called on Nichols when he needed replacement managers—at Bluefield in 1981 and Rochester in 1982.

A quiet man with a no-nonsense approach, Nichols had beaten lymph cancer in the late '70s. He was ready to take on any challenge, but could not have been prepared for what the Tidewater Tides had to offer on April 13. A crowd of 7,147 fans braved rain, temperatures in the low forties, and winds gusting at twenty-five miles per hour for the Wings' fifty-fourth home opener at Silver Stadium. By the third inning, half of them would be on their way home.

The final score was 23–1. It was Rochester's worst loss in franchise history. It was 4–0 after one, 6–0 after two, and 16–0 after three, at which point the majority of fans remaining began chanting "Rain, rain, rain." "When it's 16–0 and you've just given up 10 runs, you have only one hope left," Red Wings fan Lynn Barber told the *Democrat and Chronicle*.

The Tides outhit the Wings 20–2. Starter Mike Boddicker and his replacement, Don Welchel, left with earned-run averages of 94.50 and 40.50, respectively. The Wings, who committed four errors, scored their lone run in the fourth, when Mike Hart doubled and Tides starter Rick Ownbey walked the next three batters.

How bad was it? Tidewater's Gil Flores had four at-bats by the time Rochester's Victor Rodriguez hit for the first time.

"A disaster," Nichols said of his Red Wings debut.

"A nightmare," Welchel said.

"Numbing," shivering third baseman Rick Lisi said. "And that goes two ways, too."

Despite the embarassing debut, the '82 team made a comeback, finishing fourth at 72–68, then knocking off pennant-winning Richmond in the playoffs before losing to the Tides in the finals.

Nichols received much of the credit. The '82 Wings were hardly an offensive power. Third baseman Leo Hernandez was the lone player to hit above .300, and he recorded only 202 at-bats to finish at .317. Don Welchel (12–7), Mike Boddicker (10–5), and John Flinn (9–3) were the pitching aces.

Despite his gentlemen's one-year agreement with Giordano, Nichols agreed to return to Rochester in 1983. This time, the Wings beat Charleston 3–2 on opening day, then slipped to a sixth-place finish at 65–75. One week after the season ended, Nichols took a job as Gior-

dano's right-hand man by becoming the Orioles' director of field operations.

His replacement was former Red Wing Frank Verdi, a fiery fifty-
seven-year-old who grew up one mile away from Ebbets Field in Brooklyn. Verdi had spent seventeen years as a player and nineteen as a
manager. With Binghamton in 1949, he was credited with pulling the
hidden ball trick seven times.

Every minute of Verdi's professional career—both as player and
manager—had been spent in the minors except for one appearance at
shortstop for the 1953 New York Yankees. It was truly a bittersweet
experience. Johnny Mize pinch-hit for Phil Rizzuto in the top of the
eighth at Fenway Park, with the Red Sox leading 3–1. Mize made the
third out, and Yankees manager Casey Stengel inserted Verdi at short.
"Vic Raschi retired the Red Sox 1-2-3 in the bottom of the eighth," Verdi
recalled. "I didn't get to touch the ball except to whip it around the
infield after the first two outs." Verdi was the ninth batter due up in the
final inning, but amazingly the Yankees batted around by scoring four
runs to take the lead.

"Raschi walked to load the bases and I was due up," Verdi said. "I
got into the batter's box and the Boston manager [Lou Boudreau] decided
to change pitchers. I was anxious as hell. I knew everybody in Brooklyn
had their radios turned on and I wasn't going to let them down."

Verdi never got the chance. As he took his stance to face the new
pitcher, Stengel suddenly called time and sent Bill Renna up to pinch-hit.
"That sure took the wind out of my sails," Verdi said. "The next thing I
knew I was playing in Syracuse." Four years later, he began a three-year
stint with the Wings.

It had been twenty-five years since Verdi nearly lost his life when
shots rang out during a 1959 Red Wings game in Havana, Cuba. In that
time, he had become one of the more traveled minor-league managers,
landing jobs in ten cities over a nineteen-year period and compiling a
1,265–1,202 (.513) record. Verdi had managed in four International
League cities—Syracuse, Toledo, Tidewater, and Columbus—and captured a Junior World Series title with Syracuse in 1970 and a Governors'
Cup crown with Columbus in 1981. Verdi spent the 1983 season managing the San José Bees of the Class A California League, a co-op team
stocked by several teams, including the Orioles.

Now the self-described "strict disciplinarian" was back with the
Red Wings. Power was seen as the club's primary strength, and it was on
display in the season opener as the Wings beat the Maine Guides (the
transplanted Charleston Charlies) 6–4 on homers from left fielder Mike
Young and designated hitter Mike Calise. Bill Swaggerty picked up the

win, breaking Mike Boddicker's three-year reign as opening day starter. After the game, the exuberant Red Wings got a little carried away.

"You can't judge anything by the first game," Calise said, "but I think we've got a winner here."

"I'm happy we gave this type of game to the fans here," Young added. "I know they appreciate good baseball and we're going to try and give it to them this year."

What they gave them was the worst season since the club began playing at 500 Norton Street. By week's end, the Wings were 1–4 and had committed sixteen errors. They took a 3–2 lead into the eighth against Pawtucket but gave up six runs on two errors, two wild pitches, three walks, and a botched double play. "An abortion," Verdi said of the loss.

The Red Wings were just getting warmed up. On June 22, they lost their eleventh straight game, falling to 22–44 and moving one game shy of the sixty-four-year club record for consecutive losses. They beat Tidewater 4–0 behind Tony Arnold's pitching the next night.

The '84 Wings didn't confine their losses to just International League teams. The Orioles beat them 7–6 in the annual exhibition. The U.S. Olympic team, tuning up for its appearance at Seoul, South Korea, whipped the Wings 8–1 before 3,516 fans at Silver Stadium on June 25. The Olympians included future major-league stars Tony Gwynn, Will Clark, and Mark McGwire, who hit a two-run homer.

Finally, the International League all-stars visited on July 21 and beat the hometown zeroes 4–1. The Wings had hosted two previous all-star games, drawing 11,218 for a game against Baltimore in 1962 and 11,001 when the New York Yankees visited in 1971. This time, only 2,378 bothered to show up—the lowest attendance figure in the league's all-star game history. Of course, having a home team that was 34–63 and twenty-six games out of first didn't help. To make matters worse, Wings pitcher Joe Kucharski left with a strained shoulder after delivering just one pitch. "If anything's wrong with Joe, we've got headaches," Verdi said afterward. "But we've got headaches anyway."

Three days after the all-star game, the Wings announced that Verdi would be back in 1985. The '84 nightmare limped to its conclusion with the Wings finishing last at 52–88, their worst record since moving into Silver Stadium in 1929. Only 197,501 fans—many wearing paper bags to disguise themselves—bothered to show up. It was Rochester's lowest attendance since 1956. The biggest crowd was only 5,884 for the Orioles exhibiton May 17.

The '84 team was an equal opportunity flop. Outfielder Larry

Fans of Frank Verdi's last-place club couldn't bear to be seen in 1984.
Courtesy of the *Democrat and Chronicle/Times-Union*.

Sheets was the only starter to hit above .300 (.302) and third baseman
Leo Hernandez led with 21 homers and 83 RBI, but the rest of the
offense floundered. Joe Kucharski led the club with seven wins—and
thirteen losses. The team stole only 19 bases, hit 106 home runs, and
committed 155 errors, and the staff ERA was 4.72. There was a six-game
losing streak in May, the eleven-game tailspin in June, and an eight-game
drought in July. The Wings saved August for their big defeats, losing 21–
3 and 12–4 to Pawtucket on consecutive days. "It was," Verdi said on
the eve of the 1985 opener, "the worst exhibition of baseball playing I've
ever seen at Triple-A. Rochester's too good a town to have to put up
with that garbage. Teams didn't beat us, we beat ourselves. That won't
happen this year. I'm not promising anything except that we'll be a ball
club."

Verdi's 1985 squad was far more experienced than the '84 team,
with seven players age thirty or older. And only ten of the forty-four
players from 1984 were back. Verdi promised a club that was "150
percent better" than the previous year, but reality set in quickly. When
Rochester dropped nine straight in June and fell to 18–40, Verdi was

fired. The Red Wings offered the job to Joe Altobelli, who had been fired
as manager of the Baltimore Orioles the day before, but Altobelli declined. Pitching coach Mark Wiley was named interim manager for the
rest of the season. Verdi finished 70–128 as Red Wings manager. "I think
everyone is pretty depressed with the fact that we got Frank fired,"
pitcher Bill Swaggerty said. "That's what we did. We couldn't make him
a winner. You can't fire all of us, so you fire him."

Wiley had pitched for the Wings in 1980 and spent the next two
seasons managing at Double-A Charlotte. He had been the Wings'
pitching coach since 1983. Wiley was close to Verdi and had mixed
emotions about taking over. "This is far from a happy occasion for me,"
Wiley said. "I talked to him and he wished me all the luck in the world."

The Wings showed life under Wiley, going 40–41 the rest of the
way to finish seventh at 58–81. The Orioles had plans for Wiley, and they
didn't involve just Rochester. They wanted him to be their minor-league
pitching coach.

The new man at the Red Wings helm was John Hart. Hart's journey
to Triple-A was unusual, to say the least. A minor-league catcher for
three years in the Montreal Expos system—he never hit above .231 or
played above Double-A—the Tampa-born Hart left baseball to open a
string of Nautilus training centers in Florida. A graduate of the University of Central Florida, Hart took over the Boone High School baseball
team in Orlando and led the club to the 1981 state championship. He
was lured back into professional baseball after a nine-year absence by
Orioles farm director Tom Giordano, who made Hart his surprise manager at Baltimore's rookie club in Bluefield, Virginia, in 1982. Hart's
aggressive style and ability to define players' roles made him a hit with
the team, and Bluefield won the Appalachian League title with a 47–22
record.

Hart began working his way up the organizational ladder, winning
wherever he went: 84–52 at Class A Hagerstown in 1983; a combined
78–67 with Hagerstown and Double-A Charlotte in 1984; and a 78–65
mark with Charlotte in 1985. Hart took over a Wings roster with only
one proven .300 hitter (third baseman Tom O'Malley) and fans braced
for another long season when Rochester got off to a 3–10 start. But over
the next two month, the Wings caught fire, going an IL-best 43–28.
Paced by Ken Gerhart's twenty-eight homers, they finished second at 75–
63, eliminated Pawtucket in the playoffs, and took first-place Richmond
to a decisive fifth game in the Governors' Cup finals before losing.

Hart had given the Wings their first winning season in four years
and was an easy choice as International League Manager of the Year. His
stock, already rising in Baltimore, now went through the roof. Earl

Before he became the architect of some terrific
Cleveland Indians clubs in the mid-1990s,
John Hart managed the Wings for two seasons
in the 1980s. Reed Hoffmann photo courtesy
of the *Democrat and Chronicle/Times-Union.*

Weaver's return from retirement had been a mistake, and he was leaving
as Orioles manager for good following the '86 season. Orioles owner
Edward Bennett Williams appeared on Larry King's late-night radio
show and mentioned Hart and Baltimore third-base coach Cal Ripken,
Sr., as the top candidates. "Our best prospect isn't a player," Giordano
told a reporter. "He's the manager at Rochester." Hart tried to keep

An Arresting Night at Silver

He didn't hit a game-winning homer, bounce into a triple play, or hit a ball off the warehouse in center, but Maine Guides infielder Cory Snyder had one of the most memorable at-bats of the 1980s at Silver Stadium. It would not lead to a win or loss for his club, however. Snyder's plate appearance would result in a court appearance.

The date was May 29, 1986, and the trouble began in the fourth inning. Angry with himself after flying out to center, Snyder flung his bat in disgust toward the Guides' dugout as he ran to first base. The bat flew into the stands, hit a guard rail, and struck two women. After Snyder hit Bill Swaggerty's pitch, "he went like, 'Darn it all,' with the bat," said Blaise DiNardo, director of game security at Silver.

The twenty-three-year-old Snyder said the bat simply slipped out of his hands. "I just tried to kind of throw the bat on the ground and it got stuck on my [batting] glove," he said. "I use a lot of pine tar and it just stuck. I almost got [teammate Jim] Wilson, who was on deck. I saw it go up and yelled 'Look out, Jim.' I don't know what happened after that because I had to run [the fly ball out]."

Dorothy Matteson and her granddaughter, Deborah Shirtz were sitting in the front row behind the on-deck circle on the third-base side. The 34½-inch, 32-ounce bat glanced off a three-foot high metal fence, and the barrel of the bat hit both women in the mouth. Matteson suffered a broken denture plate and damage to the soft tissue in her mouth. She needed nineteen stitches to close the cuts. Shirtz suffered a broken nose.

Many of the 2,005 fans booed Snyder when he took his position at shortstop in the bottom of the fourth. Things got worse when Wings leadoff hitter Ken Smith walked and tried to steal second. The throw was off-target and Snyder, covering the bag, deflected the ball off his glove into Smith's face. Smith staggered off the base in a daze and was tagged out by Snyder as players from both teams raced onto the field. Order was restored—temporarily.

Before going to St. Mary's Hospital, the two injured women were rushed to the stadium's medical room. There they filled out a complaint against Snyder, charging him with two counts of third-degree assault, Class A misdemeanors punishable by up to one year in jail and/or a $1,000 fine, or three years probation. The game was delayed in the fifth inning as DiNardo entered the Guides dugout to notify Snyder he was being charged.

When Snyder came to bat in the sixth, he was drilled in the back by

Swaggerty's first pitch. Both benches emptied again, and Guides pitching coach Steve Comer tackled Swaggerty. Snyder remained at home plate but was ejected by umpire Rich Humphrey—ostensibly for his own safety—along with Swaggerty, who doffed his cap to the cheering crowd as he walked into the dugout. "Nobody told me to hit him," Swaggerty said afterward, "but you can't let stuff like that go by. Our fans are hard to come by. We want them to come back. We like them to know they can come and watch a good game without risking life and limb."

Snyder was escorted to the clubhouse by teammates, but his troubles were just beginning. The next morning, with the entire Guides team present as a show of support, he pleaded innocent to two counts of third-degree assault at an arraignment before City Judge John R. Schwartz. Now identified as James C. Snyder, Case No. 066892, of 816 Aileen St., Camarillo, California, he was released without bail, and a pretrial conference was set for June 12. Snyder thus became the first professional baseball player to be criminally charged for throwing a bat into the stands. "I can't believe there was any attempt to hurt anybody," said James Morris, attorney for the two injured women, "but at the very least, there was carelessness and recklessness." Snyder played that night at Silver Stadium, going 1-for-4 and enduring boos in each at-bat. "It was tough," he admitted, "but I wanted to play."

Snyder was called up to the parent Cleveland Indians in June, and criminal charges against him were dismissed on December 1. Snyder was again present before Judge Schwartz, and this time so were Matteson and Shirtz. In his ten-page decision to dismiss charges, Schwartz noted that, in 1958, Hall of Famer Ted Williams had struck a sixty-year-old woman after striking out and no charges had been filed. "An accident occurring every 28 years is indeed rare," Schwartz said.

Matteson and Shirtz filed a $2.3 million civil suit against Snyder, the Indians, and the Guides but the parties settled out of court in March 1988 —nearly two years after the incident—for $50,000. The Guides, who had since become affiliated with the Philadelphia Phillies, requested that they be excluded from liability because Snyder was employed by the Indians, but state Supreme Court Justice Richard C. Wesley ruled that both teams "exercised control over Snyder in areas relating to his playing ability."

Recalling the incident ten years later, DiNardo said the courtroom saga could have been avoided by Snyder. "If he had shown any remorse right after it happened, if he had just come over and apologized, those two women probably would have dropped the whole thing. But he didn't, and it just became one big mess."

Cory Snyder. Courtesy of the *Democrat and Chronicle/Times-Union*.

things in perspective, saying "It's great to be considered. If things continue on, someday I'll get a chance."

In the end, Ripken got the job and Hart returned for a second
season with the Wings, this time finishing third at 74–65. Two months
later he finally earned his big-league shot when the Orioles named him
third-base coach for 1988. Red Wings president Fred Strauss took the
loss of his talented manager in stride, saying "He's just too damn good
to keep."

The '88 season would be the longest of Hart's career. The Orioles
were 0–6 when Frank Robinson replaced Ripken on April 12. They
went on to lose their next fifteen games and never recovered, finishing a
franchise-worst 54–107. Hart was part of a coaching-staff purge that
took place one day after the season ended, but he didn't stay unemployed
for long. Hank Peters and Tom Giordano had been fired by Edward
Bennett Williams following the 1987 season. Now Peters was president
of the Cleveland Indians and Giordano was vice president of baseball
operations. Hart was hired by Cleveland as a special assignment scout
for 1989 but spent the final nineteen games of the season as interim
manager, replacing the fired Doc Edwards, and led the Indians to an 8–
11 record.

By now, Hart's focus was on higher management. He spent the next
two seasons as Cleveland's director of baseball operations, then reached
the pinnacle of his career on September 18, 1991, when he was named
the Indians' general manager. Cleveland had not reached the postseason
since 1954, but Hart began a youth movement that gradually transformed the club from cellar-dwellers into an American League powerhouse. Cleveland was 66–47 and appeared headed for the playoffs in
1994 when major-league players went on strike on August 11, eventually
forcing postponement of the World Series. Still, Hart earned one of the
highest honors in baseball when he was named Major League Baseball
Executive of the Year. He was only the second Indians executive to win
the award, the first being Bill Veeck in 1948. In 1995, the Indians soared
to baseball's best record and easily won the American League pennant.

Hart's return as Red Wings manager wasn't the only big news of
1987. Ten years after a Syracuse firm determined that Silver Stadium
needed structural repairs, the fifty-eight-year-old facility underwent a
$4.5 million renovation. Opening day on April 16 was hailed as the
beginning of a new era at Silver, complete with a motorcade that took
the Red Wings, organization officials, and city and county officials from
City Hall to the ballpark.

Silver Stadium has gone from worst to first. From
the pits to the Ritz. All it took was one busy winter at
500 Norton St. and $4.5 million worth of material and
labor.
     Rochester's "new" old baseball stadium is a won-
der to behold.
           —Bob Matthews, Times-Union, Apr. 14, 1987

New aluminum seats replaced the original wooden ones. The seats were wider and brightly colored: red for lower boxes, blue for upper boxes, green for reserved, and gold for general admission. The rotting steel beams and supports had been replaced, three new restrooms were added, and a new box office—complete with an advance ticket window —was added. New concession stands were built and expanded to accompany a wider variety of food. A wine and beer garden was built in the stadium concourse, to be open from one hour before games until midnight and featuring musical acts, magic shows, and comedians. The home clubhouse had been expanded to three times its original size, and the visitors clubhouse had been connected to the new and improved dugout.

"When I first saw the drawings, I knew we had a jewel on our hands," Wings GM Bob Goughan said. "Sometimes I'd walk late in the evening, after everyone else had left, and marvel that it finally was happening and that I was seeing it."

A curious crowd of 10,229—largest for a home opener since 1979 —watched the Wings beat Tidewater 2–1, but the novelty wore off quickly. The "new Silver" actually pulled in eight thousand fewer fans (315,807 in all) than in 1986. The seats were wider but not wide enough. Parking remained a problem on nights when attendance rose above seven thousand. Huge crowds continued to clog the concession stands. Hardly anyone used the wine and beer garden. And the expanded clubhouses meant nothing to the average fan.

Lawyers Co-op had secured the $4.5 million state loan and the Monroe County Legislature had voted to guarantee it. But as owners of Silver Stadium, the Red Wings were stuck with the payments: $33,000 a month, twelve months a year, for seventeen years. It worked out to $396,000 a year in rent for a facility that brought in revenue only six months per year. As attendance dropped over the next two years, the state debt began to be a burden on the Wings' finances. As a new decade dawned, some began to question the decision to renovate instead of replace.

15

Cups Runneth Over

Who's to say which was better? The 1988 team did what it took to win. The '90 team blew everyone away. But they were both great teams.
—Times-Union beat writer *Bill Koenig*

The introduction of interleague play between the American Association and the International League highlighted the 1988 season. In addition to home-and-home series with each opposing league member, the champions of the two leagues would meet in a best-of-seven Triple-A Classic in September.

There was a familiar face at the Rochester helm that season. Johnny Oates, the catcher on the Wings 1971 championship club, had been named to replace Hart. Oates had been a popular player in Rochester, because fans appreciated his daily commute from his army reserve base in Massachusetts for the seven-game Junior World Series. Oates spent the 1972 season with the Orioles, then was traded to Atlanta in the off-season. He also played with Philadelphia, Los Angeles, and the New York Yankees in a fifteen-year professional career that ended in 1981.

Oates managed for two years in the Yankees' minor-league system, leading Double-A Nashville to the '81 Southern League title and Triple-A Columbus to the '82 International League pennant. Oates then spent four seasons as a coach with the Chicago Cubs, but his heart was in managing. When the Orioles offered him the job in Rochester for 1988, he accepted.

On paper, the '88 Wings would be dismissed as a .500 club. Center fielder Steve Finley, who began the season at Class A Hagerstown and quickly moved up, won the IL batting title with a .314 average, outdistancing runner-up Hal Morris of Columbus by eighteen points. Third baseman Craig Worthington had mediocre numbers—a .244 average, 16 homers, and 73 RBI—but became the first Red Wing named league MVP since Rich Dauer in 1976. Rookie right-hander Bob Milacki was the pitching ace, going 12–8 with a 2.70 ERA and eleven complete games.

Oates made it work, with seemingly a different hero every night. On Memorial Day, first baseman Jim Traber belted a pair of three-run homers—including the game-winner in the bottom of the eighth—in a 12–9 win over Indianapolis. On July 10, right-hander Oswald Peraza, weakened by the flu, struck out fifteen Denver Zephyrs in seven-plus innings and pitched the Wings back into first place. On August 4, Pete Harnisch struck out seventeen batters—one shy of Roric Harrison's record set in 1971—in a 1–0 win over Toledo.

The bullpen was steady but unspectacular. Left-hander Mike Raczka led the club with ten saves but also had a 1–5 record and 5.94 ERA. Kevin Hickey, a member of the Chicago White Sox club that won the 1983 American League West, was the unsung hero. A loud prankster off the field, Hickey was all business on it in '88, posting a 2–0 record and 1.46 ERA in twenty-seven appearances. Starter Bob Milacki went seven weeks without a win, finally changing his uniform number to nine on August 5 in honor of his elusive ninth win. Milacki won that night and led the club with twelve victories.

The Red Wings and Tidewater Tides ended the season with 77–64 records and began a best-of-five series on September 2 to determine the Governors' Cup champion. Former Orioles prospect Blaine Beatty blanked the Wings 3–0 in the opener in Norfolk, but Harnisch evened the series with a 1–0 win, sending the clubs back to Rochester. Ron Salcedo's homer keyed a 4–2 Rochester win in game three, and the Wings wrapped it up on Labor Day with a 4–3 win. Shortstop Wade Rowdon knocked home the game-winning run in the eighth, then threw out pinch-runner Marcus Lawton at the plate on a one-out grounder. Curt Brown then came in and induced Craig Shipley to bounce out to Worthington, ending the Wings' longest Governors' Cup drought (fourteen years).

The inaugural Triple-A Classic was next, and the Wings appeared headed for more glory when they won the first two games of their best-of-seven series against American Association champion Indianapolis. But the Indians won game three at Silver Stadium, then swept the next three back home. Despite the loss, the Wings were welcomed back home by a parade down Main Street.

Like Hart, Oates was named International League Manager of the

Jubilant members of the 1988 Wings celebrated the club's first Governors'
Cup title in fourteen years, the longest drought in franchise history.
Courtesy of the *Democrat and Chronicle/Times-Union.*

Year in his rookie season in Rochester. And also like Hart, he was rewarded with a coaching job in Baltimore. Oates was the Orioles' first-
base coach in 1989–90, then managed the club from 1991 to 1994. He
took over as manager of the Texas Rangers in 1995. Oates became the
first person ever to play and manage in the Orioles farm system, and also
play, manage, and coach with the Orioles. His replacement in Rochester
was Greg Biagini, who had spent the previous three seasons managing at
Double-A Charlotte. Biagini was a well-traveled player during his ten-
year minor-league career, playing only 125 of his 1,017 games for United
States-based teams. He began his managerial career with Baltimore's
rookie club in Bluefield, West Virginia.

Biagini took over a young Rochester club in 1989, with most of the
stars from the Governors' Cup team gone. Curt Schilling won thirteen
games, but a light-hitting club doomed the Wings' playoff chances. Outfielder Butch Davis led the team with a .303 average and tied rookie
catcher Chris Hoiles for the home-run lead with ten. The Wings finished
72–73, missing the playoffs for the first time in four years.

Biagini would have better luck in 1990, guiding a blossoming club
overflowing with individual stories. The Red Wings wasted little time
showing the strong pitching and power hitting that would lead the club
to greatness. Two days after the season opener, Eric Bell pitched no-hit
ball for five innings and Mickey Weston tossed a one-hitter through five
as the Wings swept a pair from Scranton-Wilkes-Barre. Rookie third
baseman Leo Gomez, sent down by the Orioles on the final day of spring
training, drove in five runs, then slammed three home runs the next day
at Pawtucket. By May 17, Gomez led the league with 11 homers and 26
RBI and ranked seventh with a .336 batting average. Two days later, the
first-place Wings were in Indianapolis when Chris Hoiles, stepped in to
face Indians reliever Jim Davins in the eighth. Moments later, Hoiles's
season appeared over. A Davins fastball exploded between his left eye
and the bridge of his nose. Hoiles fell to the ground in a thud and
remained motionless, blood gushing from the wound. He remained un-
conscious and was taken from the Indianapolis field on a stretcher. X
rays at the hospital proved negative, but the area near his eye was swollen
and his vision was blurred.

"One inch over and down and who knows what might have happened," Hoiles said. "I could have lost my vision, or even worse. Some-
body up there definitely was looking out for me."

As the swelling subsided and his vision cleared, Hoiles became
eager to play again. And so eight days after the beaning, sixteen stitches
still stretched above his eye, he returned to action against Iowa. After
grounding out in his first at-bat, Hoiles homered in the ninth inning. The

next day, he went 4-for-4 with another homer, extending his hitting streak to fourteen games and raising his IL-leading average to .406. He even stole two bases as the Wings beat Pawtucket 7–3 at Silver. Hoiles was leading the league with a .398 mark when he was called up to Baltimore on June 3, the first of three stints he would experience with the big-league club that season. He finished at .348 in 74 games for Rochester, with 18 homers and 56 RBI.

Gomez and Hoiles carried the Wings' offense throughout the season, but no player could match the performance turned in by burly first baseman Sam Horn on a memorable weekend in June. Horn was an imposing hitter—six-foot-five, 240 pounds—who had spent six seasons bouncing between Boston and Pawtucket before finally being released. Prior to the 1990 season, he signed a minor-league contract with the Orioles, who were acting on a tip from former Bird and current Red Sox coach Al Bumbry. Horn couldn't field or run, but he could hit the long ball. He was expected to begin the 1990 season in Rochester, but when major-league teams expanded their rosters to twenty-seven (the owners' lockout had delayed spring training), Horn was given a reprieve by the Orioles. He made the most of his new life, hitting two three-run homers at Kansas City on opening day. But he followed that with a 1-for-12 slump, hit just one more homer in the next twenty-two games, and finally was sent to Rochester.

He continued to slump with the Wings and was batting just .211 when the Tidewater Tides came to town in late June. And then, for twenty-one hours, Sam Horn was Babe Ruth reincarnated. On Saturday, June 23, Horn homered in three consecutive at-bats, driving in eight runs as the Wings swept a doubleheader from Tidewater. His outburst included a pair of two-run homers in game one and a grand slam in the nightcap. The next day, the surge continued. Horn hit two three-run homers as Rochester rallied from a six-run deficit to beat the Tides 11–7. Horn came to bat in the eighth inning and received a standing ovation when he flied out to deep center field.

In twenty-one hours, Horn had raised his average to .345. He went 6-for-10, scored six runs, drove in fourteen, and homered five times.

He was, said Tides manager Steve Swisher, "a one-man wrecking crew." Horn tried to downplay his heroics, saying "I'm doing the best I can. Whenever they decide I'm hot, hopefully I'll be going back to where I want to be."

Horn played just seventeen games with Rochester before the Orioles decided he was hot enough, calling the slugger up on July 3. He hit .414, scored sixteen runs and drove in twenty-six with the Wings. Most impressive, he had as many homers as walks (nine). On the day Horn

The Legend of Daniel Boone

His name was Daniel Boone, and yes, he was related to the legendary pioneer of the same name (a seventh-generation nephew, to be exact). He was thirty when the Milwaukee Brewers released him on July 3, 1984, and he was certain his pitching career was over. He spent the next five years hanging drywall and painting houses in San Diego, raising a son and daughter with his wife, Marge.

In 1989, the five-foot-eight, 140-pound former knuckleballer decided to join the fledgling senior thirty-five-and-over league in Florida, just to see what he could do. There he was rediscovered by Orioles scout Birdie Tebbetts and offered a minor-league contract. Boone resumed his career in Rochester. He worked out of the bullpen at first, but on June 28 he made his first start in nine years and beat the Buffalo Bisons 8–3.

Three weeks later, his incredible comeback was chronicled in *Sports Illustrated*. And on July 23, at Silver Stadium, he really gave them something to write about by pitching a seven-inning no-hitter against the Syracuse Chiefs.

"It's a miracle," he said softly, long after the clubhouse celebration had subsided. "Before I went out the last inning, I thought to myself, 'I want this more than anything in professional baseball that I've ever wanted.'"

Boone didn't walk a batter and struck out five in the 2–0 win before 4,214 fans. The only Chief to reach base was Carlos Diaz, who got aboard on a throwing error by third baseman Leo Gomez in the third inning. In the final inning, Boone did it himself. He lunged off the mound to field Paul Runge's low shot up the middle. He struck out Derek Bell on a 3–2 knuckler. And then, with the crowd on its feet, he got Pedro Munoz to tap a one-hopper back to the mound and Boone threw him out.

The veteran pitcher was mobbed by teammates, then carried off the field by reliever Kevin Hickey and outfielder Victor Hithe. Immediately, he ran over to the box seats to kiss his wife, then hoisted his two-year-old daughter, Brittany, above his shoulders.

A devout born-again Christian, Boone was certain divine intervention had played a role in his return to organized baseball.

"I believe God put that desire back in my heart," he said. "How else could all this have come about."

Boone finished his one and only season with Rochester 11–5 with a 2.60 ERA and a Governors' Cup ring.

Dan Boone.
Karen Schiely photo courtesy of the *Democrat and Chronicle/Times-Union*.

left, Wings outfielder Tony Chance wore Horn's batting helmet and drilled two home runs in a 4–3 win at Nashville.

Horn's impact was loud, awesome, and immediate. The importance of right-hander Mickey Weston was quietly spread out over the entire season. The Michigan native was the New York Mets' twelfth pick in the 1982 draft, but it wasn't until six years later that he finally reached Triple-A with the Tidewater Tides. Weston signed with the Orioles as a six-year free agent and joined the Red Wings in 1989, going 8–3 with a 2.09 ERA. At twenty-nine, he returned to Rochester in 1990 as a jack of all trades. He was a starter, a setup man, and a closer, and he won wherever he pitched. Easygoing and likeable, Weston was never hotter than in July, when he went 6–0 and allowed only seven earned runs. On July 27, he raised his record to 10–0 with an eleven-strikeout, no-walk performance against Columbus. He was one shy of the Red Wings record for consecutive wins set by Norbert "Nubs" Kleinke in 1937. Weston would fall short, losing his only game of the season on August 21 in Syracuse, and would finish the year 11–1 with a 1.98 ERA.

"It was fun while it lasted," an upbeat Weston said after his loss. "Norbert Kleinke, wherever he is, can rest easy now."

Opponents could not. The Red Wings' lead over Scranton-Wilkes-Barre was fifteen by August 1, twenty by August 29. They would finish twenty-one and one-half games ahead with an 89–56 mark, the club's best since Harry Walker's 1953 team went 97–57. Biagini was named International League Manager of the Year, and Hoiles, Gomez, and first baseman David Segui (.336) were selected all-stars. The 1990 Wings were a powerhouse, leading the International League wire-to-wire. They were a colorful team, but it was an off-color prank that turned one of their greatest nights into one of their most embarrassing. The date was August 22, 1990, and the Wings were in Syracuse for a doubleheader needing just one win to clinch the East Division title. It was a night of anticipation, celebration—and fisticuffs.

Game one was delayed when a fourth-inning brawl between short-stop Juan Bell and outfielder Donell Nixon spilled out of the Red Wings dugout and onto the field. The scuffle left fans stunned as teammates were forced to separate the dueling teammates.

The incident began with Syracuse's Ed Sprague at bat and the Wings up 2–0. Bell, who had been on the disabled list since July 6 with a leg injury, passed in front of Nixon—and passed gas in his face. Nixon angrily warned his teammate to cease and desist, but a smiling Bell did it again a few minutes later. This time, Nixon stood up and the teammates began jawing and pushing each other.

"I could hear scuffling and swearing," said Mike Okoniewski, an Associated Press photographer who was seated next to the dugout.

"Every now and then, someone would yell 'Cut it out.' Other players would separate the two, then they would go right back at it. I just came back from covering the Mohawk uprising in Chateauguay, Quebec, and I wasn't as scared there as I was at the end of this dugout."

The verbal battle turned physical when Bell sucker-punched Nixon, cutting his teammate's mouth open. What fans saw next was Bell tumbling out of the dugout. Infielder Marty Brown lay on top of Bell, restraining him, while other teammates held Nixon back inside the dugout.

"It was without a doubt the craziest thing I've ever seen in a baseball game," *Times-Union* beat writer Bill Koenig said. "Fans were just sitting in the stands scratching their heads, saying 'What the hell is going on?'"

Order finally was restored, and Sprague hit the next pitch for a three-run homer. At the end of the inning, round two broke out as the Wings were coming off the field. This time, it spread to the box-seat railing as several players tried to separate Bell and Nixon. The three umpires rushed over, Wings general manager Dan Lunetta left his seat and raced onto the field to help, and infielder Shane Turner tried to prevent photographers from taking pictures. Finally, Brown and pitcher Kevin Hickey grabbed Bell and carried him, kicking and screaming, across the infield to the Wings' clubhouse down the right-field line. Bell, his shirt torn open by the fracas, was booed by the Syracuse crowd of 6,625; Nixon remained in the dugout holding a towel to his face. He remained in the game as the designated hitter and pounded out his third hit of the game two innings later.

The Wings won 7–5, with Rochester native and fourth-year Red Wing Chris Padget driving in the winning run to clinch the East. After the Wings lost the meaningless nightcap 2–0, both Bell and Nixon took part in the postgame champagne celebration. Players refused to comment and Biagini, who had separate talks with Bell and Nixon after the game, shrugged the incident off, saying "Something in the dugout got out of hand and it was just an unfortunate thing."

It was, wrote Koenig, "mutiny in the midst of bounty."

The Red Wings opened their best-of-five Governors' Cup series against Columbus by winning the first two games at Silver, but the Clippers rallied to win games three and four at home. That set up the decisive fifth game on Saturday night, September 9. Again the hero was Weston, who pitched six shutout innings en route to a 5–1 Cup-clinching win, the Wings' ninth overall and second in three years.

On the field, the victors raised the cup high in the air in celebration. Leo Gomez, who finished with 26 homers and 97 RBI, gazed in awe at the huge trophy and smiled. "Imagine that," he said.

As it did in 1988, the Wings' championship season ended with a loss in the Triple-A Classic series, with Rochester falling to the Omaha Royals four games to one. "The Alliance championship would have been a nice capper," Biagini said, "but I'm very satisfied with how this season has ended. This team and this city have a lot to be proud of."

Biagini's 1991 club produced the league's Rookie of the Year (out-fielder Luis Mercedes) and Pitcher of the Year (Mike Mussina) but could not produce a playoff berth, finishing second at 76–68. In the season finale against Syracuse, two players from the same team—Wings infield-ers Tommy Shields and Shane Turner—played all nine positions for the first time in professional baseball history. The Chiefs were unimpressed, but the Wings won 8–0. Biagini finally got his major-league shot follow-ing the '91 season, when he was named to Johnny Oates's coaching staff in Baltimore. His replacement was Jerry Narron, a backup catcher on the Wings' 1988 championship team. Narron was also the catcher who replaced Thurman Munson the night after the Yankees catcher was killed in a plane crash in 1979, a piece of trivia Narron never felt comfortable discussing. The Red Wings welcomed back another old face in 1992 as Joe Altobelli replaced Dan Lunetta as general manager. Altobelli's num-ber 26 was the only number retired by the Wings, and now he had set another precedent with his Rochester trifecta of player, manager, and GM.

"All of sudden, excitement has been created in me again," said Altobelli, who had been let go as a coach with the Chicago Cubs. "I think you need that to survive. It's like pressure."

Another change in 1992 was the return to a four-team International League playoff format. The IL had severed ties with the American Associ-ation following the '91 season, citing travel costs, and thus ending the Triple-A Alliance. Charlotte and Ottawa had joined the IL as expansion teams, and now the top two clubs in each five-team division would make the postseason.

On April 9, Narron's club opened with an 18–1 romp in Paw-tucket. They would not all be that easy. On June 7, Wings left-hander Arthur Rhodes had a no-hitter through seven and two-thirds innings in a scoreless game at Columbus. Amazingly, the Clippers woke up with eleven runs in the eighth to win 11–0. Three days later, the Wings re-corded an eleven-run inning and built a 13–3 lead through three against Toledo. The Mud Hens won 17–15. On May 3, Rochester played a game in which it never had the chance to blow a lead. Richmond beat the Wings 1–0 at Silver Stadium in the second game of a doubleheader, and Braves right-hander Pete Smith mowed down all twenty-one Red Wings he faced. It was the first perfect game ever thrown against Rochester.

The losses began to mount. By mid-July, the Wings had stumbled to a 33–56 record and appeared headed for their worst season since Frank Verdi's 1984 train wreck. The turning point came July 19 at Silver. Trailing Scranton-Wilkes-Barre 8–0 after six, the Wings rallied for a 10–9 win. The unlikely rally started a ten-game winning streak as the Wings moved from ten games behind second-place Pawtucket to a half game in front of the Red Sox.

With Scranton-Wilkes-Barre running away with the East—the Barons would win by thirteen and a half games—Rochester and Pawtucket battled for the final playoff spot over the next several weeks. On September 6, the Red Wings took the field in Syracuse after learning that Pawtucket had lost to Toledo 5–3. A Wings win would put them a half game behind with only one game left in the season. Rochester built a 6–0 lead, but the season's strange pattern had one more surprise left as Syracuse rallied to win 8–7 and eliminate Rochester (70–74) from the playoff race.

Like Biagini, Narron earned a promotion to the Orioles coaching staff in the off-season. The new man in Rochester was former Pittsburgh Pirates farmhand Bob Miscik, who at thirty-four became the youngest Wings manager since Cal Ripken, Sr., took over the '69 club at age thirty-three.

Miscik had a veteran team, opening the season with twelve players with major-league experience. Two weeks later, another well-traveled player joined the club. Fernando Valenzuela, who had captured the baseball world's attention during his rookie season with Los Angeles in 1981, was sent down from Baltimore to get some work in. Wearing his famous-number 34—which he borrowed from Wings outfielder Mark Smith—Valenzuela pitched three and one-third innings at Richmond on April 17, allowing six hits and four runs. He took the loss as the Braves rolled 6–3, then was sent to Double-A Bowie, Maryland, before rejoining the Orioles.

First baseman Glenn Davis, a former all-star with the Houston Astros, slumped badly in Baltimore and was sent to Rochester. It was a disastrous experience for him. Davis went 6-for-24 on the field and fared even worse off it. Following a game against the Norfolk Tides, he was involved in a scuffle at a Virginia Beach nightclub, and a bouncer (and former professional boxer) shattered Davis's jaw, sidelining him for three months.

The Wings made International League history on May 16 when Scott Coolbaugh and Bobby Dickerson hit grand slams in the same inning as Rochester romped 16–2 at Columbus. The victim was Doug Gogolewski, who allowed the shot to Coolbaugh on his first pitch in Triple-A, then surrendered Dickerson's blast four batters later.

Another highlight was right-hander Kevin McGehee, acquired from San Francisco in late April for Mercedes. McGehee would finish 7–6 with a 2.96 ERA, the first Red Wing to win the league's ERA title since Dennis Martinez in 1976. Despite ninety-two roster moves, the Wings stayed in first place for virtually the entire year and led the expansion Ottawa Lynx by six games on August 1. But in the final month Ottawa surged and Rochester slumped. When the Wings traveled to Ottawa for the final two games of the season, they were a half game out of first. Two wins would give Rochester the Eastern Division title. Anything less would give the expansion Lynx the crown. Rochester won the opener 2–1 behind left-hander Rick Krivda, just called up from Bowie. In the season finale, the Wings trailed 1–0 going into the ninth when first baseman Mel Wearing laced a two-run single with one out. Dickerson, nearing the end of his playing career, ended the game when he snared a hard shot to third and completed a double play to clinch the division, giving Rochester a 74–67 record.

Two days later, on Labor Day, the teams began a five-game playoff series at Ottawa Stadium. Mike Oquist tossed a one-hitter in a 4–0 Rochester win as the Wings went on to win the series three games to two. In the Governors' Cup finals, Mark Leonard hit two homers to key a 7–3 win at Charlotte in game one, but the Knights won the next two games to close within a game of the league title. The Red Wings rolled 15–1 in game four at Silver Stadium, setting up an all-or-nothing finale on Wednesday, September 15. It was a Knightmare for Red Wings fans, with steady rain, temperatures in the low 50s, and gusting winds throughout the game. On any other night, the game would have been postponed. But players on both teams had their bags packed and were ready to go home. International League president Randy Mobley gave the go-ahead and at 8:32—eighty-seven minutes after its scheduled start—the first pitch was thrown. Charlotte scored a first-inning run when Mark Lewis tripled and scored on a water-logged wild pitch. Sam Horn then battered his former team with a three-run homer in the third. The Knights led 6–1 by the time a lengthy rain delay set in during the fifth inning, and that's how it ended, finally, at 12:32 A.M.

Miscik returned in 1994, but with a mostly new cast. The biggest addition was third baseman Jeff Manto, who joined the club in mid-May from the Norfolk Tides. Manto had spent the previous nine seasons shuffling from one minor-league team to another, with brief stops at Cleveland and Philadelphia thrown in. He became an immediate hit with Red Wings fans, hitting a homer and driving in six runs in a 14–8 Memorial Day win over Syracuse.

It was the start of one of the greatest summers by a Red Wing in

Third baseman Jeff Manto joined the 1994 Red Wings in mid-May and became one of the city's most popular players in years, winning MVP honors with 31 homers and 100 RBI. Jamie Germano photo courtesy of the *Democrat and Chronicle/Times-Union.*

many years. Manto batted .297 and drove in his one-hundredth run on his final swing of the season, launching his thirty-first home run in Pawtucket. He became the first Red Wing to lead the league in homers and RBI since Jim Fuller in 1973. He also became the eleventh International League MVP in Wings history. Fans loved the low-key veteran. Toward the end of the season, huge lines formed behind the Red Wings dugout after each game as fans waited for Manto's autograph. He willingly obliged, spending thirty minutes on the night of his thirtieth birthday talking to a blind fan.

   Manto powered a Wings offense that led the league in runs scored (5.2 per game) and finished second in homers (141). But an inconsistent pitching staff spelled their doom, and Rochester finished 67–74, falling three and one-half games short of a playoff berth and ending a string of seven consecutive seasons with seventy or more wins.

◇

In the off-season, Orioles assistant general manager Doug Melvin left to become GM of the Texas Rangers. Melvin's duties as farm director were filled by Syd Thrift, a veteran executive most famous for building the Pittsburgh Pirates powers of the early 1990s, which featured stars such as Barry Bonds and Bobby Bonilla.

In one of his first acts, Thrift reassigned Miscik to Double-A Bowie, Maryland, and hired Marv Foley, who had worked under Thrift as bullpen coach of the Chicago Cubs the season before. Foley came to Rochester with impressive minor-league credentials, winning Triple-A titles in both the Pacific Coast League (Vancouver in 1989) and the American Association (Iowa in 1993). He was one of eleven managers who had won Triple-A titles in two leagues—the list includes former Red Wing Walter Alston and Yankees legend Casey Stengel—and was given a solid chance of completing the Triple-A Triple Crown in Rochester with a prospect-filled roster.

Foley came close, but an underachieving club in Baltimore spelled disaster for the Wings. Foley used 62 different players and the Wings were involved in 134 player moves—both club records—yet still finished 73–69 to win the International League East over Ottawa on the final day. Rochester held a 2-games-to-1 lead in the best-of-five playoffs, but the Lynx rallied to win game four and then scored three runs in the top of the ninth off reliever Jimmy Myers in game five to win 4–2 and advance to the Governors' Cup finals, where they beat the Norfolk Tides.

Despite the many moves and a so-so club, first-year general manager Dan Mason's preseason goal of 400,000 fans was fulfilled. The Wings' paid attendance was 402,127, their best since 1949.

It was an impressive turnout, but Silver's days were numbered.

16

Building Toward a New Frontier

When does Rochester get its slice of the pie?
—Sports columnist and talk-show host
Bob Matthews, June 1992

Bob Matthews first visited Silver Stadium when he was five years old, and it was love at first sight. Matthews became a regular during the late '50s and early '60s. Luke Easter was his favorite player, and Matthews would save up his allowance and paper route money each week to see his beloved Red Wings play. "I must have seen thousands of games through the years," said Matthews. "I don't think I missed a game until I went into the army."

He lauded the renovation of Silver in 1987, but when new minor-league parks began springing up throughout the nation—Buffalo's Pilot Field was the crown jewel, just eighty miles to the west—Matthews began to speak out on the need for a new stadium for Rochester. His forums were his popular daily newspaper column and his highly rated nightly talk show on WHAM, a 50,000-watt radio station.

Matthews's views didn't catch fire right away, especially with the $4.5 million renovation so fresh in people's minds. But when Major League Baseball set new minimum requirements for minor-league parks in 1991, Silver flunked the test. Moreover, the ballpark had not turned a profit since the stadium renovation. Further renovations were expected to cost up to $15 million. Why not spend $25 million and build a new stadium?

Suddenly, Matthews was not a voice in the wilderness. His push

223

for a new stadium slowly began to gain momentum, especially when Monroe County Executive Robert L. King threw his support behind the idea. The debate raged for two years. King headed the political faction supporting a downtown stadium. Assemblyman David Gantt, who had voted in favor of financing other stadiums throughout the state, was the leading proponent of renovating Silver to meet major-league requirements—which were to go into effect in April 1994—calling it a better deal for taxpayers.

Finally, in November 1992, a committee appointed by the city of Rochester and Monroe County recommended that a new stadium be built at Franklin and Pleasant streets in downtown Rochester. King endorsed the decision, but Mayor Thomas P. Ryan, Jr., refused to endorse it, saying a stadium at the proposed site "would be an absolute mistake." Ryan wanted the stadium built on West Main Street, but King held firm.

In the meantime, other suburban locations were being mentioned. Officials from Avon, located thirty miles south of Rochester, and Victor, twenty miles east, made their pitch to lure the Wings away. The political stalemate extended throughout the fall, with no end in sight. Finally, the board of directors of Rochester Community Baseball forced the issue. On January 14, 1993, the board voted 26–1 with two abstentions to endorse a wild-card site at Canal Ponds Business Park in the western suburb of Greece.

The proposed $25.8 million ballpark would be built on a three-hundred-acre site owned by Eastman Kodak. Seating capacity would be 12,500—expandable to 18,000 seats—with twenty to twenty-five luxury suites and a three-hundred-seat restaurant and sports bar. RCB president Elliot Curwin said that "a slight window" remained open for a downtown stadium, but King and Ryan held firm on their preferred downtown sites.

> *The best thing about the Greece site is that it would keep the Red Wings in Monroe County, where the base of fan support resides. The worst thing is that it is not downtown. The only way to bring life back to downtown is to offer unique attractions. Suburbanites aren't going to be lured to the city to shop or attend movies. Anyone critical of Rochester Community Baseball's board of directors for not choosing a downtown site is missing the point: The city of Rochester submitted no proposal. It is impossible to consider a site if it is not on the table.*
> —Bob Matthews,*Times-Union,* Jan. 15, 1993

Artist's rendering of Frontier Field, the Red Wings' first new home since 1929.
Courtesy of Monroe County and the Rochester Red Wings.

Despite the board's vote, city and county politicians remained
hopeful that an alternate downtown site could be found to keep the Red
Wings in the city limits, and on June 21, 1993—more than five months
after Greece was chosen as the stadium site—a compromise was reached.
King, Ryan, and the Red Wings board all agreed on a $37.3 million plan
to build a stadium on Oak Street in downtown Rochester.

The ballpark would be built just west of Eastman Kodak Company
headquarters, on land owned by Kodak, as part of a long-range plan to
develop the cultural area known as Brown's Race on the Genesee River.
The financing would come from multiple sources: $15.5 million from a
state loan, $13.55 from Monroe County, $4 million from the Red Wings,
a city contribution of $3 million for the redevelopment of Silver Stadium,
and $1.5 million in debt owed by the Wings to the state, a debt officials
hoped the state would forgive.

Officials forecast a possible opening of the new ballpark by 1995,
but said 1996 was more likely. In November 1994, Rochester Telephone

Co. announced that it was buying the naming rights to the stadium for
$1.5 million. The new ballpark would be called Frontier Field after Fron-
tier Communications, a subsidiary of Rochester Telephone. A ceremonial
groundbreaking ceremony was held at the stadium site on November 16,
and was attended by about five hundred fans, politicians, and dignitaries.
Food, music, and congratulatory speeches were the order of the day. The
celebration turned out to be premature, however. Two months later,
newly elected governor George E. Pataki released his proposed state
budget without stadium funding for Rochester and several other cities.

Demolition had begun on buildings on the stadium site, and construction was to start within weeks. Now everything came to a halt. Red
Wings fans did not take the news lightly. On February 4, 1995, nearly
three thousand of them braved bitterly cold temperatures and snow flur-
ries at Silver Stadium to show their support for Rochester's new ballpark.
It was called Stadiumstock '95, and it brought out everyone from Joe
Altobelli to Bob Matthews to International League MVP Jeff Manto,
who drove up from Philadelphia with his father to sign autographs and
address the frenzied crowd. Thousands of supporters signed a petition
and sent letters to Governor Pataki criticizing his decision to omit funding for Frontier Field.

The budget debate dragged on for five months before an agreement
including stadium funding was reached in June 1995. One month later,
a state Public Authorities Control Board gave final funding approval and
on July 24, construction on Frontier Field began.

A new era was about to begin for the Rochester Red Wings.

Extra Innings

Bibliography

Index

Rochester
Year-by-Year Standings

Year	Manager	Record	Finish	Attendance
1885	Harry Leonard	39–36	2	NA
1886	Frank Bancroft	56–39	2	NA
1887	John Humphries	49–52	7	NA
1888	Harry Leonard	64–43	3	NA
1889	Harry Leonard and			
	Patrick Powers	60–50	3	NA
1890	Patrick Powers	63–63	5	NA
1891	Tom Powers,			
	Lewis Kirstein,			
	and Charles Morton	31–61	5	NA
1892	William Watkins	42–29	3	
	Split season	27–28	4	NA
1893–94	Did not play			
1895	John C. Chapman	47–82	7	NA
1896	Daniel Shannon	69–58	3	NA
1897	Daniel Shannon and			
	George Wiedman	26–44	—	NA
1898	Charles Morton and			
	Michael Finn	32–35	—	NA
1899	Albert Buckenberger	73–44	1	NA
1900	Albert Buckenberger	77–56	2	NA
1901	Albert Buckenberger	88–49	1	NA
1902	Edward McKean and			
	Harry O'Hagan	56–74	7	NA
1903	Arthur Irwin and	34–96	8	NA
	George Smith			
1904	George Smith	28–105	8	NA

Year	Manager	Record	Finish	Attendance
1905	Albert Buckenberger	51–86	7	NA
1906	Albert Buckenberger	77–62	4	NA
1907	Albert Buckenberger	59–76	7	NA
1908	Albert Buckenberger and Edward Holley	55–82	8	NA
1909	John Ganzel	90–61	1	NA
1910	John Ganzel	92–61	1	NA
1911	John Ganzel	98–54	1	NA
1912	John Ganzel	86–67	2	NA
1913	John Ganzel	92–62	2	NA
1914	John Ganzel	91–63	3	NA
1915	John Ganzel and Robert Williams	69–69	4	NA
1916	Thomas Leach	60–78	7	NA
1917	Michael Doolan	72–82	5	NA
1918	Arthur Irwin	60–61	5	NA
1919	Arthur Irwin	76–83	6	NA
1920	Arthur Irwin	45–106	7	NA
1921	George Stallings	101–67	2	NA
1922	George Stallings	105–62	2	NA
1923	George Stallings	101–65	2	NA
1924	George Stallings	83–84	4	NA
1925	George Stallings	83–77	3	NA
1926	George Stallings	81–83	5	NA
1927	George Stallings and George Mogridge	81–86	6	NA
1928	Billy Southworth	90–74	1	235,566
1929	Bill McKechnie and Billy Southworth	103–65	1	298,303
1930	Billy Southworth	105–62	1	328,424
1931	Billy Southworth	101–67	1	293,091
1932	Billy Southworth and George Toporcer	88–78	5	153,739
1933	George Toporcer	88–77	2	152,373
1934	George Toporcer	89–64	2	162,627
1935	Ed Dyer and Burt Shotton	61–91	7	94,351
1936	Ray Blades	89–66	2	160,491
1937	Ray Blades	74–80	6	117,207
1938	Ray Blades	80–74	3	157,939
1939	Billy Southworth	84–67	GC2	170,457
1940	Billy Southworth, Estel Crabtree, and Tony Kaufmann	96–61	1	150,143

Year	Manager	Record	Finish	Attendance
1941	Tony Kaufmann	84–68	4	148,694
1942	Tony Kaufmann, Estel Crabtree, and Ray Hayworth	59–93	8	72,891
1943	Pepper Martin	74–78	5	101,382
1944	Ken Penner	71–82	7	101,163
1945	Burleigh Grimes	64–90	8	77,585
1946	Burleigh Grimes and Benny Borgmann	65–87	7	172,125
1947	Cedric Durst	68–86	5	262,891
1948	Cedric Durst	78–75	4	304,896
1949	Johnny Keane	85–67	2	443,536
1950	Johnny Keane	92–59	1	320,067
1951	Johnny Keane	83–69	2	252,538
1952	Harry Walker	80–74	GC3	232,271
1953	Harry Walker	97–57	1	252,467
1954	Harry Walker	86–68	3	195,141
1955	Harry Walker and Fred "Dixie" Walker	76–77	GC4	153,498
1956	Fred "Dixie" Walker	83–67	GC2	179,739
1957	Cot Deal	74–80	5	258,778
1958	Cot Deal and Clyde King	77–75	3	282,259
1959	Clyde King	74–80	5	256,296
1960	Clyde King	81–73	3	244,766
1961	Clyde King	76–78	4	278,157
1962	Clyde King	82–72	4	274,605
1963	Darrell Johnson	75–76	7	271,968
1964	Darrell Johnson	82–72	GC4	284,844
1965	Darrell Johnson	73–74	5	222,588
1966	Earl Weaver	83–64	1	273,247
1967	Earl Weaver	80–61	2	303,500
1968	Billy DeMars	77–69	3	243,498
1969	Cal Ripken, Sr.	71–69	5	267,987
1970	Cal Ripken, Sr.	76–64	3	306,518
1971	Joe Altobelli	86–54	GC1	361,701
1972	Joe Altobelli	76–68	4	296,864
1973	Joe Altobelli	79–67	2	302,789
1974	Joe Altobelli	88–56	GC2	269,703
1975	Joe Altobelli	85–55	2	326,072
1976	Joe Altobelli	88–50	1	258,101
1977	Ken Boyer	67–73	6	245,693
1978	Ken Boyer and Frank Robinson	68–72	6	219,814

Year	Manager	Record	Finish	Attendance
1979	Doc Edwards	53–86	8	200,013
1980	Doc Edwards	74–65	3	302,423
1981	Doc Edwards	69–70	4	359,704
1982	Lance Nichols	72–68	4	373,904
1983	Lance Nichols	65–75	6	284,046
1984	Frank Verdi	52–88	8	197,501
1985	Frank Verdi and Mark Wiley	58–81	7	214,674
1986	John Hart	75–63	2	323,463
1987	John Hart	64–65	3	315,807
1988	Johnny Oates	77–64	GC1	300,794
1989	Greg Biagini	72–73	5	284,394
1990	Greg Biagini	89–56	GC1	352,472
1991	Greg Biagini	76–68	2	345,167
1992	Jerry Narron	70–74	3	305,199
1993	Bob Miscik	74–67	1	381,061
1994	Bob Miscik	67–74	4	370,050
1995	Marv Foley	73–69	1	402,127

GC = Won Governors' Cup title

Rochester Red Wings Records

All-Time Rochester Single-Season Records

Average: George Puccinelli .391 (1932)
RBI: Rip Collins, 180 (1930)
Hits: Rip Collins, 234 (1930)
Doubles: Fred Merkle, 54 (1923)
Triples: Bill Lush, 28 (1895)
Home runs: Russ Derry, 42 (1949)
Runs: Maurice Archdeacon, 166 (1921)
Walks: Russ Derry, 134 (1949)
Stolen bases: Charles Collins, 185 (1888)
Strikeouts (batter): Jim Fuller, 197 (1973)
Wins: George McConnell 30, (1911)
Strikeouts (pitcher): Walter Beall, 227 (1924)
Shutouts: James Holmes and Edward Lafitte, 8 each (1910)

International League MVPs

1940: Mike Ryba
1943: Red Schoendienst
1950: Tom Poholsky
1966: Mike Epstein
1968: Merv Rettenmund
1970: Roger Freed

1971: Bobby Grich
1973: Jim Fuller
1976: Rich Dauer
1988: Craig Worthington
1994: Jeff Manto

International League Most Valuable Pitchers

1954: Tony Jacobs
1967: Dave Leonhard
1971: Roric Harrison

1976: Dennis Martinez
1977: Mike Parrott
1991: Mike Mussina

International League Rookies of the Year

1952: Ray Jablonski
1955: Jack Brandt
1959: Charles James
1966: Mike Epstein
1967: Curt Motton
1968: Merv Rettenmund
1970: Roger Freed

1972: Al Bumbry
1976: Rich Dauer
1980: Bobby Bonner
1981: Cal Ripken, Jr.
1988: Steve Finley
1991: Luis Mercedes

Career Batting Leaders

Batting Average

Rip Collins: .348
Red Worthington: .347
George Puccinelli: .340
Billy Southworth: .335
Don Richmond: .327

Ray Pepper: .316
Don Baylor: .315
Royle Stillman: .314
Buster Mills: .313
Estel Crabtree: .308

Home Runs

Russ Derry: 134
Tom Burgess: 93
Estel Crabtree: 91
Jim Fuller: 91
Terry Crowley: 87

Rip Collins: 85
Mike Fiore: 79
Steve Bilko: 77
Luke Easter: 66
John Valle: 66

Runs Batted In

Estel Crabtree: 542
Ray Pepper: 419
Russ Derry: 413
Tom Burgess: 383
Don Richmond: 374

Steve Demeter: 367
Allie Clark: 340
Rip Collins: 338
Harry Davis: 338
Steve Bilko: 328

Base Hits

Estel Crabtree: 1,041
George Toporcer: 950
Don Richmond: 857
Ray Pepper: 742
Joe Brown: 739

Steve Demeter: 731
Tom Burgess: 658
Jack Sturdy: 645
Harry Davis: 609
Allie Clark: 597

Runs Scored

George Toporcer: 628
Estel Crabtree: 570

Tom Burgess: 370
Ray Pepper: 345

Joe Brown: 483
Don Richmond: 480
Russ Derry: 410

Jack Sturdy: 344
Harry Davis: 341
Steve Demeter: 325

Stolen Bases

George Toporcer: 113
Damon Buford: 89
Dallas Williams: 72
Tom Shopay: 71
Joe Brown: 71

Jack Sturdy: 69
Buster Mills: 59
Don Baylor: 52
John Shelby: 52
Manny Alexander: 51

Games Played

Estel Crabtree: 934
George Toporcer: 880
Lou Ortiz: 689
Russ Derry: 683
Tom Burgess: 679

Steve Demeter: 679
Paul Florence: 648
Harry Davis: 584
Allie Clark: 579
Steve Bilko: 516

Career Pitching Leaders

Victories

Jack Faszholz: 80
Norbert Kleinke: 70
John Berly: 63
Ira Smith: 62
Cot Deal: 61

Max Surkont: 59
Tony Kaufmann: 51
Herman Bell: 48
Glenn Gardner: 47
Bill Kirkpatrick: 47

ERA (Minimum 150 Innings)

Mickey Weston: 1.95
Mike Flanagan: 2.39
Dennis Martinez: 2.58
Dyar Miller: 2.64
Roric Harrison: 2.81
Mike Ryba: 2.82

Mickey Scott: 2.89
Ira Hutchinson: 2.90
Bill Trotter: 2.93
Bob Tiefenhauer: 2.94
Tom Poholsky: 2.94

Strikeouts

Frank Bertaina: 501
Dick Ricketts: 501
Tom Phoebus: 482

Billy Short: 443
Bill Kirkpatrick: 419

Victories, One Season

George McConnell: 30 (1911)
Robert Barr: 29 (1888)
Robert Barr: 29 (1889)
Robert Barr: 29 (1890)
Don McFarlan: 27 (1896)

John Malarkey: 27 (1901)
John Wisner: 26 (1923)
George Harper: 25 (1895)
Walter Beall: 25 (1924)

Strikeouts, One Season

Walter Beall: 227 (1924)
Tom Phoebus: 208 (1966)
Frank Bertaina: 188 (1965)
Roric Harrison: 182 (1971)
Ed Barnowski: 176 (1966)
Cal Browning: 173 (1958)

Bob Weiland: 171 (1936)
Paul Derringer: 164 (1930)
Art Quirk: 162 (1961)
Herb Moford: 158 (1961)
Darold Knowles: 155 (1965)
Richie Lewis: 154 (1992)

Rochester Twenty-Game Winners

1887: Edward Bakely, 22
1888: Robert Barr, 29
1889: Robert Barr, 29
1890: Robert Barr, 29
1892: George Meakin, 23
1895: George Harper, 25
1896: Don McFarlan, 27
1899: Robert Becker, 22
1899: Charles Morse, 21
1900: Charles Morse, 24
1901: John Malarkey, 27
1909: Eros Barger, 23
1910: Edward Lafitte, 23
1910: Frank McPartlin, 22

1911: George McConnell, 30
1913: Robert Keefe, 21
1914: Eldon Upham, 21
1917: Charles Lohman, 24
1921: John Wisner, 22
1921: Fred Blake, 21
1923: John Wisner, 26
1924: Walter Beall, 24
1928: Herman Bell, 21
1930: Paul Derringer, 23
1931: Raymond Starr, 20
1936: Robert Weiland, 23
1939: Silas Johnson, 22
1940: Mike Ryba, 24

Rochester No-Hitters

Date	Pitcher	Opponent	Score
July 6, 1888	George Hays	London	6–0
June 30, 1908	Sandy Bannister	Buffalo	L1–0 (7)
Sept. 5, 1910	George McConnell	Toronto	5–0
Sept. 1, 1924	Frank Karpp	Syracuse	8–0 (7)
Sept. 27, 1924	William Moore	Syracuse	4–0

Sept. 14, 1929	Tex Carleton	Toronto	3–1
Aug. 20, 1941	Matt Surkont	Jersey City	1–0 (7)
Aug. 17, 1943	Blix Donnelly	Jersey City	4–0
Sept. 5, 1952	Jack Collum	Ottawa	9–0
Apr. 29, 1955	Duke Markell	Columbus	9–0
July 4, 1961	Art Quirk	Syracuse	5–0 (7)
June 9, 1963	Nat Martinez	Jacksonville	5–0 (7)
July 26, 1964	John Miller	Columbus	2–0 (7)
July 28, 1966	Dave Vineyard	Toledo	1–0
Aug. 15, 1966	Tom Phoebus	Buffalo	1–0 (7)
May 4, 1969	Marcelino Lopez	Richmond	5–1 (7)
May 28, 1971	Greg Arnold	Charleston	2–0 (7)
Apr. 20, 1974	Wayne Garland	Charleston	5–0
Aug. 16, 1974	Gary Robson	Charleston	2–0 (7, perfect)
July 23, 1990	Dan Boone	Syracuse	2–0 (7)

No-Hitters Against Rochester

Date	Pitcher	Opponent	Score
Aug. 28, 1885	Prendergrass	Utica	4–1
June 18, 1889	Edward Cushman	Toledo	8–0
June 4, 1907	George McQuillen	Providence	2–0
Sept. 12, 1907	John McCloskey	Baltimore	7–1
Aug. 21, 1909	Charles Kissinger	Buffalo	5–0
July 6, 1910	James Wiggs	Montreal	3–0
July 22, 1916	Urban Shocker	Toronto	1–0 (11)
Aug. 17, 1958	Rudolfo Arias	Havana	7–0 (7)
May 23, 1967	Dave Vineyard	Toronto	2–1
Aug. 31, 1971	Mike Pazik	Syracuse	5–0
Aug. 6, 1972	Tommie Moore	Tidewater	2–0 (7)
June 7, 1974	Hank Webb	Tidewater	1–0 (7)
July 21, 1974	Charles Ross	Pawtucket	4–0 (7)
May 3, 1992	Pete Smith	Richmond	1–0 (7, perfect)

Other Red Wings Marks

Consecutive wins by pitcher: William Horner (1886) and Norbert Kleinke (1937), 11 each

Longest game: 33 innings, April 18–19 and June 23, 1981 (3–2 loss to Pawtucket)

Highest score: 30–2 win over Newark, April 21, 1924

Longest winning streak: 19 games in 1953

Longest losing streak: 12 games in 1920

Hitting streak: George Puccinelli 31 (1932)

Former Rochester Players/Managers/General Managers
in Baseball Hall of Fame

Name	Hall	Years in Rochester	Highlights
Buck Ewing	1939	1880	Top 19th century player; hit .311 in 18 seasons
George Sisler	1939	1931	Hit .340 with 1180 RBI; eclipsed .400 mark twice
Dan Brouthers	1945	1899	.349 average in 19 years
Rabbit Maranville	1954	1927	Played 23 seasons; ranks third with 2,670 games
Dazzy Vance	1955	1918	Led NL in strikeouts for seven straight seasons
Bill McKechnie	1962	1929	Only NL manager to win pennants with three clubs
Burleigh Grimes	1964	1945–46	Last legal spitballer, won 270 games
Stan Musial	1969	1941	3,630 hits, 475 HRs, .331 career average
Ross Youngs	1972	1917	Hit .322 in 10 seasons; died at age 30
George Kelly	1973	1917	.297 average in 16 years
Jocko Conlan	1974	1924–26	Hit .321 for Rochester in 1924; inducted as umpire
Warren Giles	1979	1929–36	Wings GM, president, then NL president
Bob Gibson	1981	1958	251 wins, 2 Cy Youngs
Johnny Mize	1981	1933–35	Hit 359 HRs, 1,337 RBI
Frank Robinson	1982	1978 Mgr.	Hit 586 HRs; only MVP in both AL and NL
Walter Alston	1983	1937, 1943–44	managed Dodgers to seven pennants, 3 world titles
Red Schoendienst	1989	1943–44	10-time All-star with Cardinals; 2,449 hits
Jim Palmer	1990	1967–68	268 wins, 2.86 ERA; won three Cy Young Awards
Earl Weaver	1996	1966–67	Won 1970 World Series

Red Wings Hall of Fame

1989: Joe Altobelli, Rip Collins, Estel Crabtree, Russ Derry, Luke Easter, Bobby Grich, Morrie Silver, Billy Southworth, George Toporcer, Harry Walker

1990: Don Baylor, George Beahon, Steve Demeter, Jack Faszholz, Tom Poholsky, Don Richmond, Red Schoendienst

1991: Fred Beene, Ray Pepper, Mike Ryba, Dick Sierens

1992: Tom Burgess, Roger Freed, Tony Jacobs, George Sisler, Jr., Jay Stalker,
    Danny Whelan
1993: Tom Decker, Bob Keegan, Boog Powell
1994: Cot Deal, Bing Devine, Jim Fuller
1995: Earl Weaver, Joe Cullinane, Pat Santillo

Shuffling the Lineup

Cardinals Era

First base: Rip Collins
Second base: Specs Toporcer
Shortstop: Red Schoendienst
Third base: Don Richmond
Outfield: Ray Pepper, Russ Derry, Pepper Martin
Catcher: Paul Florence
Pitcher (R): Paul Derringer
Pitcher (L): Fritz Ostermueller
Reliever: Tony Jacobs
Manager: Billy Southworth
Graduate: Stan Musial
Personality: Morrie Silver
Greatest moment: Estel Crabtree's home run in the 1939 Governors' Cup final

Orioles Era

First base: Boog Powell
Second base: Rich Dauer
Shortstop: Bobby Grich
Third base: Steve Demeter
Outfield: Don Baylor, Roger Freed, Jim Fuller
Catcher: Chris Hoiles
Pitcher (R): Fred Beene
Pitcher (L): Frank Bertaina
Reliever: Mickey Scott
Manager: Joe Altobelli
Graduate: Cal Ripken, Jr.

Personality: Luke Easter
Greatest moment: "Finigan's Rainbow," home run in 1961 playoff

Fred's Lists

Trick question: Who is the only man to play for the Red Wings and the Rochester Americans professional hockey team?

Answer: Fred Costello. Costello is the organist for both teams. He has entertained fans at Silver Stadium since 1977 with his music and his trivia questions and lists. Here are some of his favorite lists.

Favorite Red Wing Names

Frank "Noodles" Zupo   Luco Lancelotti
Drungo Hazewood   Sidney Stringfellow
Lester Fusselman   Stanley Partenheimer
Lynn Lovenguth   Maurice Mozzah
Carden Gillenwater   Stan Jok

Red Wings Most Feared Home-Run Hitters

Russ Derry   Allie Clark
Jim Fuller   Tommy Burgess
Luke Easter   Terry Crowley
Steve Bilko   Rip Collins
Boog Powell   Mike Epstein

Fabulous Fifteen: Red Wings Who Made It Big in the Majors

Stan Musial   Boog Powell
Johnny Mize   Mike Flanagan
Cal Ripken, Jr.   Rip Collins
Bobby Grich   Jim Palmer
Don Baylor   Bob Gibson
Doug DeCinces   Red Schoendienst
Marty Marion   Tim McCarver
Eddie Murray

Five Greatest Red Wings Teams in History

1971, Joe Altobelli, manager
1930, Billy Southworth, manager
1976, Joe Altobelli, manager
1950, Johnny Keane, manager
1953, Harry Walker, manager

Bob Brown's All-Time Red Wings–Orioles Team

Authors' note:
During a thirty-five-year career with the Baltimore Orioles, Bob Brown was
at various times traveling secretary, public relations director, and director of
publications. He currently is vice president, communications, for Maryland Base-
ball Limited Partnership, which owns and operates the Bowie Baysox, Frederick
Keys, and Salisbury Shorebirds.

Over the last thirty-five years, nearly two of every three players who have played
with the Orioles have also worn a Rochester Red Wings uniform. In that period,
Orioles box scores have carried close to 420 different names—270 of them
Rochester graduates. To establish an all-time Orioles team from Red Wings
alumni, we had to establish a series of ground rules. We limited the choices to
those who played a substantial number of games for Rochester and who were
still working their way up to the majors at the time. In some cases, players
changed positions while they were in Baltimore and we based our position
choices on where they settled defensively after they joined the list.

This is a very subjective list. It is based on one person's close observations
during a long exposure to Orioles baseball. You'll probably disagree with at least
some of the selections. You wouldn't be a real baseball fan if you didn't.

First base: Right off the bat there is a very difficult choice to be made
between Eddie Murray and Boog Powell. Boog's season in Rochester (1961, the
first year of the working agreement) was the more sensational. He batted .321,
crashed 32 homers, and 92 RBI—and he met his future wife, Rochester native
Jan Swinton.

Murray spent less than half a season in Rochester. He was called up from
Double-A Charlotte in mid-July 1976 after Jim Fuller broke his thumb. His
numbers were more modest than Powell's (11 homers, 40 RBI, .274), but you
can't argue with three thousand hits and nearly five hundred homers in the big
leagues.

The choice is Murray.

Second base: Though he was primarily a shortstop for the Red Wings,
Bobby Grich was the best defensive second baseman in the American League for
three years with the Orioles, on a par with the great former Pirate Bill Mazeroski.
Twice he accepted more than 900 chances defensively, a level reserved only for
those with great range, and in 1973 he committed only five errors in 945 chances.
That computes to a .995 fielding percentage, still an American League record.

Grich perhaps never matched his International League promise as a hitter.
In 1970, he hit .383 for the Wings in sixty-three games before being called up to
Baltimore and in 1971 he batted .336-32-83, but he was always a formidable
presence at the plate and averaged fourteen homers in five full seasons with
Baltimore.

Dave Johnson is the runner-up in our balloting, slightly ahead of Rich
Dauer, who was remarkably consistent defensively but lacked range and didn't
have quite as much power as Grich and Johnson.

Shortstop: The Orioles have had three world-class shortstops in their forty-two seasons—Luis Aparicio, Mark Belanger, and Cal Ripken, Jr.—and Belanger and Ripken played for the Wings.

Ripken actually played more third base at Rochester (Bob Bonner was the regular shortstop in 1981) but in Baltimore, Earl Weaver moved him to shortstop on July 1, 1982, one month into his consecutive games streak. The move was highly controversial at the time, but Earl was right. He usually was.

Belanger probably had more range than Cal and he won eight Gold Gloves, but Ripken has hit more homers than any shortstop in history. He'll own most of the Orioles career offensive records before he's through and he's a lock for the Hall of Fame.

Ripken one, Belanger two.

Third base: Doug DeCinces by a landslide. He played two years with the Red Wings before succeeding Brooks Robinson in Baltimore. DeCinces still ranks as the Orioles' second-best third baseman of all time. He was one of those players who became far more productive with the bat as a big leaguer than he ever was in the minors. In other words, he rose to the challenge.

Outfield: I'm taking the liberty of naming a four-man outfield: Paul Blair, the club's best-ever center fielder and an eight-time Gold Glover, who occasionally hit for surprising power; Al Bumbry, the fastest runner in Orioles history (at least until rookie Curtis Goodwin made the scene in June 1995) and a man who made himself into a fine hitter and fielder; Merv Rettenmund, who led the Orioles in hitting in two of their three consecutive American League championship seasons (1969–71) after batting .331 and winning International League MVP honors for Rochester in 1968; and Gary Roenicke, an unspectacular but highly competent left fielder who put up some big numbers for the Orioles back in the days when winning was the name of the game. He hit .307 for the Wings in 1978.

Brady Anderson would be on this list except he played only twenty-eight games for Rochester spread over two years. He's the best left fielder and one of the two best leadoff men (along with Don Buford) the Orioles have ever had.

Designated hitter: Don't get mad at me for leaving Don Baylor off the list of outfielders. He's up next. He was a fair outfielder with a weak arm caused by a football injury, but my-oh-my what he added to the offense and to the character of his ball club. What a shame he couldn't have spent his entire career in the Baltimore organization as he so desperately wanted to.

Pinch hitter: Terry Crowley, all by himself.

Catcher: Over the years, the Orioles' biggest weakness from a player development standpoint has been catching. The O's have won more Gold Gloves than any other American League club, but no Baltimore catcher has ever been so honored.

The three who have created the most impact have been Gus Triandos, Rick Dempsey, and Chris Hoiles. Triandos and Dempsey came to the O's directly from the Yankees. Hoiles originally was a Tiger but played the better part of two years for the Red Wings—and hit .348 for the 1990 Governors' Cup champions—before he was ready to move up. Hoiles gets my vote.

Starting pitchers: Jim Palmer was unquestionably the best pitcher the Orioles have ever had, but he isn't eligible for this team. In two stints for the Wings in 1967–78 he pitched only eleven innings while recovering from shoulder injuries. The only thing memorable about his Rochester tour was that he gave up the lone grand slam of his career, to Buffalo's Johnny Bench.

For our purposes, the top left-handers were Mike Flanagan and Scott McGregor, who won 141 and 138 games for Baltimore, respectively. Among right-handers, the remarkable Nicaraguan Dennis Martinez, who has overcome alcoholism and gone on to win more than 200 games in the majors, is the first choice. He's followed by big-game winner Mike Boddicker, a twenty-game winner for Baltimore in 1984.

Relief pitchers: Among the Orioles' career saves leaders through 1995, only three—Eddie Watt, Tim Stoddard, and Sammy Stewart—ever pitched for the Wings. We'll take Stoddard because he had one dominant year, 1980, when he set what then was a club record with 26 saves.

The best of the bunch turned out to be Darold Knowles, who saved 143 games in 747 relief appearances spread over sixteen seasons, while compiling a 3.12 ERA for eight different clubs.

Manager: This is an easy one. Earl Weaver was one of the best and most creative managers in modern history. Many of his players disliked him when they played for him. Ask them now, and most will tell you they were the happiest days of their baseball careers. Winning will do that to you. Weaver led the 1966 Red Wings to the International League pennant and captured four AL flags (and one World Series) with the O's. The runner-up is Joe Altobelli, a legend in Rochester and the last man to bring the Orioles a World Series title.

Rochester Red Wings
All-Time Roster: 1928–1995

The statistics below were supplied by the Rochester Red Wings. In cases where the number of games is limited and no statistics are available, the category has been left blank.

All-Time Batters Roster

Name	Year	Avg.	HR	RBI
Adams, Earl "Sparky"	1935	.167	1	1
Adams, Elvin "Buster"	1940	.190	3	21
Aleno, Charles	1942	.270	0	5
Alexander, Manny	1992	.292	0	3
	1993	.244	6	51
	1994	.249	6	39
Alfaro, Jesus	1982	.250	0	0
Alfonzo, Edgar	1995	.185	1	5
Allen, Harold "Hank"	1970	.348	2	24
Allen, Kim	1978	.288	2	14
Allen, Rod	1985	.234	7	32
Allietta, Bob	1977	.226	3	19
Alomar, Antonio	1957	.274	3	26
	1958	.224	0	9
Alstead, Jason	1993	.178	0	4
Alston, Tom	1954	.297	7	42
Alston, Walter	1937	.246	6	36
	1943	.240	5	40
	1944	.158	0	2

Name		Year	Avg.	HR	RBI
Altobelli, Joe		1963	.244	15	44
		1964	.249	11	52
		1965	.295	20	59
		1966	.233	1	5
Alvarez, Oswald		1964	.000	0	0
Amaro, Ruben		1958	.200	1	20
Anderson, Brady		1989	.200	1	8
		1991	.400	0	2
Anderson, George		1930	.293	1	14
Andrew, Kim		1977	.313	0	4
Andrews, Robert		1974	.306	5	55
Ankenman, Fred "Pat"		1939	.219	0	11
Asbell, Jim		1939	.291	8	58
Asbury, Tom	(Roch.-Tor.)	1944	.252	4	42
Ashford, Tucker		1984	.247	7	40
Ayala, Benny		1979	.355	1	7
Babe, Loren		1958	.267	3	30
Backer, Leonard		1936	.269	0	32
Baez, Kevin		1994	.237	2	42
Baich, Dan		1953	.185	0	2
Bailor, Bob		1973	.277	1	4
		1974	.230	1	25
		1975	.293	5	39
		1976	.311	1	12
Baranca, German		1983	.230	9	27
Barker, Ray		1961	.248	15	63
		1967	.242	12	47
Barnes, Bill		1943	.235	2	14
Baron, Charley		1945	.221	3	33
		1946	.284	7	50
		1947	.243	0	5
Barrios, José		1983	.265	10	30
Bartee, Kimera		1995	.154	0	3
Bartholomei, Francis		1943	.143		
Barton, Larry		1932	.097	0	1
		1933	.000	0	0
		1935	.197	0	4
		1936	.246	3	10
Bates, Del	(Rich.-Roch.)	1968	.268	5	24
Batiste, Kim		1995	.281	3	28
Baugh, Ray		1945	.280	0	45
Baugh, Sammy		1938	.183	1	11
Baylor, Don		1968	.217	0	4
		1970	.327	22	107
		1971	.313	20	95

Name		Year	Avg.	HR	RBI
Beal, Floyd		1938	.400	0	
		1939	.267	4	36
		1940	.200	1	5
		1943	.000	0	0
Belanger, Mark		1966	.262	6	38
Bell, Juan		1989	.262	2	32
		1990	.285	6	35
		1992	.196	2	14
Benson, Vernon		1947	.274	6	30
		1948	.246	4	38
		1949	.204	1	10
		1953	.303	6	34
		1954	.240	6	31
		1955	.227	14	45
Bentley, John		1931	.306	1	8
Bergamo, August		1940	.286	6	68
		1941	.273	3	27
Berra, Dale		1988	.181	3	13
Bessent, Donald		1962	.333	0	3
Bianco, Tom		1978	.286	7	44
		1979	.219	2	26
Bilko, Steve		1948	.146	0	3
		1949	.310	34	125
		1950	.290	15	58
		1951	.282	8	50
		1952	.322	12	55
		1963	.261	8	37
Binder, George		1931	.257	0	22
Bjorkman, George		1985	.242	5	14
Blackberry, George		1937	.263	1	24
Blades, Ray		1929	.146	0	2
Bladt, Richard		1977	.226	6	32
Blair, Horace		1937	.400		
Blair, Paul		1964	.130	2	5
		1965	.329	4	21
Blakely, Lincoln		1940	.256	1	22
Blatnik, John	(Syr.-Roch.)	1952	.274	17	66
Blattner, Bob "Buddy"		1942	.244	4	25
Blefary, Curt		1964	.287	31	80
Bollweg, Don		1950	.313	17	60
Bonaparte, Elijah		1983	.273	4	48
Bonner, Bobby		1979	.273	0	0
		1980	.241	2	41
		1981	.229	3	35
		1982	.206	2	18

Name		Year	Avg.	HR	RBI
Bonner, Bobby *(cont.)*		1983	.222	1	15
		1984	.277	1	26
Borgmann, Ben		1933	.341	0	9
		1934	.279	1	42
Bourjos, Chris		1981	.249	4	16
		1982	.261	5	33
Bowa, Frank		1945	.233	0	32
Bowens, Sam		1962	.269	11	49
		1963	.287	22	70
		1965	.275	3	19
Brandt, Jack		1955	.305	12	70
Breeding, Marv		1964	.222	0	5
		1965	.263	10	54
Breese, Eldon		1938	.224	0	7
Brewster, Charles		1947	.236	4	58
Broome, Roy		1950	.271	1	21
Brown, Darrell		1985	.180	0	0
Brown, Donald		1958	.196	1	4
Brown, James		1934	.259	1	41
		1935	.241	3	51
		1936	.309	5	45
Brown, Jarvis		1995	.314	0	4
Brown, Joe	(Jer.Cty.-Roch.)	1928	.313	6	74
		1929	.284	4	81
		1930	.313	10	68
		1932	.277	4	60
	(Roch.-Buf.-Jer.Cty.)	1933	.289	3	48
Brown, Marty		1990	.242	5	25
Brown, Randy		1973	.223	2	14
Brummer, Don		1963	.219	4	26
Brunsberg, Arlo	(Roch.-Tol.)	1969	.228	13	48
Bucha, John		1946	.211	0	11
		1948	.303	2	24
		1949	.289	8	47
		1951	.261	3	45
		1952	.284	6	72
Buchek, Gerald		1960	.226	5	22
Buddin, Donald		1964	.246	0	5
Buford, Damon		1992	.284	1	12
		1993	.284	1	4
		1994	.270	16	66
		1995	.309	4	18
Bumbry, Al		1972	.345	6	47
		1993	.284	1	4

Name		Year	Avg.	HR	RBI
Burbrink, Nelson		1954	.256	0	45
		1955	.245	0	13
Burda, Robert		1959	.250	0	4
Burgess, Tom		1953	.346	22	93
		1954	.236	10	34
		1955	.285	10	50
		1956	.281	10	71
		1957	.289	22	72
		1958	.276	19	63
Burgett, Dick		1948	.406	0	7
		1949	.277	4	54
Burman, John		1944	.280	1	39
Burmeister, Gerald		1943	.239	4	44
Burnett, Ora		1942	.253	3	35
		1944	.251	4	36
Burright, Larry		1964	.229	1	11
Burton, Ellis		1960	.257	14	40
Busco, John		1974	.000	0	0
Bush, Loll		1936	.365	1	8
Byrd, Samuel		1937		vol. retired	
Byrne, Clayton		1994	.000	0	0
Byrne, James	(Syr.-Roch.)	1936	.235	0	13
Cabell, Enos		1972	.269	8	66
		1973	.354	2	24
Calise, Mike		1983	.254	13	34
		1984	.235	17	45
Campbell, Darrin		1993	.183	1	11
Campbell, James		1969	.274	20	76
Cannizzaro, Chris		1960	.251	5	44
		1962	.244	1	12
Cardoza, Donald		1978	.255	11	63
Carey, Paul		1992	.230	1	7
		1993	.311	12	50
		1994	.250	8	28
		1995	.236	9	50
Carey, Tom		1933	.297	6	61
		1934	.287	3	81
		1935	.301	3	39
Carmel, Leon "Duke"		1958	.222	7	19
		1959	.172	0	1
		1960	.211	3	15
Carpenter, William		1960	.000	0	0
Carreon, Camilo	(Roch.-Jck.)	1966	.264	3	11
		1967	.145	0	8

Name		Year	Avg.	HR	RBI
Caufield, John		1947	.182		
Cazen, Walter		1940	.327	4	33
Chance, Tony		1990	.269	14	75
		1991	.251	14	55
Chism, Tom		1978	.317	10	62
		1979	.312	11	60
		1980	.257	8	29
		1981	.255	12	44
Chiti, Harry		1961	.326	11	25
Christian, Joe		1958	.245	3	26
		1959	.238	1	4
		1962	.188	0	6
Ciaffone, Larry		1947	.231	2	11
		1950	.324	10	53
		1951	.240	5	28
		1952	.279	4	62
Cijntje, Sherwin		1987	.286	0	7
		1988	.227	2	12
		1989	.200	0	7
Cimo, Matt		1988	.253	8	20
Cimoli, Gino		1964	.315	4	23
Clapp, Terry		1974	.000	0	0
Clark, Allie		1953	.328	7	43
		1954	.323	18	81
		1955	.308	23	84
		1956	.289	15	75
		1957	.285	12	57
Clark, Earl	(Roch.-Balt.)	1934	.244	2	24
Clark, J. C.		1936	.322	1	9
Clay, Dain		1940	.150	0	1
		1941	.234	4	24
		1943	.264	0	6
Clayton, Larry		1965	.114	2	9
		1968	.222	0	0
Cobb, Bernie		1938	.284	3	37
		1939	.000		
Cochran, Nielsen		1965	.200	1	10
Coggins, Richie		1970	.279	3	19
		1971	.282	20	53
		1972	.322	10	45
Cole, Dick		1948	.252	4	22
		1949	.236	7	43
		1950	.278	4	44
Coleman, David		1965	.500	0	0

Name		Year	Avg.	HR	RBI
Collins, James "Rip"		1928	.375	4	
		1929	.315	38	134
		1930	.376	40	180
Collins, Steve		1943	.000		
Connally, Fritz		1985	.214	6	22
Connell, Truman		1937	.200	0	4
Contreras, Joaquin		1990	.250	1	29
		1991	.000	0	0
Cooke, Allen Lindsay		1939	.340	4	74
		1942	.232	2	33
Coolbaugh, Scott		1993	.245	18	67
Corbett, Ray		1985	.222	0	1
Corey, Mark		1978	.324	5	40
		1979	.249	10	30
		1980	.230	3	25
		1981	.239	1	5
		1982	.000	0	0
Cosgrove, Francis		1944	.200	1	9
Cosmidis, Alex		1958	.174	1	9
Costa, Billy		1946	.167		
Cotelle, Como	(Roch.-J.Cty.)	1931	.307	5	44
Courtney, Clinton		1961	.217	0	4
Crabtree, Estel		1933	.299	3	27
		1934	.313	15	89
		1935	.279	15	68
		1936	.346	14	65
		1937	.281	15	86
		1938	.300	12	82
		1939	.337	14	94
		1940	.314	3	30
Craig, Rodney		1987	.179	0	5
Cregar, Bernard		1945	.286		
		1946	.256	0	5
		1947	.229	0	36
Crespi, Frank "Creepy"		1939	.259	0	1
		1940	.301	6	80
Criscione, Dave		1977	.285	7	45
		1978	.261	7	22
Cross, Joffre		1942	.131	0	2
Crouch, John		1937	.342	1	8
Crowley, Jim		1995	.173	1	6
Crowley, Terry		1968	.262	8	34
		1969	.282	28	83
		1971	.282	19	63

Name	Year	Avg.	HR	RBI
Crowley, Terry *(cont.)*	1976	.261	2	7
	1977	.308	30	80
Crumling, Eugene	1945	.257	0	10
Cruz, Todd	1985	.091	0	1
Cuccinello, Al	1936	.311	8	82
	1937	.239	6	30
Cullop, Nick	1932	.267	14	
Cunningham, Joe	1954	.318	8	42
	1955	.275	10	70
	1956	.319	11	73
Cunningham, Ray	1929	.206	0	2
Dagres, Angelo	1962	.111	0	0
Dauer, Rich	1975	.170	0	0
	1976	.336	11	78
Davis, Butch	1988	.143	0	0
	1989	.303	10	64
Davis, Glenn	1993	.250	0	3
Davis, Harry	1939	.297	21	92
	1940	.304	17	101
	1941	.296	14	88
	1942	.246	7	57
Davis, Otis	1944	.270	4	41
	1945	.195	0	13
DaVanon, Jerry	1972	.206	1	18
Deal, Ellis "Cot"	1952	.277	5	22
	1953	.279	2	30
	1955	.231	0	2
	1956	.311	7	22
	1957	.265	4	23
	1958	.286		
DeCinces, Doug	1973	.267	19	79
	1974	.282	11	66
DeJardin, Bobby	1995	.314	0	3
DelBusto, Oscar	1972	.000	0	0
Delker, Ed	1930	.360	0	8
	1931	.252	1	37
	1936	.000	0	0
Demeter, Steve	1964	.266	16	65
	1965	.299	15	90
	1966	.313	18	82
	1967	.317	5	67
	1968	.301	10	63
Dempsey, Pat	1983	.000	0	0

Name		Year	Avg.	HR	RBI
Derry, Russ		1947	.269	26	89
		1948	.215	16	42
		1949	.279	42	122
		1950	.281	30	102
		1951	.249	19	53
		1952	.141	1	5
Derryberry, Tim		1980	.098	2	5
		1981	.234	17	49
Derucki, Walter		1954	.237	5	33
Detweiler, Bob		1946	.236	5	30
Devarez, Cesar		1995	.250	1	21
Devlin, Jim	(Balt.-Roch.)	1945	.247	4	29
Dickerson, Bobby		1991	.333	0	0
		1992	.241	4	29
		1993	.250	3	18
Dieffenbach, Ray		1938	.207		
Diering, Charles		1946	.266	10	60
		1948	.267	5	61
Diggle, Ronnie		1979	.255	13	38
Dimmel, Mike		1978	.246	8	42
Distefano, Benny		1991	.267	18	83
Dixon, Siverwin		1956	.236	1	8
Dodd, Tom		1986	.163	2	6
Doljack, Frank		1936	.200	1	6
Dostal, Bruce		1993	.294	3	30
		1994	.287	1	36
Downs, Ben		1953	.000	0	0
Doyle, Blake		1977	.234	1	36
		1978	.280	1	23
		1979	.260	0	21
Dulin, Tim		1988	.333	2	6
		1989	.252	5	38
		1990	.238	3	46
Duncan, Louis		1928	.252	0	25
Duncan, Taylor		1975	.284	6	54
		1976	.271	11	69
		1977	.301	27	76
		1979	.235	2	16
Durham, Joseph		1961	.263	10	47
		1962	.281	17	73
		1964	.239	6	18
Durnbaugh, Bobby		1957	.221	0	4
Dusak, Ervin		1941	.304	5	33
		1942	.296	16	57
		1949	.241	4	15

Name		Year	Avg.	HR	RBI
Dwyer, Jim		1988	.296	0	4
Easter, Luke	(Buff.-Roch.)	1959	.262	22	76
		1960	.302	14	57
		1961	.291	10	51
		1962	.281	15	60
		1963	.271	6	35
		1964	.200	0	1
Eaton, Tommy		1981	.216	1	26
Eberle, Mike		1990	.233	0	4
		1991	.178	0	5
Echols, Clint		1946	.000		
Eckenrode, Larry		1972	.216	2	12
Eden, Mike		1979	.270	5	36
		1980	.257	4	31
Emery, Calvin		1962	.292	14	62
Epps, Harold		1935	.295	1	7
		1940	.306	4	36
Epstein, Mike		1966	.309	29	102
Escalera, Nino		1962	.239	4	25
Essegian, Charles		1959	.297	4	5
Estrada, Francisco		1972	.252	6	15
Etchebarren, Andy		1965	.247	6	42
Falcone, Dave		1983	.250	0	2
		1984	.213	5	15
		1985	.237	7	17
		1986	.333	1	4
		1987	.091	0	1
Fallon, George		1940	.273	4	53
		1941	.228	4	51
		1942	.240	2	49
Farson, George		1967	.125	0	0
		1969	.310	2	7
		1970	.237	0	10
		1971	.217	1	3
Fassler, Wally		1951	.114	0	0
		1952	.175	0	2
		1957	.218	1	14
Faulkner, Craig		1989	.000	0	0
		1994	.217	2	10
Fazio, Don		1971	.272	4	37
		1972	.248	2	30
Felix, August	(Buff.-Roch.)	1928	.315	9	94
		1929	.288	5	56
Fernandez, Lorenzo "Chico"		1969	.250	0	0

Name	Year	Avg.	HR	RBI
Ferraro, Mike	1969	.279	4	40
	1970	.304	6	70
	1971	.272	7	65
Finigan, Jim	1961	.234	3	20
Finley, Steve	1988	.314	5	54
	1989	.160	0	2
Fiore, Mike	1966	.244	9	22
	1968	.271	19	62
	1974	.265	15	63
	1975	.268	5	40
	1976	.268	12	64
	1977	.284	19	57
Fisher, George "Showboat"	1931	.325	17	78
	1932	.286	6	29
Flesner, Paul	1972	.252	0	9
Florence, Paul	1929	.265	5	49
	1930	.298	7	54
	1931	.272	10	67
	1932	.256	8	51
	1933	.277	9	40
	1934	.312	5	25
	1935	.314	4	24
Flowers, D'Arcy "Jake"	1935	.275	15	62
Floyd, Bob	1967	.243	1	25
	1968	.287	6	52
	1970	.290	1	14
Fourroux, Lloyd	1967	.114	1	2
Frantz, Art	1945	.211	0	17
Frazier, Fred	1973	.230	2	32
Freed, Roger	1970	.334	24	130
Frey, Jim	1959	.296	11	42
	1960	.317	16	66
Friedman, Jason	1995	.377	4	9
Fuller, Jim	1972	.228	11	37
	1973	.247	39	108
	1974	.278	5	16
	1975	.213	17	50
	1976	.227	19	55
Fusselman, Lester	1948	.230	1	15
	1953	.249	5	25
Gainer, Del	1928	.328	0	8
Galliher, Marv	1974	.265	3	31
Garcia, Alfonso "Kiko"	1975	.244	3	32
	1976	.276	3	44

Name		Year	Avg.	HR	RBI
Garriott, Cecil		1938	.000		
Gates, Mike		1984	.206	0	1
Geiger, Gary		1957	.223	9	24
Gelbert, Charley		1928	.340	21	116
Gerhart, Ken		1986	.274	28	72
Gibson, Bob		1937	.235	3	16
Gibson, John		1947	.000		
Gilbert, Jerome		1965	.278	0	1
Gilbert, Walter		1933	.300	2	32
Gillenwater, Carden		1938	.278	1	46
		1939	.252	3	28
		1941	.283	0	7
Glenn, John		1960	.233	2	7
Gomez, Leo		1990	.277	26	97
		1991	.257	6	19
		1993	.200	0	1
Gonzales, Dan		1980	.294	6	31
Gonzales, Rene		1987	.300	0	24
Goodman, Ival "Goodie"		1933	.266	3	11
		1934	.331	19	122
Goodwin, Curtis		1995	.264	0	7
Gotay, Julio		1960	.224	1	12
Gowdy, Harry		1928	.252	3	22
Graham, Dan		1980	.346	4	12
		1982	.272	11	50
Grandcolas, Al		1956	.000	0	0
		1957	.000	0	0
	(Roch.-Havana)	1958	.211	3	19
Granger, Lee		1984	.222	0	1
		1985	.245	5	18
Gravino, Frank		1948	.277	18	74
Green, Gene		1956	.300	23	96
		1957	.299	20	87
		1959	.305	19	71
Green, Lee		1965	.000	0	0
Green, Leonard		1958	.261	1	10
Gresham, Kris		1995	.250	0	4
Grich, Bobby		1970	.383	10	42
		1971	.336	32	83
Griffin, John		1963	.204	1	11
		1964	.240	8	33
Gulliver, Glenn		1982	.295	12	35
		1983	.309	11	62
		1984	.216	3	13
		1986	.118	1	1

Name		Year	Avg.	HR	RBI
Gutierrez, Jackie		1986	.303	1	22
		1987	.255	2	25
Gutierrez, Ricky		1991	.306	0	15
		1992	.253	0	41
Hale, John		1981	.220	5	16
Halkard, Jim		1946	.265	0	6
Hamlin, Ken		1963	.249	13	50
Hammonds, Jeffrey		1993	.311	5	23
Haney, Larry		1966	.213	7	7
Harlow, Larry		1974	.200	0	0
		1975	.255	2	31
		1976	.247	7	47
		1977	.335	9	50
Harrell, Billy		1959	.266	17	69
		1960	.293	15	78
Harris, Dunray		1966	.000	0	0
Harris, Walt		1989	.219	1	24
		1990	.154	0	1
Hart, Mike	(Tol.-Roch.)	1981	.258	10	33
		1982	.237	3	7
		1986	.256	13	50
		1987	.257	20	61
Hayworth, Ray		1942	.192	0	
Hazen, Vaughn		1944	.192	0	6
		1949	.184	1	3
Hazewood, Drungo		1981	.094	1	6
		1983	.224	3	18
Healy, Francis		1935	.271	0	14
Heath, Minor "Mickey"		1932	.267	7	18
		1933	.283	9	42
Heil, Charles	(Tide.-Roch.)	1976	.187	0	7
Held, Herschel		1943	.225	0	13
		1944	.254	5	67
Henderson, W.	(Buff.-Roch.)	1928	.138	1	5
Hernandez, Enzo		1970	.266	1	39
Hernandez, Leo		1982	.317	11	43
		1983	.343	8	25
		1984	.275	21	83
		1985	.269	17	69
Herrera, Roberto	(Roc.-Atl.)	1962	.236	1	15
Herring, Allen		1959	.125	0	0
Hertweck, Neal		1956	.227	2	9
Hickey, Don		1974	.209	2	19
		1975	.231	3	17
Hickman, James		1960	.200	1	2

Name		Year	Avg.	HR	RBI
Hinkle, Gordon		1930	.321	0	3
		1933	.324	2	39
Hinzo, Tommy		1993	.271	6	69
Hitchcock, Jim		1940	.105		
Hithe, Victor		1990	.274	0	15
Hockenberry, Charles		1946	.278	2	21
Hoiles, Chris		1989	.245	10	51
		1990	.348	18	56
Holland, Tim		1993	.107	0	0
Holm, Roscoe "Watty"		1931	.278	1	30
		1932	.311	0	11
Hood, Dennis		1994	.111	0	0
Hopkins, Clifford		1942	.267	0	1
Hopp, Johnny		1937	.307	9	69
		1938	.299	9	48
Hopper, Robert Clay		1928	.444	1	7
Horn, Sam		1990	.414	9	26
House, Frank		1961	.260	3	21
Hovley, Steve		1969	.294	8	24
		1974	.203	3	18
Hudler, Rex		1986	.260	2	13
		1987	.255	5	10
Huesman, John		1953	.204	0	14
		1956	.209	2	9
Hughes, Keith		1988	.270	7	49
		1989	.274	2	43
Hulett, Tim		1989	.280	3	50
		1990	.372	2	4
Hunnefield, Bill (Jer.Cty.-Alb.-Roch.)		1932	.266	4	36
		1935	.158	0	1
Hunt, Joel		1931	.252	1	18
Huppert, Dave	(Tol.-Roch.)	1981	.182	2	12
		1983	.199	0	11
Hurst, Frank		1928	.308	1	16
Huson, Jeff		1995	.251	3	21
Hussey, John	(Buff.-Roch.)	1950	.250	4	11
Hutto, Jim		1971	.285	15	73
		1973	.206	4	28
		1974	.220	15	49
		1975	.239	12	42
		1976	.243	7	32
Irving, James		1935	.271	0	7
Isherwood, Norman		1936	.000		

Name		Year	Avg.	HR	RBI
Jablonski, Ray		1952	.299	18	103
Jackson, Lou		1964	.262	23	71
		1965	.248	18	61
Jackson, Ron		1984	.161	0	1
James, Arthur		1979	.261	3	21
James, Charles		1959	.300	18	79
		1960	.248	3	12
Jarquin, G. "Skeeter"		1977	.278	0	7
		1978	.150	0	1
Jarrell, Joe		1989	.125	0	3
Javet, Lloyd		1933	.220	1	2
Jefferson, Stanley		1989	.259	3	36
Jeltz, Steve		1991	.189	1	24
Jennings, Doug		1992	.275	14	76
Jimenez, Manuel		1965	.296	13	59
Johnson, David		1963	.246	6	22
		1964	.264	19	73
		1965	.301	4	22
Johnson, Elijah		1969	.301	14	63
		1970	.271	20	104
Johnson, Larry		1971	.307	5	39
		1972	.268	5	24
		1973	.248	5	60
Johnson, Larry Doby		1979	.313	3	14
Johnson, Owen		1967	.214	5	30
		1968	.188	0	2
Johnson, Robert Wallace		1961	.332	16	65
Jok, Stan	(Jer.Cty.-Roch.)	1955	.290	16	84
		1956	.253	4	17
		1961	.175	0	0
Jones, Rick		1982	.230	13	51
		1983	.232	7	38
		1984	.224	6	16
		1985	.173	0	4
		1986	.251	9	56
Jones, Vernal "Nippy"		1946	.344	5	55
		1947	.337	10	81
		1951	.305	5	24
Jonnard, Clarence "Bubber"		1930	.234	0	22
		1931	.293	1	28
	(Roch.-Jer.Cty.)	1932	.263	1	25
Joost, Ed		1946	.276	19	101
Jordan, Jim	(Roch.-Jer.Cty.)	1931	.276	4	37

Name		Year	Avg.	HR	RBI
Juelich, Jack		1937	.309	5	52
		1938	.262	2	60
Kabbes, Ron		1959	.177	0	8
		1960	.187	0	7
		1961	.264	5	41
		1962	.215	3	45
		1963	.211	2	15
Kahn, Lou		1952	.273	0	8
		1953	.278	0	5
Kasko, Eddie		1956	.303	9	67
Katt, Ray		1958	.285	11	42
		1960	.261	0	3
Kaufmann, Tony		1928	.402	0	30
Kazak, Ed		1947	.125	0	1
		1948	.309	12	85
Keane, Johnny		1935	.000	0	0
Kelley, William	(Roch.-Buff.)	1928	.279	10	73
Kelly, Jay Thomas		1976	.289	18	70
Kennedy, Junior		1972	.240	3	33
		1973	.219	1	15
Kennedy, Kevin		1977	.279	0	3
		1978	.254	4	58
		1979	.197	3	32
		1980	.263	1	28
		1981	.183	0	5
Kimm, Bruce		1977	.167	0	11
King, Joe		1943	.279	0	32
		1945	.255	1	68
King, Lewis		1944	.000		
Kingwood, Tyrone		1991	.312	1	18
Kluch, William		1932	.246	0	4
Knapp, Mike		1995	.183	1	12
Komminsk, Brad		1990	.291	1	8
Koval, Tom		1943	.242	5	37
Kravitz, Dan	(Rich.-Roch.)	1962	.274	18	60
		1963	.235	8	28
Krenchicki, Wayne		1978	.296	12	71
		1979	.261	0	22
		1980	.264	2	39
		1981	.214	0	6
Kress, Charles		1947	.281	7	42
		1951	.261	12	42
		1952	.226	0	6
		1953	.317	25	121

Name		Year	Avg.	HR	RBI
Krug, Everett "Chris"		1963	.133	0	1
Kubski, Al		1946	.276	19	101
Kunes, Edward		1932	.231	2	10
Kurowski, George "Whitey"		1939	.291	11	68
		1940	.279	15	73
		1941	.288	13	69
Lachemann, Rene		1968	.000	0	0
Lammers, Wally		1952	.287	1	11
		1953	.180	1	19
Lancelotti, Luco		1944	.220	0	17
		1945	.199	0	18
Landreaux, Ken		1988	.272	7	23
Landrum, Tito		1988	.235	1	4
LaPointe, Ralph		1949	.273	3	35
Lassetter, Don		1955	.268	3	8
		1958	.269	16	73
Layne, Harry		1928	.312	6	56
	(Roch.-Balt.)	1929	.304	10	74
Leahy, Clifford		1936	.000		
LeBlanc, Rolland		1942	.267	0	4
Lehman, Mike		1992	.190	0	1
Leonard, Charles		1967	.222	0	4
Leonard, Mark		1993	.276	17	58
Lewis, T. R.		1994	.305	6	31
		1995	.295	4	19
Lewis, William "Bud"		1934	.317	3	69
Liddell, David		1992	.107	1	2
Liggett, Jim		1964	.275	10	35
		1965	.222	3	19
Lillard, Eugene		1940	.222	1	8
		1941	.262	12	49
		1942	.261	11	62
Liranzo, Rafael		1977	.251	6	26
		1978	.220	11	56
Lisi, Rick		1981	.231	6	40
		1983	.252	3	7
Lofton, Rodney		1990	.143	0	0
		1991	.000	0	1
		1992	.235	0	8
Logan, Dan		1980	.195	2	16
		1981	.255	23	73
		1982	.288	19	68
		1983	.269	11	56
Lomastro, Gerry		1987	.264	2	12

Name		Year	Avg.	HR	RBI
Lonnett, Joe	(Buff.-Roch.)	1962	.182	6	24
Lopez, Carlos		1979	.282	6	30
Lucas, Fred		1930	.293	1	16
Lund, Gordon		1968	.275	1	15
		1969	.280	0	8
Machemer, David		1979	.292	1	31
Mack, Joe	(Tor.-Roch.)	1942	.231	4	36
		1943	.263	9	51
Madden, Bill	(Tol.-Roch.)	1966	.229	11	30
Maddern, Clarence	(Mi.-Roch.)	1957	.290	4	25
Magrann, Tom		1988	.294	0	0
Malinosky, Anthony		1937	.342	0	10
		1938	.160		
Malone, Edward		1944	.269	1	23
Mancuso, Gustave		1929	.310	9	35
Manto, Jeff	(Nor.-Roch.)	1994	.297	31	100
Marion, Marty		1937	.246	4	37
		1938	.249	2	21
		1939	.272	5	53
Marsh, Fred		1945	.267	0	32
Marshall, Charles		1946	.217	0	9
		1947	.228	2	19
		1948	.208	6	34
		1949	.260	3	22
		1950	.203	0	17
Martin, Frank		1945	.182	0	2
Martin, John "Pepper"		1930	.363	20	114
		1943	.280	1	12
Martinez, Chito		1991	.322	20	50
		1993	.262	5	23
Martinez, Pedro		1966	.000	0	0
Mason, John		1965	.277	2	29
		1966	.298	5	51
		1967	.254	5	31
		1968	.198	0	6
Mata, Vic		1988	.224	1	14
Matchick, Tom		1972	.252	11	59
		1975	.276	2	33
		1976	.265	4	44
Mateosky, Bernard		1960	.304	12	48
May, Dave		1966	.274	11	34
		1967	.317	11	57
		1968	.310	4	17
Mayer, Hector		1953	.188	1	6

Name		Year	Avg.	HR	RBI
McAllister, Fred		1952	.230	3	21
McArdle, James		1954	.094	0	2
McCardell, Roger		1961	.143	1	2
McCarver, Tim		1959	.357	0	8
McClain, Scott		1995	.251	8	22
McDowell, Oddibe		1991	.231	4	22
McGinnis, Russ		1995	.182	3	11
McGrew, Alvin	(Roch.-Tol.)	1975	.257	6	25
	(Roch.-Syr.)	1976	.183		
McGuire, Mickey		1961	.186	0	1
		1964	.215	2	19
		1966	.307	3	38
		1967	.255	3	46
		1968	.148	0	2
		1969	.292	8	63
McKnight, Jeff		1990	.280	7	45
		1991	.383	1	18
McKnight, Jim		1959	.197	2	10
McLemore, Mark		1991	.281	1	18
McMillan, Tom		1977	.274	0	12
McWeeney, Jack	(Jack.-Roch.)	1945	.202	4	17
Meadows, Scott		1991	.339	5	42
		1992	.259	1	9
Melendez, Francisco		1989	.258	9	78
Mercedes, Luis		1991	.334	2	36
		1992	.313	3	29
Mesner, Steve		1941	.271	0	9
Mickelson, Ed		1952	.269	2	27
Mierkowicz, Ed		1949	.293	15	88
		1950	.293	7	64
		1951	.287	5	35
		1953	.303	9	53
Miller, Brent		1994	.000	0	0
Miller, Darrell		1990	.204	0	0
Miller, Lemmie		1985	.250	1	10
Mills, Colonel "Buster"		1932	.360	1	8
		1933	.309	7	64
		1934	.269	4	40
		1935	.313	8	75
		1936	.331	18	134
Miranda, Art		1969	.271	1	34
		1970	.172	0	5
		1971	.194	0	4

Name		Year	Avg.	HR	RBI
Mize, Johnny		1933	.352	8	32
		1934	.339	17	66
		1935	.317	12	44
		1953	.307	12	61
Mizerak, Steve		1943	.212	1	17
		1944	.240	0	
		1945	.249	4	23
Mokan, John	(Buff.-Roch.)	1928	.317	8	63
Molinaro, Bob		1985	.250	12	35
Monahan, Peter	(Buff.-Roch.)	1928	.282	9	55
Montgomery, Reggie		1988	.000	0	0
Moore, Al		1931	.317	0	58
		1932	.311	2	23
Moore, Billy		1989	.199	4	28
Moore, Eugene		1935	.324	16	81
Moore, Howard		1934	.250		
Moore, Jim		1934	.188	0	4
	(Roch.-Syr.)	1935	.329	4	40
Moore, Wilcy		1958	.240	1	3
Mora, Andres		1976	.328	6	15
		1977	.301	11	45
		1978	.227	4	10
Morehouse, Frank		1937	.267	3	17
		1938	.282	5	38
Morrow, Boyce		1928	.288	2	48
		1929	.293	3	18
Morrow, John		1943	.136	0	1
Motton, Curt		1966	.337	4	13
		1967	.323	18	70
		1973	.222	2	11
		1974	.300	8	46
Mozzah, Maurice		1957	.270	5	40
Mueller, Ray		1940	.240	5	34
		1941	.240	7	47
Murray, Eddie		1976	.274	11	40
Murtaugh, Danny		1939	.326	0	6
		1946	.322	0	62
Musial, Stan		1941	.326	3	21
Myers, Frank		1937	.129	0	1
Myers, Fred		1929	.324	0	0
Myers, Lynn		1940	.189	2	10
		1941	.305	1	33
Myers, William		1931	.225	3	15
		1932	.223	1	13

Name		Year	Avg.	HR	RBI
Narron, Jerry		1988	.250	8	33
Narron, Sam		1938	.311	7	49
		1939	.302	9	62
		1942	.257	5	19
Naylor, Earl		1943	.255	4	57
		1944	.288	4	37
Neis, Bernard		1933	.192	0	3
Nelson, Glenn "Rocky"		1947	.056	0	2
Nelson, Melvin		1956	.244	4	35
		1957	.133	0	0
Nichols, Carl		1987	.255	11	52
		1988	.228	3	16
Nichols, Leroy		1944	.290	2	26
		1945	.303	4	87
		1946	.232	0	8
Nicholson, David		1961	.091	0	3
Nietopski, Ed		1950	.210	3	35
Nixon, Donell		1990	.247	2	26
Noboa, Junior		1995	.100	0	2
Nordbrook, Tim		1973	.210	0	10
Norman, Nelson		1985	.186	2	11
Oates, Johnny		1970	.375	0	4
		1971	.277	7	44
Obando, Sherman		1994	.330	20	69
		1995	.293	9	53
O'Brien, John		1958	.323	1	9
		1959	.208	2	7
O'Brien, Tom		1947	.239	5	42
Ochoa, Alex		1995	.274	8	46
O'Donnell, Harry	(Buff.-Roch.)	1928	.284		
Oertel, Charles		1961	.277	2	25
O'Farrell, Bob		1936	.276	2	43
		1937	.232	0	20
Ogrodowski, Bruce		1938	.214	2	30
Olivares, Ed		1958	.167		
Oliver, Gene		1958	.282	18	64
		1959	.283	15	57
		1960	.263	12	40
Olsen, Bernard		1949	.143	0	3
O'Malley, Tom		1985	.302	10	44
		1986	.307	9	30
O'Neill, Paul		1980	.194	0	6
Oquendo, Ismael		1984	.230	2	11

Name	Year	Avg.	HR	RBI
O'Rear, John	1977	.251	5	40
Ortiz, Alejandro	1987	.167	0	1
Ortiz, Lou	1950	.227	12	54
	1951	.245	7	50
	1952	.263	9	73
	1953	.298	11	81
	1954	.225	4	49
Ott, William	1965	.264	2	33
Overman, Joe	1943	.186	0	5
	1944	.255	0	23
Owens, Billy	1995	.143	0	1
Padget, Chris	1987	.257	7	29
	1988	.220	10	44
	1989	.245	9	51
	1990	.279	6	43
Palacios, Rey	1993	.000	0	0
Pardo, Al	1983	.255	1	31
	1985	.253	8	35
	1986	.213	8	34
Parent, Mark	1992	.287	17	69
	1993	.247	14	56
Parham, Robert	1932	.302	5	39
	1933	.286	6	38
Paris, Kelly	1985	.275	18	67
	1986	.249	11	48
Parrill, Marty	1977	.286	0	0
	1978	.172	2	12
Parrilla, Sam	1971	.333	11	70
	1972	.236	0	12
Payne, Jim "Zip"	1945	.302	1	34
Peel, Homer	1935	.291	3	36
Peete, Charles	1955	.280	1	10
Pellino, Michael	1935	.154		
Pepper, Ray	1929	.278	3	35
	1930	.347	4	78
	1931	.356	8	121
	1932	.298	9	85
	1933	.295	11	100
Perkins, Harold	1989	.282	3	11
Peters, Francis	1967	.241	7	49
	1968	.247	10	60
	1969	.282	3	15
Pfleger, Roy	1942	.282	2	20

Name		Year	Avg.	HR	RBI
Phillips, Howard		1955	.258	2	45
		1956	.238	6	24
Pignatano, Joe	(Roch.-Buff.)	1963	.237	3	27
		1964	.203	4	19
Pinkston, Roy		1943	.143		
Plaskett, Elmo		1968	.212	1	8
Plaza, Ron		1956	.297	5	30
		1957	.221	14	49
Poland, Hugh		1936	.255	13	51
		1937	.242	12	49
Powell, John "Boog"		1961	.321	32	92
Pratt, George		1946	.240	0	10
Puccinelli, George		1931	.295	16	73
		1932	.391	28	115
	(Roch.-New.)	1933	.292	15	92
Purpura, Dan		1983	.239	0	6
Putman, Ed		1980	.256	5	32
		1981	.289	2	8
Pyznarski, Tim		1988	.125	2	5
Rabe, William		1940	.250	2	7
Rac, Russell	(Tor.-Roch.)	1957	.273	9	41
Rand, Bob		1955	.259	1	16
		1956	.278	12	44
Rand, Richard		1959	.244	3	28
Ransom, Jeff		1984	.185	2	8
Rapp, Vern		1954	.133		
Rausch, Bob		1944	.197	0	7
		1945	.324	1	62
		1946	.204	0	9
Rayford, Floyd		1980	.230	9	46
		1981	.248	11	45
		1982	.250	1	2
		1983	.361	2	38
		1984	.056	1	1
		1986	.285	4	17
		1987	.277	10	28
Ready, Randy		1993	.289	9	46
Rebel, Arthur		1946	.251	12	80
Reddish, Mike		1985	.271	13	37
		1986	.295	4	18
Redmond, Henry		1940	.111		
		1941	.324	0	5
Reinbach, Mike		1972	.389	1	4
		1973	.255	11	33

Name		Year	Avg.	HR	RBI
Reinbach, Mike *(cont.)*		1974	.233	5	29
		1975	.290	11	62
Rensa, George		1932	.200	0	11
Repoz, Roger		1972	.251	13	46
Repulski, Eldon "Rip"		1952	.296	13	65
Rettenmund, Merv		1968	.331	22	59
Retzer, Ken		1967	.236	1	13
Rice, Delbert		1943	.198	0	18
		1944	.264	6	50
		1960	.233	1	11
Rice, Harold		1947	.248	5	50
		1948	.321	7	73
		1950	.310	17	79
		1951	.330	12	36
Richmond, Don	(Balt.-Roch.)	1949	.301	8	65
		1950	.333	18	99
		1951	.350	5	49
		1952	.329	6	62
		1953	.312	15	89
	(Roch.-Syr.)	1954	.296	7	50
Richter, Allen		1954	.260	0	46
		1955	.277	0	40
Ricketts, David		1957	.306	0	29
		1960	.091	0	1
Riggan, Percy		1952	.263	13	39
		1954	.229	5	22
Riley, Leon		1932	.277	5	36
Ripken, Billy		1987	.286	0	11
Ripken, Cal, Jr.		1981	.288	23	75
Ripken, Cal, Sr.		1961	.083	1	2
Ripple, Jim		1941	.378	5	22
	(Roch.-Tor.)	1942	.249	14	72
Robbins, Doug		1992	.309	6	46
Robertson, Rod		1995	.278	15	58
Robinson, Earl		1962	.250	0	0
		1963	.262	8	42
		1964	.307	11	39
Robinson, Warren		1941	.219	0	12
		1942	.255	3	36
		1946	.250	0	2
		1947	.172	7	22
Robles, Sergio		1972	.266	5	29
		1973	.207	1	34

Name		Year	Avg.	HR	RBI
Rodriguez, Victor		1982	.247	0	18
		1984	.274	6	46
Roenicke, Gary		1978	.307	13	64
Roettger, Oscar		1937	.253	1	22
		1938	.000		
Rojas, Hilario	(Syr.-Roch.)	1966	.241	1	8
Rollings, Russell		1931	.196	1	5
Romano, Tom		1989	.202	1	12
Rosado, Luis		1984	.291	5	48
		1985	.200	0	4
Roth, Greg		1992	.217	1	2
Rothrock, Jack		1936	.299	5	51
Rowdon, Wade		1988	.252	7	33
Royster, Willie		1979	.281	3	13
		1980	.264	3	35
		1982	.198	1	10
Roznovsky, Vic	(Roch.-Buff.)	1966	.286	2	15
		1968	.238	4	34
Ryan, John	(Tor.-Syr.-Roch.)	1966	.256	3	12
Sadowski, Bob Frank		1960	.223	4	13
Saferight, Harry	(Rich.-Roch.)	1981	.218	2	22
Sainford, Ronald		1961	.227	5	35
St. Clair, Ed	(Roch.-Rich.)	1955	.238	10	43
Sakata, Lenn		1980	.344	3	8
		1985	.214	0	2
Salcedo, Ron		1987	.232	4	28
		1988	.246	3	27
Salmone, William		1933	1.000		
Sanchez, Orlando		1984	.305	3	34
Sand, John Henry "Heinie"		1929	.248	14	101
Saverine, Bobby		1962	.285	11	50
		1965	.267	2	30
Sax, Oliver	(Tor.-Roch.)	1934	.194	1	13
Scarsone, Steve	(SWB.-Roch.)	1992	.256	1	12
Schaefer, Jeff		1984	.264	0	3
		1985	.198	2	12
		1994	.216	0	1
Schaffer, Jim		1970	.253	13	48
Scheffing, Robert		1940	.268	4	38
Schoendienst, Albert "Red"		1943	.337	6	37
		1944	.372	2	14
Schreiber, Ted	(Buff.-Roch.)	1965	.223	1	16
Schu, Rick		1989	.223	1	10
Schuble, Henry		1936	.323	0	3

Name	Year	Avg.	HR	RBI
Scoffic, Louis	1936	.320	10	67
	1937	.326	6	77
	1938	.253	1	19
	1941	.258	1	18
Scott, Donnie	1986	.272	1	16
Scott, Legrant	1941	.298	3	28
Scripture, Bill	1968	.230	8	51
	1969	.265	9	52
Scruggs, John	1966	.207	9	31
	1967	.229	13	44
Segui, David	1990	.336	2	51
	1991	.271	1	10
Selkirk, George	1933	.306	22	108
Seltz, Rolland	1944	.088	0	1
Sepich, John	1967	.143	0	1
Shamburg, Ken	1990	.333	0	0
	1991	.150	0	3
	1992	.209	5	34
Shannon, Wally, Jr.	1959	.290	13	50
	1960	.251	15	58
Shantz, Wilmer	1957	.239	5	36
Sheets, Larry	1983	.154	0	2
	1984	.302	13	67
Shelby, John	1981	.264	3	32
	1982	.279	16	52
	1985	.286	8	21
	1987	.250	1	2
Shelton, Ron	1970	.207	0	1
	1971	.260	1	9
Sher, Robert	1947	.253	8	42
Shetrone, Barry	1961	.277	15	44
Shevlin, James	1932	.274	0	22
Shields, Tommy	1991	.289	6	52
	1992	.302	10	59
Shires, Art	1933	.277	2	24
Shopay, Tommy	1970	.324	7	34
	1973	.266	7	33
	1974	.313	10	36
	1976	.347	4	19
	1977	.350	0	7
Simmons, Nelson	1986	.273	8	37
	1987	.271	3	21
Sisler, George	1931	.303	3	81

Name		Year	Avg.	HR	RBI
Skaggs, Dave		1975	.222	0	10
		1976	.242	2	27
Smalley, Roy		1958	.216	12	51
Smith, Bobby Gene		1959	.252	3	11
Smith, Dana		1989	.000	0	0
Smith, D. L.		1987	.188	1	6
		1988	.230	0	19
Smith, Earl		1930	.239	0	11
Smith, Forest Elwood		1962	.077	0	0
Smith, Greg		1995	.229	4	21
Smith, Ira		1928	.276	4	66
		1930	.198	1	13
		1931	.203	0	9
		1932	.290	0	18
		1933	.231	1	9
		1934	.261	0	8
		1937	.242	0	5
Smith, Jim		1978	.221	5	26
		1979	.238	4	34
	(Tide.-Roch.)	1980	.245	5	34
Smith, Keith	(Tide.-Roch.)	1981	.215	2	21
Smith, Ken		1986	.154	3	6
Smith, Mark		1993	.280	12	68
		1994	.247	19	66
		1995	.277	12	66
Smith, Raymond		1939	1.000		
Smith, Tommy		1978	.284	5	24
		1979	.164	1	9
		1980	.200	0	1
Southworth, Billy		1928	.361	6	81
		1929	.349	4	25
		1930	.370	6	58
		1931	.267	2	18
		1932	.220	1	21
Spalding, Dick (Buff.-Roch.)		1929	.301	1	30
Stanicek, Pete		1987	.297	2	16
		1988	.174	2	8
		1990	.174	0	6
Staniland, Chuck		1959	.216	8	36
Stefero, John		1983	.196	2	5
		1984	.067	0	1
		1985	.188	10	23
		1986	.258	2	7
Stein, Justin	(Balt.-Roch.)	1938	.145	0	6

Name		Year	Avg.	HR	RBI
Stephenson, Henry		1945	.288	2	6
Stevens, Ed		1957	.273	12	25
		1958	.263	14	47
Stillman, Royle		1973	.354	1	41
		1974	.292	7	49
		1975	.313	14	75
		1976	.292	5	44
Stone, Jeff		1988	.277	3	27
Stone, Ronald		1967	.283	9	33
		1968	.252	5	42
Stopa, John		1939	.207	0	10
Stringer, Al	(Buff.-Roch.)	1949	.268	3	36
		1950	.303	0	24
Stringfellow, Sid		1936	.300		
Sturdy, Maurice "Jack"		1936	.289	2	82
		1937	.279	1	6
		1938	.299	10	64
		1939	.314	8	83
		1943	.238	0	7
		1944	.279	3	68
		1945	.255	0	17
Stuvengen, J.	(Roch.-Buff.)	1928	.206	1	7
Sullivan, John		1969	.253	4	44
Tackett, Jeff		1989	.181	2	17
		1990	.239	4	33
		1991	.236	6	50
		1993	.320	0	2
Tate, Lee		1959	.234	2	16
Taylor, Howard		1937	1.000		
Teed, Dick		1957	.129	0	0
Tellinger, Emil		1954	.216	1	5
Tettleton, Mickey		1988	.244	1	4
Tevlin, Creighton		1976	.278	0	2
		1977	.278	4	31
Thomas, David		1949			
Thomas, Vern		1980	.259	1	35
Thompson, Donald		1949	.242	3	42
Timko, Andy		1943	.140	0	4
Toporcer, George "Specs"		1928	.298	0	30
		1929	.262	2	46
		1930	.307	1	61
	(Jer.Cty.-Roch.)	1931	.277	2	52
		1932	.298	1	77
		1933	.297	1	40
		1934	.291	1	30

Name		Year	Avg.	HR	RBI
Torve, Kelvin		1986	.242	4	41
		1987	.262	9	32
Towns, Jimmy		1944	.294	0	9
		1945	.252	0	8
Traber, Jim		1985	.265	7	37
		1986	.279	12	55
		1987	.274	21	71
		1988	.285	6	23
Tracy, Jack		1970	.219	1	11
Trail, Chet	(Roch.-Tide.)	1968	.265	9	24
		1969	.244	3	3
Triplett, Hooper		1942	.272	3	35
Turner, Shane		1989	.222	2	19
		1990	.282	1	19
		1991	.282	1	57
		1994	.195	0	9
Tutt, Johnny		1984	.305	1	9
Tyler, Brad		1994	.261	7	43
		1995	.258	17	52
Tyler, John		1931	.000	0	0
Tyrone, Wayne		1979	.237	5	21
Ullger, Scott		1987	.277	12	38
Urban, Karl		1928	.258	1	25
Valentine, Fred		1961	.267	17	64
		1962	.291	3	20
		1963	.309	8	34
		1969	.287	18	70
Valle, John		1980	.260	18	70
		1981	.249	9	39
		1982	.269	12	51
		1983	.222	20	52
		1984	.190	7	28
VanGorder, Dave		1987	.136	1	5
Van Noy, Jay		1951	.225	14	38
		1955	.244	6	46
		1956	.212	3	19
Vanzin, Frank		1970	.095	1	3
Verdi, Frank		1957	.284	2	31
		1958	.237	2	31
		1959	.295	2	41
Vezilich, Lou		1938	.285	6	78
Virdon, Bill		1954	.333	22	98
Virgil, Osvaldo		1962	.268	12	58
		1963	.307	11	75

Name		Year	Avg.	HR	RBI
Voigt, Jack		1991	.270	6	35
		1992	.284	16	64
		1993	.361	3	11
Vollmer, Clyde		1946	.275	9	58
Wagner, Leon		1960	.265	16	48
Wagner, Sebastian		1935	.000		
Waldron, George		1937	.000		
Walker, Greg		1990	.303	2	11
Walker, Harry		1940	.300	0	1
		1952	.365	4	36
		1953	.303	7	37
		1954	.310	0	13
		1955	.429		
Wallin, Larry		1972	.242	0	5
Ward, Pete		1962	.328	22	90
Wargo, Paul		1943	.271	3	43
Washington, U. L.		1981	.225	2	25
Washington, Ron		1987	.320	15	43
Watkins, George "Watty"		1929	.337	20	119
Watlington, Neal		1958	.169	2	6
Watts, Ed "Pete"	(Rich.-Roch.)	1972	.271	6	21
		1973	.245	4	28
		1974	.265	5	38
Watwood, John		1937	.284	2	20
Wawruck, Jim		1994	.300	9	53
		1995	.302	1	23
Wayton, Henry		1935	.000		
Wearing, Mel		1992	.326	4	45
		1993	.235	14	61
		1994	.233	6	11
Weekly, John		1964	.200	1	6
Weintraub, Phil		1936	.371	20	98
West, Tom		1935	.257	2	32
Wetherby, Jeff		1991	.143	1	5
White, Charlie		1955	.207	2	14
White, Don		1945	.274	6	23
		1946	.300	0	4
White, Doug		1943	.188	2	13
Whitehead, Lewis		1934	.250	2	34
Wiggins, Alan		1985	.182	0	1
		1986	.205	0	3
Wilber, Delbert		1950	.295	11	80
Wilborn, Ted		1986	.289	1	10
		1987	.000	0	0
Williams, Babe		1943	.200		

Name	Year	Avg.	HR	RBI
Williams, Dallas	1980	.270	11	54
	1981	.283	9	48
	1984	.242	2	17
Williams, Dewey	1947	.221	0	10
Williams, Jeff	1986	.100	0	1
Williamson, Howard	1930	.202	1	23
Wilson, Charley	1930	.300	8	100
	1931	.276	7	71
	1932	.298	9	69
	1933	.230	7	26
	1935	.246	2	31
Wilson, George	1959	.270	12	36
Windle, Willis	1932	.224	3	23
Winsett, John Tom	1934	.356	21	74
	1941	.160	0	3
Witte, Jerome	1950	.270	2	9
Wood, Bill	1972	.500	0	0
Wood, James	1962	.225	11	32
Woods, Tyrone	1995	.261	8	31
Woodson, Tracy	1994	.237	5	36
Worthington, Craig	1987	.258	7	50
	1988	.244	16	73
Worthington, Robert	1929	.327	8	113
	1930	.375	8	113
Wright, Claude	1947	.254	1	22
Wyrostek, John	1939	.267	0	9
	1941	.252	3	39
Yacopino, Ed	1992	.282	4	61
	1993	.149	0	5
Young, Floyd	1941	.263	4	18
Young, Mike	1981	.333	0	0
	1982	.265	16	62
	1983	.284	14	66
	1984	.333	4	15
	1986	.278	5	21
Young, Robert	1947	.315	0	33
	1948	.268	4	38
	1949	.268	6	46
Youngbauer, Jeff	1979	.270	5	43
Youngdahl, Raynor	1962	.122	1	28
	1963	.210	13	46
Zaun, Gregg	1993	.256	1	11
	1994	.237	7	43
	1995	.293	6	18
Zupo, Frank "Noodles"	1961	.206	0	8

All-Time Pitchers Roster (1928–95)

Name		Year	W	L	ERA
Aase, Don		1988	0	0	1.23
Adamson, Michael		1967	3	4	1.95
		1968	8	4	3.07
		1969	11	8	4.17
		1970	4	5	4.36
		1971	0	1	9.00
Adkins, Steve		1994	0	7	4.69
Aldrich, Jay		1990	4	1	5.37
Alicea, Miguel		1987	0	1	6.48
Anderson, Harley		1966	5	6	5.00
		1967	0	0	5.50
Anderson, John Charles		1961	14	9	3.65
		1962	4	7	4.03
Andrews, Nathan		1935	0	0	6.43
		1937	9	13	3.13
Appleton, Peter	(Roch.-Bal.)	1934	11	13	4.59
Arnold, Greg		1971	2	7	4.78
Arnold, Tony		1983	0	1	3.52
		1984	5	6	4.53
		1986	4	3	1.95
		1987	2	1	3.03
Arruda, Tom		1967	5	7	3.60
		1968	5	9	4.19
Augustine, Jerry		1985	6	3	3.96
		1986	0	0	10.50
Babcock, Bob	(Memph.-Roch.)	1974	0	5	6.68
		1975	2	2	4.85
		1976	7	6	5.04
Baczewski, Fred		1957	0	2	4.95
Baker, Tom		1962	10	9	4.20
		1963	0	1	4.50
Bakkelund, Don		1946	0	0	
Ballard, Jeff		1986	0	2	7.11
		1987	13	4	3.09
		1988	4	3	2.97
		1991	3	3	4.41
Baney, Dick		1970	4	4	5.27
		1971	1	0	5.79
Bare, Raymond		1978	7	13	4.05
Barnes, Frank		1960	1	1	

Name		Year	W	L	ERA
Barnowski, Ed		1966	17	8	3.23
		1967	4	7	4.92
	(Roch.-Buff.-Rich.)	1968	1	8	4.30
		1969	1	1	9.64
Barr, Jim		1984	1	4	5.71
Barrett, Francis "Red"		1938	0	4	
Bastian, Jose		1978	0	1	3.86
		1979	3	3	3.73
Bauta, Eduardo	(Roch.-Buff.)	1965	5	7	3.42
Bautista, Jose		1989	4	4	2.83
		1990	7	8	4.06
		1990	1	0	0.59
Beard, Ralph		1953	0	1	
		1955	3	4	4.19
Beckman, Bill	(Tor.-Roch.)	1942	11	6	3.62
Beene, Fred		1966	2	1	2.57
		1967	5	1	2.95
		1968	8	7	2.68
		1969	15	7	2.98
		1970	9	3	3.20
		1971	7	1	4.44
Belcher, Maywood		1935	2	5	5.25
Bell, Eric		1985	7	3	3.05
		1988	3	1	1.98
		1989	1	2	4.99
		1990	9	6	4.86
Bell, Herman		1928	21	8	3.38
		1929	11	5	3.54
		1931	16	11	3.26
Benitez, Armando		1995	2	2	1.25
Berly, John		1928	5	3	5.07
		1929	12	11	3.85
		1930	16	8	2.49
		1934	14	8	3.89
	(Roch.-Balt.)	1935	6	8	5.70
	(Tor.-Roch.)	1940	5	4	2.66
		1941	6	4	3.43
Bernal, Vic		1979	4	1	3.64
Bertaina, Frank		1963	3	3	4.50
		1965	13	9	3.88
		1966	9	2	2.33
	(Roch.-Buff.)	1969	7	3	3.56
		1970	12	3	3.67
Bielecki, Mike		1993	5	3	5.03

Name		Year	W	L	ERA
Biercevicz, Greg		1985	0	3	3.72
Blair, Dennis		1977	4	3	3.63
		1978	0	6	7.96
Blake, Ed		1948	7	6	3.88
	(Roch.-Syr.)	1949	5	4	4.78
Blake, John F.		1933	11	7	4.03
Blaylock, Bob		1955	0	0	
		1956	9	4	1.67
		1957	4	10	4.20
		1959	0	1	
Blaylock, Gary		1954	10	12	3.34
		1955	4	4	5.14
		1956	8	5	3.02
		1957	10	11	3.74
		1958	14	10	3.21
Boddicker, Mike		1978	1	0	1.80
		1979	4	6	6.00
		1980	12	9	2.18
		1981	10	10	4.20
		1982	10	5	3.58
		1983	3	1	1.90
Bokelmann, Dick		1949	4	4	4.29
		1950			
		1952			
Bolton, Tom		1994	2	0	2.25
Boone, Daniel		1990	11	5	2.60
Borowski, Joe		1995	1	3	4.04
Boswell, Dave		1971	3	0	3.00
Bowden, Mark		1988	9	5	3.38
Bowman, Billy Joe		1957	2	1	
Bowman, Bob		1938	11	7	3.11
Boyer, Cloyd		1949	15	10	3.13
		1954	0	0	
Brabender, Gene		1967	8	6	2.77
Bridges, Marshall		1959	3	3	3.55
Brito, Jose		1984	3	5	4.04
		1985	0	1	7.30
Brown, Curt		1988	2	0	1.19
Brown, Mark		1982	1	0	1.42
		1983	6	1	3.54
		1984	4	4	3.74
Brown, Mike		1987	0	0	1.80
Brown, Virgil		1934	1	1	

Name		Year	W	L	ERA
Browning, Calvin		1957	0	0	15.00
		1958	13	12	3.54
		1959	13	11	4.89
		1960	5	9	3.50
Brumbeloe, Charles		1940	18	11	2.58
		1941	3	5	4.96
Bruner, Roy		1941	3	6	5.31
		1946	3	9	3.97
Brunet, George		1964	0	1	9.00
Budny, Joe	(Roch.-Syr.)	1953	1	0	
Bunker, Wally		1968	6	1	2.70
Burbach, Bill		1971	7	2	4.84
Byerly, Eldred "Bud"		1944	3	9	3.83
		1946	15	14	3.89
		1947	5	13	4.88
Camacho, Ernie		1982	0	1	2.04
Campbell, Paul	(Roch.-Buff.)	1968	2	1	3.91
		1969	7	11	4.98
Carey, Brooks		1981	10	9	3.37
Carleton, James "Tex"		1929	18	7	2.71
		1930	13	13	5.01
Carlucci, Rich		1984	4	6	3.70
Castro, Alejandro		1961	1	1	
		1962	6	7	2.94
		1963	3	5	4.42
Cayll, Ron		1969	1	2	6.33
Chapman, Ed		1930	0	0	
		1933	10	5	2.69
Chavez, Carlos		1995	0	0	10.80
Chevez, Tony		1977	5	9	4.46
		1978	6	11	4.20
		1979	2	1	5.16
Chitren, Steve		1995	0	0	2.45
Chittum, Nelson		1963	13	3	3.18
		1964	11	11	3.35
Chucka, Joe		1950			
Ciola, Louis	(Roch.-Syr.)	1953	0	0	
Clark, Michael		1942	0	2	7.83
Clark, Terry		1995	1	2	2.70
Cleary, Al		1946	0	2	6.23
Clements, Pat		1993	0	0	5.91
Codiroli, Chris		1990	0	0	13.50

Name	Year	W	L	ERA
Collum, Jack	1949	3	2	3.86
	1950	8	6	3.03
	1951	15	8	2.80
	1952	9	10	3.77
Conboy, James	1943	0	0	
Concepcion, Carlos	1984	0	0	12.96
Condrick, George	1952	10	9	3.35
	1953	11	4	3.88
Connelly, Bill	1954	2	2	4.50
Cook, Mike	1993	6	7	3.10
	1994	0	1	3.12
Cooper, Don	1987	2	2	3.82
Copeland, George	1948	5	3	2.94
	1949	11	7	4.03
	1950	8	8	5.35
Coppinger, Rocky	1995	3	0	1.04
Cosgrove, Stephen	1964	0	0	
	1965	1	5	4.43
Couchee, Mike	1985	1	4	6.49
Cozart, Charles	1945	4	6	4.88
Crimian, John	1952	8	3	2.10
	1953	13	5	2.85
Cross, Ward	1935	4	6	4.76
Culkar, Steven	1989	2	2	3.99
Curlee, Bill	1941	4	4	4.20
Dalkowski, Steve	1963	0	2	6.00
Davis, Storm	1982	2	1	3.71
Deal, Ellis "Cot"	1952	14	9	3.56
	1953	16	9	3.72
	1955	7	4	2.73
	1956	15	7	4.39
	1957	9	9	4.57
	1958	0	0	
Decatur, Arthur	1928	15	13	3.60
Dedrick, Jim	1993	1	0	2.57
	1994	3	6	3.82
	1995	4	0	1.77
De la Rosa, Francisco	1990	0	0	0.00
	1991	4	1	2.67
DeLeon, Luis	1986	4	8	3.48
	1987	3	3	2.66
Delgado, Richardo	1966	3	7	4.50
	1967	9	4	3.43
	1968	9	5	3.87
	1969	3	4	3.06

Name	Year	W	L	ERA
	1970	7	8	3.19
	1971	0	2	4.00
Derringer, Paul	1929	17	12	3.91
	1930	23	11	2.89
DeSilva, John	1995	11	9	4.18
Dettmer, John	1995	4	7	4.68
DiCecco, Joe	1946	0	0	
Dillard, Gordon	1988	0	2	2.45
Dillman, Bill	1966	0	0	
	1968	11	11	4.29
	1969	5	6	4.95
Dixon, Ken	1983	3	6	4.48
	1987	4	0	3.27
Donnelly, Ed	1956	2	2	5.75
	1957	2	1	4.24
Donnelly, Sylvester	1943	17	8	2.40
Donohue, James	1959	0	0	
Dooner, Glenn	1984	0	0	1.24
Doyle, Andrew	1936	1	2	6.85
	1937	3	3	5.69
Doyle, Bob	1938	0	1	
	1941	0	2	
Doyle, Carl	1941	3	2	
Dreisewerd, Clem	1941	15	6	2.91
	1942	1	14	5.19
Drummond, Tim	1992	1	0	1.98
DuBois, Brian	1993	0	2	9.00
	1994	0	4	7.24
Dukes, Tom	1972	2	2	3.48
Dusak, Erv	1949	11	8	4.57
Dwyer, Art	1945	0	0	5.59
Echols, Clint	1946	0	0	
Eckert, Al	1932	12	12	4.66
	1933	0	0	
	1935	0	2	
Edgerton, Bill	1969	3	2	4.50
Ellis, Nicholas	1944	0	0	
Emmerich, Bill	1944	12	13	3.17
Estrada, Chuck	1965	7	14	4.45
Farmer, Ed	1977	11	5	4.47
Faszholz, Jack	1950	5	3	4.03
	1951	12	9	3.41
	1952	15	8	3.67
	1953	10	6	3.69

Name		Year	W	L	ERA
Faszholz, Jack *(cont.)*		1954	18	9	3.20
		1955	13	11	3.96
		1956	7	13	4.86
Fernandez, Sid		1994	0	0	4.50
Fierbaugh, Randy		1979	1	1	3.60
		1980	1	0	5.88
Fisher, Albert		1935	6	8	4.18
		1936	0	0	
Fisher, Jack		1970	4	4	4.41
Fisher, Tom		1967	10	6	3.04
		1968	2	4	3.65
Flanagan, Mike		1975	13	4	2.50
		1976	6	1	2.12
		1987	0	0	3.00
Flinn, John		1977	10	7	3.55
		1978	1	0	5.17
		1979	6	6	2.70
		1981	9	3	3.61
		1982	5	7	4.89
Ford, Dave		1977	9	14	4.81
		1978	11	6	3.80
		1979	6	5	3.55
		1981	1	0	1.50
		1982	5	5	3.93
		1983	3	2	6.54
Ford, Willard		1929	2	2	7.25
Foreman, Charles	(Roch.-Bal.)	1928	2	2	
		1930	10	6	3.36
		1931	7	6	4.30
		1932	6	6	7.00
Forney, Rick		1995	0	0	3.94
Fourroux, Lloyd		1967	1	5	4.00
Fowlkes, Alan		1986	0	1	15.00
Freeman, Jimmy	(Rich.-Roch.)	1975	7	6	3.13
		1976	2	3	3.83
Frohwirth, Todd		1991	1	3	3.65
Fussell, Fred		1939	2	0	
Galasso, Bob		1975	9	7	2.85
		1976	13	5	3.45
Gardner, Glenn		1944	15	14	3.80
		1945	8	8	3.58
		1946	14	15	3.98
		1947	8	18	3.89
		1948	2	4	5.09

Name		Year	W	L	ERA
Garland, Wayne		1972	7	9	3.79
		1973	10	11	3.57
		1974	2	2	5.40
Gatewood, Aubrey		1968	4	10	4.32
		1969	0	0	4.50
Geiger, Gary		1956	3	2	3.78
Gibson, Bob		1958	5	5	2.45
		1960	2	3	2.85
Gibson, Bob		1988	2	2	1.21
Giggie, Robert		1961	1	3	4.50
Gillick, Patrick	(Roch.-Col.)	1962	2	4	6.50
		1963	0	0	1.29
Glick, Norm		1945	0	1	
Gonzalez, Julian		1983	5	3	4.43
		1984	2	7	6.02
Gornicki, Hank		1939	3	3	5.16
		1940	19	10	3.21
		1941	12	9	2.83
Grabowski, Al		1931	4	4	5.06
Grant, George	(Jer.Cty.-Roch.)	1930	11	14	4.58
Greason, Bill		1956	2	1	
		1957	5	6	3.43
		1958	7	10	4.00
		1959	2	1	5.59
Green, Chris		1987	0	2	3.00
Green, Ed		1947	3	1	4.28
		1948	2	5	6.16
Griffin, Mike		1987	5	1	3.28
		1988	4	8	3.85
Grilli, Steve	(Syr.-Roch.)	1981	4	5	6.26
Grimsley, Ross		1982	1	0	8.71
Grodzicki, John		1939	8	7	4.50
		1940	3	3	3.79
Habenicht, Bob		1951	11	6	4.33
Habyan, John		1986	12	7	4.29
		1987	3	2	3.86
		1988	9	9	4.46
Hahn, Fred		1951	7	8	3.83
		1952	5	9	3.76
		1953	5	6	3.82
Hall, Grady		1992	0	0	13.50
Hanrahan, Tom		1944	0	0	
Hanrahan, Vern	(Jack.-Roch.)	1964	5	4	2.45
		1965	2	6	4.10

Name		Year	W	L	ERA
Hardin, Jim		1967	5	3	2.04
Harnisch, Pete		1988	4	1	2.16
		1989	5	5	2.58
Harper, Dave		1977	0	1	3.27
Harrell, Ray		1934	12	9	4.06
		1935	6	10	4.98
		1936	14	13	4.80
Harrison, Roric		1971	15	5	2.81
Hartley, Mike		1995	0	1	0.82
Hartzell, Paul		1980	10	4	3.20
Havens, Brad		1985	8	10	4.85
		1987	2	3	6.03
Haynes, Jimmy		1994	1	0	6.75
		1995	12	8	3.29
Hearn, James		1949	8	3	4.25
Heim, Millard		1955	8	9	4.68
Heise, Clarence		1935	0	1	
Heise, Larry		1984	0	0	20.25
Heitzman, Sylvester		1928	3	3	6.30
Henry, Frank		1933	8	4	5.42
Henshaw, Roy		1939	6	8	5.41
Hernandez, Julio		1991	0	0	10.50
Herron, Gerald		1967	1	4	7.13
		1968	6	3	4.50
		1969	8	7	3.57
Herson, Mike		1969	3	10	3.87
Heusser, Ed		1933	4	5	8.51
Heving, Joseph		1931	0	2	
Hickey, Kevin		1988	2	0	1.46
		1990	2	1	5.79
Hiland, Jim		1959	1	6	5.35
Hill, Carmen		1931	18	12	3.03
Hill, Delano		1967	4	5	4.42
		1968	1	2	3.44
Hobaugh, Ed	(Tor.-Atl.-Roch.)	1963	6	7	4.11
Hoch, Robert		1953	1	1	4.06
		1954	0	0	
Hofferd, John		1969	1	2	4.20
Hogg, John		1965	0	3	7.62
Hoitsma, Harry		1953	0	3	5.68
		1954	3	5	4.50
Holdsworth, Fred		1975	4	9	3.24
Holman, Brad		1995	0	1	0.00
Holton, Brian		1990	1	4	9.19

Name		Year	W	L	ERA
Hood, Don		1972	9	10	3.48
		1973	4	7	3.16
Hoover, John		1984	2	3	5.21
Householder, Brian		1987	1	2	4.91
Huffman, Phil		1985	10	10	3.49
		1986	10	9	5.11
		1987	5	6	4.78
Hughes, Richard		1959	0	0	
Huismann, Mark		1989	2	1	1.71
Humphries, Bertram		1943	0	2	
Hunt, Kenneth		1965	0	0	15.00
Hurd, Tom		1959	2	2	3.58
		1960	2	2	5.25
Hurst, James		1995	1	1	3.79
Hutchinson, Ira		1942	13	13	3.73
		1943	17	11	2.21
Hutson, George Herbert		1973	5	6	3.43
Hyde, Dick		1961	1	1	1.04
		1962	0	0	10.29
Irvin, Larry		1928	7	1	3.05
		1929	14	9	3.10
		1930	7	4	5.71
		1931	7	3	4.30
Ivan, Alexander		1935	0	0	
Jackson, Larry		1954	12	6	3.19
Jackson, Roy Lee		1985	1	1	3.00
Jacobs, Anthony	(Sprng.-Roch.)	1953	12	3	2.63
		1954	16	1	2.91
		1955	8	7	3.71
Jacobs, Arthur		1929	2	0	
Jaworski, Edwin		1944	0	0	
Jefferson, Jesse		1972	6	3	2.45
		1973	6	2	3.41
Johnson, David Charles		1973	8	5	3.18
		1974	7	4	2.36
		1975	3	1	5.67
		1976	11	5	2.80
Johnson, David Wayne		1989	7	6	3.26
		1991	0	1	4.15
Johnson, Jerry		1985	4	11	5.14
Johnson, Kenneth		1946	1	4	5.02
		1948	6	9	4.23
Johnson, Silas Ken		1938	14	11	3.03
		1939	22	12	4.32

Name	Year	W	L	ERA
Jones, Gordon	1961	8	8	4.53
Jones, Larry	1979	1	7	3.00
	1980	13	14	4.35
	1981	9	9	3.77
Jones, Mike	1989	9	7	3.35
	1990	2	3	6.00
Jones, Odell	1985	4	6	4.20
	1986	7	3	3.66
Jones, Stacy	1991	4	4	3.38
	1992	0	0	6.75
Jones, Steven	1970	1	0	6.88
	1971	0	0	18.00
Jordan, Niles	1953	8	1	3.55
	1954	6	6	5.11
Judd, Oscar	1937	11	11	5.19
	1938	6	5	4.66
Judd, Ralph	1931	7	6	5.47
Jurisch, Al	1942	4	8	4.19
Kaufmann, Tony	1928	3	2	4.40
	1932	10	8	4.46
	1933	13	15	4.19
	1934	5	7	4.04
	1935	8	13	4.47
	1936	11	9	4.64
	1937	1	6	4.22
Kay, Art	1960	8	6	3.26
	1961	9	10	2.86
Keegan, Bob	1959	18	10	3.04
	1960	6	9	3.73
Keen, Howard "Vic"	1928	12	11	4.05
Kelley, Anthony	1990	1	0	5.14
Kelly, Robert	1955	1	2	7.20
Kerrigan, Joe	1979	10	6	3.51
	1980	3	3	2.78
Kilgus, Paul	1991	2	2	5.76
King, Jerry	1983	0	2	11.57
Kinnunen, Mike	1986	1	3	2.35
	1987	6	4	1.75
Kirkpatrick, Bill	1970	7	8	4.50
	1971	11	10	3.28
	1972	11	9	3.51
	1973	2	2	6.00
	1974	15	7	2.83
	1976	1	0	3.86

Name		Year	W	L	ERA
Kleinke, Norbert		1934	19	7	3.27
		1935	3	9	5.00
		1936	16	12	4.16
		1937	19	8	3.47
		1938	13	9	4.05
Kline, Steve	(Roch.-Rich.)	1977	2	2	3.45
Klingenbeck, Scott		1995	3	1	2.72
Klinger, Robert		1932	0	1	
		1936	7	4	4.79
Knechtges, Paul		1964	1	1	15.00
		1966	2	2	4.64
		1967	2	1	3.64
		1968	3	3	3.21
Knight, John		1954	1	0	
Knowles, Darold		1964	6	7	3.04
		1965	11	5	2.53
Koby, George		1945	0	0	
		1946	0	0	
Koch, Henry		1945	0	1	
Krieger, Kurt	(Roch.-Syr.)	1951	6	6	5.66
		1953	1	2	5.32
Krist, Howard		1935	0	0	4.50
		1937	13	15	3.14
		1938	6	11	5.09
		1947	2	4	4.94
Krivda, Rick		1993	3	0	1.89
		1994	9	10	3.53
		1995	6	5	3.19
Kucharski, Joe		1984	7	13	4.99
		1985	6	13	4.36
		1986	0	2	21.13
		1987	4	6	5.79
Kucks, John		1961	10	14	3.72
Kuipers, Sam		1944	5	6	4.13
		1945	0	1	
Kunkel, Bill		1965	3	4	3.71
Kuzava, Bob		1958	5	3	3.31
Lane, Aaron		1995	0	0	6.30
Layana, Tim		1992	3	3	5.35
Lee, Mark		1995	4	2	1.57
Lehew, Jim		1962	0	0	8.53
Leinen, Pat		1992	3	4	5.86
Lemp, Chris		1995	0	1	11.25

Name		Year	W	L	ERA
Leonhard, Dave		1966	9	7	3.88
		1967	15	3	2.61
		1971	7	4	3.76
		1973	3	1	4.24
Leopold, Bob		1961	1	6	4.86
Lewis, Jim		1992	2	5	4.92
Lewis, Richie		1991	1	0	2.81
		1992	10	9	3.28
Lillard, Eugene		1940	1	3	7.33
Lindsey, Jim		1933	3	9	5.66
Lingrel, Ray		1929	9	6	4.17
Linskey, Mike		1990	7	9	3.58
		1991	1	5	7.24
Lisenbee, Horace	(Mon.-Roch.)	1938	0	0	9.00
Liska, Ad	(Roch.-Syr.)	1934	6	11	4.90
List, Robert		1959	1	0	
Littlejohn, Carlisle		1929	14	7	3.97
		1930	8	1	4.99
		1931	2	3	3.96
Long, Bob		1987	1	0	4.32
Lopez, Marcelino		1969	2	1	2.91
Lovenguth, Lynn	(Roch.-Col.)	1957	14	15	3.69
		1958	11	13	4.02
Ludwig, Ed		1954	3	3	5.09
		1955	7	5	4.77
Luebber, Steve		1980	13	8	3.59
		1981	5	5	1.80
Luebke, Dick		1961	3	2	3.20
		1962	10	7	1.77
Lugos, Frank		1949	0	0	
Luna, Memo		1954	9	11	3.50
Lyons, Hershel		1939	1	4	3.56
		1940	19	12	3.38
		1941	12	11	3.96
Lyons, Jim		1935	2	1	4.81
Mackinson, John	(Roch.-Col.)	1955	9	7	3.41
		1956	14	7	4.01
		1957	3	2	3.56
		1958	0	0	
Macon, Max		1935	0	0	
MacPherson, Bruce		1982	1	1	10.24
Magee, Bo		1995	0	0	13.50
Manuel, Barry		1993	1	1	3.66
		1994	11	8	5.48

Name		Year	W	L	ERA
Manz, George		1971	8	5	5.10
		1972	3	4	3.58
		1973	11	5	3.60
		1975	6	5	4.78
Maras, Ed		1970	5	2	3.46
	(Roch.-Winn.)	1971	9	10	6.06
Markell, Harry "Duke"	(Syr.-Roch.)	1954	8	12	3.04
		1955	13	13	4.43
		1956	10	10	3.07
		1957	3	4	5.29
Martin, Fred		1952	8	14	4.25
Martinez, David		1991	0	5	5.48
Martinez, Dennis		1975	0	0	5.40
		1976	14	8	2.50
		1986	2	1	6.05
Martinez, Nativadad		1962	6	8	4.70
		1963	6	6	4.89
Martinez, Tippy		1986	0	1	6.00
Mayer, Edwin		1956	1	4	
Mayo, Ricky		1978	0	0	4.50
McAfee, William		1933	1	4	5.37
McCall, Larry		1974	2	4	5.36
McClain, Joe		1958	6	4	4.50
		1959	3	8	4.43
McCormick, Mike		1964	12	8	3.29
McCracken, Ovid		1928	7	7	4.61
McDonald, Ben		1990	3	3	2.86
		1991	0	1	7.71
		1995	0	0	2.45
McGehee, Kevin		1993	7	6	2.96
		1994	10	8	4.76
		1995	11	9	5.83
McGraw, Bob		1930	10	8	4.05
McGregor, Scott	(Syr.-Roch.)	1976	12	6	3.06
		1987	0	2	3.06
McKeon, Joel		1990	4	2	4.68
		1991	0	1	9.00
McLaughlin, Bill		1940	1	1	
McQueen, Mike	(Rich.-Roch.)	1974	0	1	6.16
Mejia, Cesar		1989	3	6	4.86
Melliere, Floyd		1953	2	4	4.60
Meriwether, Conklyn "Al"		1945	0	2	
Merritt, Lloyd		1959	0	0	

Name	Year	W	L	ERA
Mesa, José	1988	0	3	8.62
	1989	0	2	5.40
	1990	1	2	2.42
Michaels, John	1934	16	10	3.35
	1935	9	10	4.42
	1936	4	2	3.86
Mikan, John	1946	10	6	4.08
	1947	16	13	3.90
	1948	9	9	4.47
Milacki, Bob	1988	12	8	2.70
	1992	7	1	4.57
Miller, Dave	1991	0	0	0.00
	1992	4	0	3.81
Miller, Dyar	1973	6	3	2.75
	1974	12	8	2.70
	1975	5	0	2.20
Miller, John	1962	2	1	3.69
	1963	8	15	3.85
	1964	8	9	4.30
Miller, Randy	1977	2	5	3.54
Miller, Ray	1971	3	2	3.16
	1972	7	5	3.21
	1973	1	1	1.38
Miller, Robert Lane	1958	1	1	6.60
	1959	8	12	3.50
Milliken, Bob	1960	3	1	1.59
Mills, Alan	1992	0	1	5.40
	1995	0	1	0.00
Minetto, Craig	1982	4	5	3.27
	1983	3	6	3.59
Mirabella, Paul	1983	3	5	3.66
Mitchell, John	1990	5	0	1.57
Mitchell, Paul	1973	8	7	4.14
	1974	14	6	2.89
	1975	10	1	2.06
Moford, Herb	1955	1	6	4.71
	1956	1	1	
	1961	15	13	3.16
	1962	10	11	4.47
	1963	1	1	10.29
Montague, John	1970	6	9	4.86
	1971	8	6	4.46
Mooney, Jim	1933	2	3	
Moore, Daryl	1992	0	0	2.95

Name		Year	W	L	ERA
Moore, Herb		1937	2	2	4.02
		1938	0	1	
		1947	0	0	6.00
Moore, Lloyd		1946	2	7	5.89
Morgan, Mike		1988	0	2	4.76
Morogiello, Dan		1983	1	1	5.73
Morris, John W.		1968	3	0	3.67
Moss, Ray		1931	4	3	3.09
Moulden, C. Carroll		1969	1	1	6.48
Moyer, Jamie		1993	6	0	1.67
Munns, Les		1936	1	4	7.04
Murray, George	(Tor.-Roch.)	1936	13	8	5.38
Musselman, Ron		1987	6	6	3.04
Mussina, Mike		1990	0	0	1.35
		1991	10	4	2.87
Myers, Chris		1991	8	7	4.49
Myers, Jimmy		1995	0	4	3.06
Narum, Leslie "Buster"		1962	12	4	3.83
		1963	6	12	4.88
Naylor, Earl		1943	0	0	
Naymick, Michael		1944	1	6	3.69
Nelson, Roger Eugene		1968	3	0	1.29
Neuberger, Herman		1945	1	2	4.50
Newsome, Art		1932	2	0	6.26
		1933	0	0	
Noles, Dickie		1988	10	5	3.12
Nunn, Howard		1959	8	9	4.03
O'Brien, Bob		1972	5	9	4.50
O'Connor, Jack		1987	3	0	2.67
O'Donoghue, John, Sr.		1968	2	4	2.38
		1969	0	1	2.00
O'Donoghue, John, Jr.		1992	5	4	3.23
		1993	7	4	3.88
		1994	4	7	5.72
Ogden, John	(Roch.-Bal.)	1933	7	5	3.76
Oliveras, Francisco		1984	1	2	7.97
		1987	3	0	4.33
Oquist, Mike		1992	10	12	4.11
		1993	9	8	3.50
		1994	3	2	3.73
		1995	0	0	5.25
Osborne, Bill		1946	6	4	3.86
Ostermueller, Fred "Fritz"		1930	2	2	6.21
		1933	16	7	2.44

Name		Year	W	L	ERA
Pacella, John		1984	6	3	3.11
		1988	0	0	0.00
Pagnozzi, Mike		1978	2	5	5.89
Pakron, John		1945	1	0	
Palmer, Jim		1967	0	0	11.57
		1968	0	0	13.50
Palmieri, Ernest		1955	0	1	
Papa, John		1964	0	1	4.66
Papai, Al		1948	5	6	4.37
		1953	1	0	
		1961	0	1	
Parrott, Mike		1975	1	0	0.00
		1977	15	7	3.42
Partenheimer, Stan		1945	4	3	4.24
Pearce, Frank	(Roch.-Bal.)	1935	7	9	4.68
		1942	0	6	5.72
Pena, Orlando		1971	2	1	2.45
		1972	7	9	0.96
Pennington, Brad		1992	1	3	2.08
		1993	1	2	3.45
		1994	6	8	5.32
Pepper, Hugh "Laurin"		1958	9	14	4.29
Peraza, Oswald		1988	3	0	2.89
		1991	3	4	5.20
Perkins, Gerald		1974	1	2	3.60
Phoebus, Tom		1964	11	9	3.39
		1965	3	3	3.89
		1966	13	9	3.02
Picone, Mario		1954	4	4	3.29
	(Roch.-Tor.)	1955	7	16	4.10
Pirtle, Gerry		1979	2	9	4.89
Poholsky, Tom		1949	14	10	3.69
		1950	18	6	2.17
Poole, Jim		1991	3	2	2.79
Porter, Robert		1941	0	0	
		1992	1	6	5.31
Portocarrero, Arnie		1961	1	1	
Poslask, Michael		1935	2	0	
Potter, Dykes		1932	0	0	
		1933	0	1	
		1934	0	4	6.00
		1935	0	0	
Quirk, Arthur		1961	10	8	3.58
		1962	7	6	4.71

Name	Year	W	L	ERA
Raczka, Mike	1987	4	8	6.39
	1988	1	5	5.94
	1989	1	6	5.13
Radler, Frank	1945	6	23	4.91
Raffensberger, Ken	1938	15	10	2.91
	1939	15	15	3.20
Rajsich, Dave	1985	0	2	5.40
Ramirez, Allan	1981	1	3	4.17
	1982	6	10	4.86
	1983	4	5	3.90
	1984	4	10	4.36
Rampola, John	1935	0	1	
Rasmussen, Dennis	1992	0	7	5.67
Rasmussen, Eric	1986	4	3	1.98
	1987	6	8	4.80
Reeder, Bill	1947	5	5	4.43
	1948	12	12	3.17
	1950	9	8	4.60
	1951	0	0	9.00
Reeder, Dennis	1953	10	9	3.22
	1954	0	0	
Reinhart, Art	1929	3	4	6.65
Reynolds, Robert	1972	8	7	1.71
Rhodes, Arthur	1992	6	6	3.72
	1993	1	1	4.05
	1994	7	5	2.79
	1995	2	1	2.70
Ricci, Chuck	1993	0	0	5.65
Ricketts, Dick	1957	12	9	3.66
	1958	15	13	3.30
	1959	6	10	3.48
	1960	9	13	4.21
Riel, Francis	1940	1	1	
Riley, Edward	1978	0	0	3.00
Rineer, Jeff	1978	9	4	4.70
	1979	5	15	4.39
	1980	4	4	5.07
Roberts, James	1956	1	0	
Robinson, Jeff	1991	1	2	6.43
Robson, Gary	1974	5	3	3.96
	1975	1	2	2.16
Roe, Elwin "Preacher"	1939	7	4	4.35
	1940	5	8	3.94

Name		Year	W	L	ERA
Rowe, Ken		1965	5	9	4.35
		1966	4	5	3.20
		1967	8	5	3.66
Rowe, Tommy		1980	6	7	4.60
		1981	8	9	4.34
		1982	1	2	7.36
Roy, Jean-Pierre		1942	3	5	3.62
		1943	2	8	5.61
	(Roch.-Mon.)	1944	12	11	3.78
Rubert, Octavio		1953	7	4	2.40
		1954	0	1	
Russell, Kelton		1956	5	5	4.21
		1957	5	5	3.69
Rusteck, Richard		1969	0	1	8.00
Ryan, Kevin		1995	0	3	9.35
Ryba, Mike		1939	18	12	2.69
		1940	24	8	2.94
Sackinsky, Brian		1995	3	3	4.60
Sadecki, Ray		1960	2	1	1.76
Sadowski, Bob		1960	4	5	2.70
Sakas, Lou		1942	5	3	2.72
		1943	3	3	3.33
		1944	7	3	4.45
		1945	4	6	3.65
		1946	0	2	12.00
Sanchez, Israel		1991	6	2	3.42
		1992	0	0	2.35
Satre, Jason		1993	4	5	5.85
		1994	6	7	4.97
Savoe, Dick		1962	2	0	1.93
Schelberg, John		1928	1	2	9.44
Scherrer, Bill		1988	0	0	0.00
Schilling, Curt		1989	13	11	3.21
		1990	4	4	3.92
Schmidt, Fred		1943	13	10	2.42
Schmidt, Willard		1952	1	1	
		1960	11	5	3.83
Schneider, Jeff		1980	2	4	4.86
		1981	5	1	2.35
Schoen, Gerald	(Roch.-Syr.)	1969	2	2	5.80
		1970	5	2	3.50
Schultz, Michael	(Syr.-Roch.)	1949	4	10	4.57
		1950	8	5	4.50
	(Roch.-Buff.)	1951	4	4	3.49

Name	Year	W	L	ERA
Schulze, Don	1993	8	5	4.10
Schwarz, Jeff	1989	0	2	5.84
	1990	0	0	7.11
Scott, Ralph "Mickey"	1970	6	3	4.98
	1971	9	1	3.38
	1974	8	2	0.99
Scott, Robert	1963	4	2	3.07
	1964	5	4	4.50
Searcy, Steve	1993	2	1	6.00
Seinsoth, William	1938	1	0	
	1940	0	1	
Sekel, Bob	1974	3	5	3.45
	1975	1	6	2.29
Seminara, Frank	1995	1	0	3.28
Severinsen, Al	1968	2	0	1.42
	1969	3	4	2.03
	1970	4	6	3.22
Shea, John	1995	0	1	2.95
Sherer, Al	1934	0	0	
	1938	8	12	5.20
Sherrill, Lee	1938	1	0	
Shirley, Jack	1954	0	0	
Shope, Norman	1945	10	6	5.07
Short, Billy	1962	3	4	4.29
	1963	13	8	3.38
	1964	8	11	3.39
	1965	13	4	2.92
	1966	3	5	2.78
Sisk, Doug	1988	0	2	5.91
Skinner, Mike	1986	10	8	4.18
	1987	1	2	6.39
Smith, Harold	1928	9	15	4.16
Smith, Ira	1930	12	7	4.27
	1931	15	9	3.26
	1932	16	10	4.15
	1933	11	11	4.58
	1934	6	6	4.72
	1937	2	7	4.89
Smith, James	1941	0	0	
Smith, Mark	1978	0	3	9.20
	1982	0	0	2.45
	1983	2	3	5.33
Smith, Mike "Mississippi"	1989	1	4	5.75

Name	Year	W	L	ERA
Smith, Mike "Texas"	1989	2	4	3.21
	1990	9	6	4.96
Smith, Myrl	1975	0	2	9.00
	1977	1	5	5.91
Smith, Robert Gilchrist (Col.-Roch.)	1961	4	3	5.07
Smith, Roy	1991	6	2	3.50
Smith, Rufus (Roch.-Jer.Cty.)	1931	7	8	4.73
Smith, William	1955	1	1	
Smith, William Garland	1959	9	7	3.82
Snell, Nate	1979	4	7	4.38
	1981	1	3	2.63
	1982	4	6	3.67
	1983	6	2	3.60
	1984	0	2	4.82
	1985	0	0	0.00
	1986	2	2	4.44
Snider, Maynard	1939	0	0	
Snyder, Bob (Char.-Roch.)	1973	8	7	3.45
	1974	7	5	3.55
	1975	1	1	3.43
Sommer, Tim	1968	2	2	4.95
	1969	1	0	5.32
Speck, Cliff	1981	6	3	3.79
	1982	8	10	3.45
	1983	8	12	5.04
Spencer, Glenn	1935	3	5	4.75
Spier, Dale	1972	5	7	5.40
Staab, Larry	1970	4	6	4.50
Stanhope, Chuck	1988	2	1	4.34
	1989	5	4	4.25
	1990	1	0	4.09
Stanhouse, Don	1982	2	3	4.12
Starr, Ray	1931	20	7	2.83
	1932	9	12	5.08
Starrette, Herman	1963	6	2	1.13
	1964	5	2	1.96
	1965	3	3	2.88
	1966	0	1	8.57
Stathos, Tony	1954	1	1	
Stein, Wm. Randolph	1973	1	2	3.50
	1974	3	1	4.24
	1975	8	2	3.11
	1976	5	6	5.48

Name	Year	W	L	ERA
Stephan, Todd	1992	5	6	3.96
	1993	3	7	5.10
Stephen, Lou "Buzz"	1969	1	0	6.10
	1970	0	1	7.20
Stephenson, Earl	1976	4	3	1.17
	1977	5	6	4.44
	1978	7	5	3.68
(Roch.-Tide.)	1979	2	6	3.72
Stethers, Howard	1964	0	0	0.00
	1965	0	2	14.40
Stewart, Sammy	1977	0	5	6.33
	1978	13	10	3.79
Stoddard, Tim	1978	7	3	2.62
Stone, Dean	1960	9	7	3.67
	1963	1	1	4.36
Stranski, Scott	1986	0	0	0.00
Strode, Les	1987	0	1	8.57
Strohmeyer, Fred	1944	0	1	
Strommen, Clair	1944	0	5	4.96
	1945	0	1	
Sumey, George	1944	0	1	
Sunkel, Tom	1937	0	3	12.00
Surkont, Matthew "Max"	1941	10	6	3.20
	1942	10	18	5.04
	1946	9	17	5.47
	1947	15	10	3.55
	1948	15	11	4.16
Swaggerty, Bill	1983	9	6	4.64
	1984	6	2	2.66
	1985	11	13	3.24
	1986	12	7	4.25
Swanson, Harold	1937	1	0	
	1938	0	0	
Talavera, Jorge	1958	0	1	
Taylor, Howard	1937	0	0	
	1944	0	0	
Teachout, Arthur "Bud"	1932	14	7	4.15
Telford, Anthony	1987	0	0	0.00
	1991	12	9	3.95
	1992	12	7	4.18
	1993	7	7	4.27
Templeton, Archie	1938	0	0	
	1940	0	1	
Terpko, Jeff	1978	3	3	5.00

Name	Year	W	L	ERA
Theim, Theodore	1960	1	1	5.14
Thoms, Richard	1971	0	0	3.27
Thorpe, Paul	1989	2	1	2.66
Thurmond, Mark	1988	5	3	2.65
Tibbs, Jay	1988	3	1	2.84
	1989	3	0	0.93
Tiefenauer, Bob	1951	9	9	2.66
	1952	5	4	4.26
	1953	9	3	2.31
	1960	11	4	3.14
Tirado, Aris	1990	1	0	7.43
Toms, Thomas	1978	1	2	6.08
Torrez, Pete	1979	3	2	5.27
	1980	2	4	4.40
	1981	2	4	3.41
	1982	0	1	17.61
Tortora, Louis	1945	0	0	
Trine, Bill	1944	0	2	
Trotter, William	1943	12	16	2.59
	1944	14	12	2.55
	1945	9	13	3.83
Umbarger, Jim	1981	6	9	4.18
Underwood, Pat	1984	0	2	9.00
Valenzuela, Fernando	1993	0	1	10.80
Van Bommel, Bill	1976	0	2	4.76
	1977	3	6	7.26
Vandenberg, Hal	1941	11	10	3.38
Vetter, Bob	1943	0	0	
Vicino, Rocco	1935	0	0	
Vineyard, Dave	1962	7	2	3.90
	1963	8	6	3.70
	1964	10	4	2.65
	1965	0	4	5.40
	1966	6	9	4.12
Wagner, Frank	1945	6	4	3.71
Wahonick, John	1937	0	0	9.00
	1938	1	1	3.21
	1939	2	2	6.75
Walker, William	1937	12	11	3.93
Wallace, Mike	1979	0	6	6.34
Ward, Richard	1935	3	3	
Wargo, Paul	1943	0	2	5.46
	1946	1	3	5.07
Washburn, Ray	1960	5	4	4.45

Name		Year	W	L	ERA
Watt, Ed		1965	6	4	3.52
Weems, Mark		1971	0	1	6.88
		1972	0	0	0.00
		1973	9	7	3.91
Wegmann, Tom		1994	5	1	3.69
		1995	3	2	3.44
Weiland, Robert	(Alb.-Roch.)	1935	9	10	2.74
		1936	23	13	3.50
Welchel, Don		1981	1	1	2.25
		1982	12	7	4.64
		1983	4	12	4.64
		1984	4	5	4.42
		1985	7	4	3.75
Weldon, Larry		1944	0	0	
Wentz, Carl		1941	1	0	
Werly, Jamie		1984	1	6	9.80
Weston, Mickey		1989	8	3	2.09
		1990	11	1	1.98
Wetherell, Delano		1932	11	9	3.51
		1933	2	2	5.00
White, Adel		1937	1	1	3.00
Wicker, Kemp		1943	10	18	2.79
		1944	13	9	2.80
		1945	11	12	4.02
Wild, Ken		1950	12	1	4.86
		1951	6	8	3.64
Wiley, Mark		1980	8	7	4.05
Wilks, Ted		1938	4	2	3.92
Williams, Jeff		1993	2	5	5.76
Williams, Jimmy		1995	1	2	7.11
Williamson, Mark		1987	0	1	6.75
		1988	2	3	3.34
		1992	0	0	0.00
Willis, Mike		1974	9	4	2.64
		1975	14	8	2.57
		1976	12	6	4.21
Willsher, Chris		1984	0	4	20.25
Wilshusen, Terry		1970	2	2	6.88
		1972	6	3	3.40
Wilson, Roger		1986	0	0	2.54
Winford, Jim		1932	8	10	3.64
		1933	6	3	3.60
		1934	2	7	5.96
Wirth, Alan		1982	0	3	5.49

Name		Year	W	L	ERA
Wissman, Ed		1941	4	3	2.61
		1942	10	12	4.45
Wittig, John	(Bal.-Roch.)	1950	8	6	5.48
		1951	0	0	
Wood, Brian		1993	1	2	2.70
Woodward, Rob		1990	6	1	3.00
		1991	7	7	4.11
Wooldridge, Floyd		1953	2	0	2.81
		1955	0	2	3.48
Wright, Melvin		1955	1	1	2.76
		1956	5	7	3.07
		1957	5	5	2.90
		1958	1	2	2.87
Wysong, Harlan		1932	2	4	4.89
Yarewick, William		1941	0	0	
Yochim, Ray		1946	4	4	3.81
		1947	14	15	3.57
		1948	1	4	6.40
Yuhas, John		1949	8	9	4.45
		1950	15	6	4.54
		1951	13	11	3.04
Zornow, Gerry		1937	0	0	

Bibliography

Baseball Files

Baseball Hall of Fame, Cooperstown, N.Y.
Gannett Rochester Newspapers Library, Rochester, N.Y.
Rochester Public Library, Rochester, N.Y.

Books

Astifan, Priscilla. 1990. *Baseball in the 19th Century.* Rochester, N.Y.: Rochester City Historical Department.

Baylor, Don. 1989. *Don Baylor: It's the Whole Truth—A Baseball Player's Life.* New York: Simon and Schuster.

Bilovsky, Frank, and Rich Westscott. 1993. *The New Phillies Encyclopedia.* Philadelphia: Temple Univ. Press.

Fox, Stephen. 1995. *Big Leagues.* New York: William Morrow.

Karst, Gene, and Martin J. Jones. 1973. *Who's Who in Professional Baseball.* New Rochelle, N.Y.: Arlington House.

Hagen, Walter. 1956. *The Walter Hagen Story.* New York: Simon and Schuster.

McCarthy, Bill. 1949. *Rochester Diamond Echoes: From the Hop Bitters of 1880 to the Red Wings of '49.* Rochester, N.Y.: self-published.

O'Neal, Bill. 1992. *The International League: A Baseball History.* Austin: Eakin Press.

Reichler, Joseph. 1985. *The Baseball Encyclopedia.* New York: Macmillan.

Remington, John. 1969. *The Red Wings—A Love Story: A Pictorial History of Professional Baseball in Rochester.* New York: Christopher Press.

Robinson, Jackie, and Alfred Duckett. 1972. *I Never Had It Made.* New York: G. P. Putnam's Sons.

Smith, Curt. 1992. *Voices of the Game.* Rev. ed. New York: Simon and Schuster.
Society for American Baseball Research. 1984–92. *Minor League Baseball Stars.* 3 vols. Manhattan, Kansas: Society for American Baseball Research.
———. 1992–94. *Minor League History Journal.* 3 vols. Cleveland: Society for American Baseball Research.
Thorn, John, with Peter Palmer and Michael Gershman. 1993. *Total Baseball.* 3rd ed. New York: Harper Perennial.
Ward, Geoffrey, C., and Ken Burns. 1994. *Baseball: An Illustrated History.* New York: Knopf.

Guides

Baltimore Orioles media guides, 1989, 1991–95.
Cleveland Indians media guide, 1995.
Colorado Rockies media guide, 1995.
Reach Guide, 1890.
Rochester Red Wings media guides, 1979, 1985, 1989–95.
Rochester Red Wings yearbooks, 1939, 1940, 1978, 1981–95.
St. Louis Cardinals media guides, 1992–95.
The Sporting News official baseball guides, 1972, 1975–77.
The Sporting News official baseball registers, 1977, 1978, 1984, 1985, 1986, 1987, 1990.

Newspapers and Magazines

Baseball America
Rochester Democrat and American, 1858, 1860, 1877
Rochester Democrat and Chronicle, 1900–95
Rochester Evening Express, 1869
Rochester Times-Union, 1949, 1956–57, 1982–95
Rochester Union and Advertiser, 1858, 1877
The Smithsonian
The Sporting Life
The Sporting News
Sports Illustrated
Upstate Magazine
USA Today Baseball Weekly

Index